GEARR… E A BHFU…
… ACU

GRANDMOTHER AND WOLFE TONE

FOR PEGGY

By the same author

ESSAYS

Escape from the Anthill (Mullingar: The Lilliput Press, 1985, paperback, 1986)
Wolfe Tone and the Common Name of Irishman (Mullingar: Lilliput Pamphlets/The Lilliput Press, 1985)
The Children of Drancy (Mullingar: The Lilliput Press, 1988)

HISTORY

Ten Thousand Saints: A Study in Irish and European Origins (Kilkenny: Wellbrook Press, 1972)

TRANSLATION

The Thief by Leonid Leonov (London: Martin Secker, 1931)
The Cherry Orchard by Chekhov (London: H. W. Deane, 1934)

GRANDMOTHER AND WOLFE TONE

HUBERT BUTLER

With a Foreword by
DERVLA MURPHY

THE LILLIPUT PRESS
DUBLIN
1990

First published in 1990 by
THE LILLIPUT PRESS LTD
4 Rosemount Terrace, Arbour Hill,
Dublin 7, Ireland

A CIP record for this book is available
from the British Library.

ISBN 0-946640-44-0

Jacket design by Jarlath Hayes
Set in 10 on 12 Palatino by
Koinonia Ltd of Manchester
and printed in England by
Billings & Sons of Worcester

CONTENTS

ACKNOWLEDGMENTS

Thanks and acknowledgments are due to the editors and publishers of the following periodicals and newspapers in which various parts of this volume first appeared. All other material is previously unpublished.

'The Barriers': *The Bell*, July 1941.

'Otway Cuffe': *Dublin Magazine*, October 1948.

'The County Libraries: Sex, Religion, and Censorship': *Irish Writing*, July 1949, under title 'The County Libraries and The Censorship'.

'Midland Perspectives': Sections I and II, *Irish Press*, 20 July 1948 and 8 July 1949; sections III, IV and V, *The Irish Times*, 10 May, 27 July and 6 August 1956.

'Grandmother and Wolfe Tone': *The Kilkenny Magazine*, Spring and Autumn 1963.

'The City': *The Irish Times*, 10 April 1948.

'The Final Solution': *The Irish Times*, 3-6 June 1963.

'Escape to Spain': *The Irish Times*, 1-2 December 1958.

'American Impressions': Sections I and II, *The Irish Times*, 4-5 June 1962; section III, *The Irish Times*, 18-20 June 1968.

FOREWORD

This volume, like its predecessors, will sharpen the temporal sense of the middle-aged; we have lived through decades during which humankind suddenly reached a watershed. And there we now stand, hesitating about the best way forward. We need good guidebooks, such as *Grandmother and Wolfe Tone*.

In a gentle essay near the beginning, 'The Auction', Hubert Butler recalls his early adolescence when tuberculosis 'seemed a sordid, almost shameful secret between the doctors and the dying' and his mother started a branch of the Women's National Health Association in Bennettsbridge. Seventy years later he was vigorously addressing a Kilkenny anti-Amendment meeting during Ireland's tendentiously named 'Pro-Life' Referendum campaign. In between stretched a long, rich lifetime of travel, study and strenuous activity on behalf of threatened Jews. There were also occasional public controversies, reluctantly entered into but pursued with skill, dignity and tenacity. The most celebrated of these, concerning the barbarously enforced 'conversion' to Roman Catholicism of Serbian Orthodox Christians, had an outcome of which Ireland should have felt deeply ashamed – but didn't.

Seeing the proofs of this book on my desk, an acquaintance exclaimed, 'That crank! *Now* what's he on about?'

Outraged, I protested that for most of this century Hubert Butler has been among this country's tiny minority of balanced, liberal and fearless thinkers.

'But you're just another crank,' said my visitor, 'so it's no wonder you imagine he's sane.'

Examining this involuntary compliment, I could see that if you're in the business of crude categorizing, Hubert and I might indeed be graded together – if only because of our loyalty to our rural birthplaces and our distaste for the hectic artificiality of contemporary urban life. Although a generation (thirty-one years) separates us, it is not the 'dividing generation' of twentieth-century Ireland. My childhood overlaps with the era in which Hubert matured and we share memories that I do not share with today's thirty-year-olds. A few of my primary school classmates walked barefooted for miles, then pulled on their nail-studded boots by the convent gate. On Sunday mornings pony-traps and donkey-carts lined the streets around the church.

On fair-days scores of cattle, sheep, horses and pigs were driven into the town centre. Lismore then supported seven bakeries, four dressmakers, two tailors, two cobblers, three basket-makers and twenty-three pubs; now only the pubs (and several fewer of those) remain. Too often one heard of whole families being rapidly wiped out by tuberculosis. Puritanical paranoia was rampant and library books were censored according to the revulsions of manic local spinsters. The majority of my contemporaries had no alternative in their teens but to emigrate. Many small farms were occupied only by an unmarried couple – a brother and sister. Most local roads were untarred. All the local rivers were unpolluted. Election campaigns were physically gruelling, emotionally exciting and mentally exhilarating; people walked or cycled for miles to hear Dev speaking outside the Town Hall and afterwards debated important issues rather than the colour of his suit. Everyone knew – and meant not to forget – which side who was on during the Civil War. The clergy ruled O.K.

Life in rural Ireland was incomparably more agreeable then than now – for those of us who did not have to walk barefooted, die of tuberculosis, emigrate to Birmingham or be cowed by the P.P. Discarding all selfish and romantic prejudices, no humane person could regret our present affluence despite its aesthetically offensive side-effects. Yet there are numerous new hazards around. An abrupt transition to comparative material prosperity, especially when it is unevenly experienced, inevitably spreads dangerous viruses throughout society. To combat these we need strong medicine, such as Hubert Butler provides. Many of his essays encourage readers to dose themselves with honesty about modern Ireland, to confront what has gone wrong in this century and to have faith that much can be put right in the next.

In 1943 Hubert wrote 'The Two Languages' for *The Bell*: but only now do we have an opportunity to benefit from this remarkable probing of the Irish psyche. Inexplicably, Geoffrey Taylor, then *The Bell*'s literary editor, considered it too obscure for publication: too compressed, allusive and idiosyncratic. Here the relevant correspondence between author and editor is perspicaciously included. Taylor pleaded for more 'FACTS' and complained, 'The whole article stimulates my interest and imagination, but it does *not* illuminate my understanding.' In a characteristic reply – urbane and kindly, yet unrelenting – Hubert pointed out that 'before one . . . agrees to suspend a certain kind of criticism (some sort of suspension accompanies all reading), one must want to arrive at the same place as the writer does, and you probably don't. I have a picture of the sort of society I would like, so have you; if either of us could describe it we should be almighty geniuses.'

This exchange helps to explain why, until recently, Hubert's writings reached so few. In 1943, and for long after, your average Irish reader did not want to accompany him on his intellectual journeys. The road he chose was rough and unpredictable; the toll-fees had to be paid in the coinage of courage; the destination was uncertain but bound to demand difficult adjustments when/if the traveller arrived. Happily there is by now a bolder generation eager to explore the unknown.

The Bell expired in December 1954, perhaps because it had mislaid its guts. Then a new literary magazine, to be called *The Bridge*, was suggested. Hubert wrote a wise and sensitive draft editorial, published here for the first time as 'Crossing the Border'. Thirty-six years later it makes sad reading, though we can still learn much from it if we will. *The Bridge* never was built, for lack of a paltry £2000, which fact itself reveals how urgently such a link was needed.

Another hitherto unpublished essay, 'Abortion', was prompted by the harrowing Cadden case. In 1956 Nurse Mary Ann Cadden was charged with the murder of a young married woman from Co. Kilkenny and, on largely circumstantial evidence, sentenced to death – a sentence later commuted to life imprisonment. This case deeply distressed Hubert and 'Abortion' is not his usual shapely essay. It reads like an extract from a private journal in which the writer is striving to determine his own true feelings and convictions. Thus it has a peculiarly moving poignancy which more than makes up for its lack of polish. Presumably it went unpublished (and therefore unpolished) because thirty-four years ago in Ireland it was impossible publicly to debate such sex-related problems. But by 1983 that taboo was no more and in the course of his powerful address to Kilkenny's anti-Amendment meeting Hubert proclaimed: 'I am speaking for myself alone when I say that we have no right, as outsiders, to put pressure on others to bear children against their will, against their judgment and maybe against their consciences. Abortion is always an evil but best seen as a symptom of a far greater evil, the total uncaringness of our society.'

It delighted me to come upon 'Influenza in Aran', an entertaining recent essay on a subject about which Hubert has for long had buzzing insects in his headgear. This swarm is best described by himself: 'My guess would be that the [Irish] saints were the fabulous pre-Christian ancestors of pre-Celtic and proto-Celtic tribes and amalgamations of tribes, and that in their pilgrimages and pedigrees and in the multiplicity of their names, nicknames, cult-centres, we can read the true story of the wanderings of tribes. But since on this early pattern of history-writing later patterns have been superimposed, we have a palimpsest that is very hard to decipher.' On Aranmore we meet our hero as a diligent but light-hearted scholar who has been invigorated by the challenge of deciphering a remote corner of this palimpsest and revels in subtly mocking the pretensions of pompous or myopic experts. As an elegant amateur, he recoils from that professional jargon which reflects minds long since reduced, by the use of 'scientific methods', to mere cerebral machines. No doubt those academics also think him a crank; in most modern university departments there is little room left for intuition or imagination.

Escape from the Anthill and *The Children of Drancy* have brought Hubert belated international acclaim (and literary awards) as an essayist of remarkable range and talent. As a human being he is no less remarkable: detached but never cold or cynical, assured and sometimes over-dogmatic but never arrogant, erudite but unstodgy, compassionate but unsentimental, hard-hitting but never spiteful. Although a resolute crusader for honesty in every area of life, he is tolerant of individuals who have been conditioned by Church or State (or both) to operate within a cocoon of hypocrisy. For decades he has been condemning the intellectual and emotional sleaziness of modern society, yet he remains consistently positive and optimistic about the future.

AE wrote of Standish O'Grady: 'When a man is in advance of his age, a generation, unborn when he speaks, is born in due time and finds in him its inspiration. O'Grady may have failed in his appeal to the aristocracy of his own time but he may yet create an aristocracy of intellect and character in Ireland.'

The same could be written of Hubert Butler.

Dervla Murphy
Lismore, January 1990

PART ONE

IRELAND

It will be some time perhaps before many of the Anglo-Irish drop that rather provocative hyphen and call themselves simply Irish. First of all there are misunderstandings to be cleared up, suspicions to be allayed. Reconciliation will not, I think, be complete in the South till it has happened in the North too. It may develop out of those regional loyalties which the men and women to whom I have referred (Flood, O'Grady, Otway Cuffe) tried to foster. The Kilkenny Archaeological Society took as its motto a sentence from Camden: 'If any there be', he wrote, 'which are desirous to be strangers in their owne soile, and forrainers in their owne citie, they may so continue, and therein flatter themselves. For such like I have not written these lines, nor taken these paines.'

HUBERT BUTLER
Maidenhall, 10 January 1950
on Radio Éireann

1

OTWAY CUFFE

Many Irish historians who do not like political nationalism trace its growth in Ireland to the contagion of the Anglo-Irish. They contrast the noisy and narrow provincialism of the colonist with the broad universalism which should be congenital in the Catholic Irish native. The paradox is arresting but unfair. It is true that the Anglo-Irish have played a part out of all proportion to their numbers in shaping the idea of an Irish nation, but within their own group they have been, except for two decades under Grattan, a tiny, despised and neglected minority, and, when self-government came, they were very quickly pushed on one side. If there are provincial and demagogic traits in the Irish state today displeasing to the Catholic historian, it does not seem just to blame the Anglo-Irish nationalist.

It is difficult to think of anyone less of a provincial or a demagogue than Otway Cuffe, the younger brother of the Earl of Desart, who for a dozen years was the exponent of Irish nationalism in Kilkenny, and yet he seems to me to be typical of many Anglo-Irish nationalists of a generation ago. He was no politician and scarcely ever appeared on a public platform. He never said or did the kind of things that attract attention and headlines. He took so little trouble about publicity for himself or his work that it is only by searching through the local newpapers that it is possible to glean a few facts about his life. Yet it was realized on his death in 1912 that a notable Irishman had died, whose failure to make a permanent mark on his country was Ireland's failure and tragedy as well as his own.

Most of those who knew him intimately are now dead and almost nothing has been printed about his private life outside the memoirs of his niece, Lady Sybil Lubbock. She writes well enough and was fond of her uncle, but everything he thought and did was a mystery to her, and it is plain that the rest of his family found all his activities equally mystifying and embarrassing. Behind all her praise a single refrain is audible. Why, with his gifts and advantages, did he choose to sacrifice himself for people who would only exploit him and ridicule him behind his back?

When Cuffe came back to Ireland in the late 1890s there was probably a greater gulf of sympathy and experience between the various Irish groups than had ever existed before. The successors of Grattan and Flood had become completely anglicized and neither hoped nor wished for a recovery of influence in their own country except as representatives of England. Anyone who tried to bridge the gulf did so at his peril. Lady Sybil's father, Lord Desart, kept to the safer bank, not without regrets. It is curious how ignorant they had become of the land in which they had grown to consequence. Lady Sybil believed that Kilkenny was on the Suire (*sic*), repeating this mistake in two books. Her father was a distinguished lawyer, her mother was related closely to the English royal family, and their attitude to their Callan neighbours was benevolent and correct but very cautious. They seemed to have lived at Desart Court the life not merely of a garrison, but of a beleaguered garrison. Finding the local tradesmen unreliable, they were in the habit of getting their groceries by hamper from London. They did not believe in spreading frivolous ideas among the labouring classes, and Lady Desart was seriously annoyed when a neighbour offered a prize for country dancing in Desart village school. 'A course in cleanliness and practical housewifery would be more to the point,' she said. When her brother-in-law, Otway, said that what the Irish country people needed was 'poetry, poetry and music', she retorted, 'In my opinion what the villagers need most are buttons and teeth.'

This was Cuffe's family background, and against it it is easy for Lady Sybil to represent him, in an affectionate but purblind way, as a versatile but unrealistic person who pandered to the whims of the disaffected. She relates how embarrassing they found Otway's 'peasant arts and crafts, his folk-lore and his classes in the Irish language'. Lord Desart considered that these things, 'though innocuous in themselves were in Ireland inevitably flavoured with political and nationalist controversy and therefore to be eschewed'. 'Of course,' he said with mild amusement, 'the Kilkenny County Council may be genuinely interested in his fairy tales and theosophy and admirable bookbinding but I should hardly have expected it.' He was particularly hostile to the new interest in Irish legend and folklore, which Standish O'Grady, the editor of *The Kilkenny Moderator,* had aroused in Ireland.

All country folk [he said] tell the same tales and a backward people like the Irish keep theirs longest. There is nothing wonderful in that. The harm begins when men like Yeats come and make solemn pilgrimages to see the fairies for themselves and then write seriously about them and encourage all the world to think that ignorance and superstition are better than reason and common sense. Of course, there is charm in these fancies but there is cruelty too and there is a danger in any denial of reason.

The wrongness of these views, which are shrewd enough, lies in their complacency and detachment. To O'Grady and to Otway Cuffe it seemed that the Irish landlords were already becoming as obsolete as the fairies; objects, sometimes, of superstitious veneration but seldom seen and of no practical use. Their criticisms could be of value only if they were ready to receive criticism in turn, but they were not.

I have quoted Lord Desart, an astute man eminent in his profession, to show what a lonely furrow an Anglo-Irish nationalist had to plough, and how easily what he did could be misinterpreted and ridiculed even by those who were fond of him. It is strange to find that W. B. Yeats and Desart both later became senators, but unquestionably it was Yeats, the student of theosophy and the fairies, and not the lawyer, who played the greater part in the senate and proved the more staunch and formidable champion of Anglo-Irish culture.

Otway Cuffe had led an adventurous life. He had worked on the railways in America, had learnt bullfighting in Spain, woodcarving and bookbinding in Italy. From India he had acquired an interest in Indian thought which his relations dubbed theosophy, and on a visit to Iceland had met William Morris and been captivated by his social philosophy. But the serious occupations for an Irish gentleman were still hunting, shooting and fishing, and Cuffe's mild, extraneous enthusiasms were regarded as evidence of affectation and frivolity. I suppose that his neighbours sensed in his enthusiasm an implied criticism of their own apathy, and protected themselves by representing him as a harmless eccentric. In fact he was an able and diplomatic member of committees and councils and he certainly never teased the Kilkenny County Council with bookbinding or theosophy.

In *Escape from the Anthill* ('Anglo-Irish Twilight', pp. 75ff) I have told how Cuffe and his sister-in-law, Ellen, Lady Desart, supported Standish O'Grady in his war upon Lord Ormond and the local potentates of Kilkenny. Soon after that Cuffe became an alderman and then Mayor of Kilkenny. His ancestors had frequently been mayors of Kilkenny but in 1906 it was so strange for a Cuffe to wish to be on the Kilkenny Corporation as to seem sinister. At his first meeting a polite alderman drew attention to the part his great-grandfather had once played in Kilkenny municipal affairs. This seemed sycophantic to another alderman who shouted out: 'Don't go on about his great-grandfather or I'll put you out on your head!' In fact Cuffe played his part by effacing not only his great-grandfather but himself as well, using his great influence and intelligence indirectly and through others, avoiding always the impression that he was pushing himself forward or trying to recover for his class an influence which it had lost.

King Edward VII had lately visited Ireland and stayed at Kilkenny Castle. The town had been sumptuously decorated by Messrs Womersley of Leeds. If you leant over John's Bridge and watched the gas jets reflected on the placid Nore from Messrs Womersley's Venetian Masts, you could easily, it was said, fancy yourself on the Rialto. Because it was Ireland there were banners with 'God bless our Sporting Monarch!' on them as well as Union Jacks and shamrocks and harps and triumphal arches. One reporter noted that on the gorgeous banners which spanned the streets, 'Kilkenny' stood out fresh and clear, while 'Welcome to' was rather faint. Messrs Womersley, like the King, had done this sort of thing hundreds of times before and could produce an overwhelming effect on the inexperienced townsfolk with a wise economy of effort.

The King had been genial, the Queen beautiful. Reluctantly, perhaps regrettably, all had enjoyed themselves, and the psychological reaction when it came was more than usually complex and inarticulate. In thousands of Rural District Councils there were neurotic scenes which even the local reporters were unable to represent as debates. Thus at Callan, near Desart, the Board of Guardians passed a vote of condemnation on itself for passing a vote of condemnation on the Waterford Corporation for presenting an address to King Edward. One of the Board boasted that in Kilmoganny he had himself prevented Earl Spencer, the Lord Lieutenant, from being cheered, but now, he added, he would lead the cheers. An opposition member cried out: 'Was that the time they had the streets of Kilmoganny covered with beer and porter?'

'No, no! He came as an accidental gentleman hunting with his red coat on his back.'

'You'll get people to sell their bodies and souls for beer anywhere and in Kilmoganny too.'

'I saw no beer.'

The Callan Board of Guardians ultimately got itself into such a hysterical state about these matters as to attract the attention of 'The World Animated Picture Company', which was looking for material for a high-spirited Irish farce. It claimed to be The World's First Fireproof Model and it was drawing huge crowds to Kilkenny by its pictures of the Gordon Bennett Race and the King's visit. It had settled for a moment on Cuffe's young theatre like a beautiful freshly hatched butterfly laying its eggs wherever it saw new growth. In a few years its progeny would take over Cuffe's theatre and every other theatre and devastate the independent drama in every Irish provincial town.

At the next meeting of the Callan Board of Guardians the chairman read out a letter from the Company asking permission to take their picture in action, 'if possible, wearing any local or characteristic costumes they may adopt when attending meetings. We are prepared to pay them each £5 and guarantee a royalty of 15 per cent on gross receipt of pictures.'

Cuffe had been equerry to the King but his views did not seem to be those of a monarchist. He seems to have taken no part in these embarrassing festivities or in the remorse that followed on them. He tried always as far as possible to be an 'accidental gentleman' but this was not always easy for one who had been an officer in the British army. The Kilkenny Corporation, like the Callan Guardians, spent much time passing passionate resolutions of congratulation or condemnation. I cannot agree that these were as petty and ridiculous as they read now in retrospect, though undoubtedly they consumed energy and enthusiasm that could have been spent on the wise conduct of local affairs. There were then very few sensational injustices in the relations of England and Ireland but the old hatred, which in a few years was to burst out in rebellion and civil war, was kept alive by small sneers and sophistries, by unimaginative civil servants and pointless insults to Irish pride.

Whatever Cuffe did or said was bound to be found wrong by someone, and his Kilkenny activities were watched suspiciously by the Dublin press. In one week he was attacked violently by both the unionist *Evening Mail* and the nationalist *United Irishman*. There was the affair of G. R. Symes's play, *The Dandy Fifth,* and that of the Gortnahoe District Council's notepaper. There had been rowdy demonstrations against the play because it was thought to contain sneers against the Irish nation and propaganda for the British army. Kilkenny Corporation passed a vote of congratulation for the demonstrators, and Cuffe, who had not voted, was reproved sternly by the *Evening Mail* because 'though holding the King's Commission' he had allowed 'these insults to the Army and its Uniform' to be uttered.

As for the Gortnahoe District Council, they had in the interests of economy used OHMS notepaper and been censured by the Kilkenny Gaelic League. Cuffe, who maintained that 'loyalty' was compatible with an Irish Ireland, threatened to resign from the Gaelic League and for this threat he was severely censured in his turn by the *United Irishman*. Was he right or wrong? I do not know, but at least he took the problem seriously.

A generation ago these squabbles seemed even more futile than they do today. Yet the problems of the Gortnahoe District Council were real ones and Cuffe was right not to scorn them. Multiplied a millionfold and debated with armies and atom bombs, rather than with simple acrimony, they have become the insoluble enigmas of modern Europe. O'Grady and Cuffe were probably wise in thinking that in a political problem, as in an equation, the solution will come most easily when the numbers on both sides are reduced to their smallest. They believed in the small community, even when it disappointed them.

Cuffe went ahead in his own way. He brought down Douglas Hyde, who was met by a drum and fife band and who spoke to the Kilkenny branch of the Gaelic League of which Cuffe was the president and moving spirit. Hyde told them that no act of parliament could recover their nationality. He said that with her 'shilling shockers' England was pelting them with the mud of her streets: 'If we do not work on Irish lines, we shall become the Japanese of western Europe, capable only of imitation and lost to native initiative.' He told them that they were all of them deeply conscious of their inadequacy.

If we take hold of that feeling and elevate it, we shall increase Irishmen's sense of self-respect, of individuality and honour, and that is what the Gaelic League wants to do. The more divergence of thought, of characteristics, habit and customs that obtains in the Commonwealth, the better for the races. Ours is the least reading and most unlettered of peoples. Our art is distinguished above all others by its hideousness.

In all this he showed how very little there was in the early Gaelic League of that spirit of complacency, arrogance and provincialism which invaded it later.

One of Standish O'Grady's ideas had been that if there was a trained volunteer force, like Charlemont's Volunteers, the British garrison could withdraw and leave Ireland to defend itself. Cuffe drilled a Kilkenny brigade and started a gymnasium and a club. To advertise and pay for his schemes there were frequent concerts at which Irish songs and dances alternated with gymnastic displays. They were ecstatically described in the local press. 'Mr Dawson', we read, 'brought down the house with his Indian clubs.' Cuffe himself recited Thomas Davis's poem 'Owen Roe O'Neill'. 'The fine stately figure of this noble and true Irishman, attired in Irish dress, pouring forth his feelings over such a leader and chieftain as Owen Roe O'Neill was decidedly an unusual sight.' Many jeered at the obvious incongruities and he was suspected of exhibitionism, whereas he was really making his protest against banality. His enterprises were found irresistibly ludicrous by people who find nothing funny in the long patient queues that today wind down the streets of our provincial towns to see some travesty of Irish history concocted in Hollywood or Elstree.

One of Cuffe's enterprises that is still remembered is the Sheestown play. O'Grady never tired of saying that it was only by the friendly alliance of north and south that Ireland could become a vigorous and civilized land. He was a southerner and yet he believed that all the great and significant movements in Irish history, from the time of Cuchulainn and Owen Roe

O'Neill to the '98, had drawn strength and inspiration from the north. The visit of the Cave Hill Players from Belfast to Kilkenny, on Cuffe's invitation, was a symbol of this belief. They acted a play of O'Grady's on Red Hugh O'Donnell at Sheestown, Cuffe's home on the banks of the Nore. O'Grady had long left *The Kilkenny Moderator* and all Cuffe's activities are recorded only in the shoddiest provincial journalism, but through all the clichés it is possible to see that he stirred men's minds in a way they had not been stirred before. The Belfast men camped upon the banks of the Nore and their huge bonfires lit the woods upon the opposite shore, where Chinese lanterns hung from the trees and pipers played as they marched. The harvest moon cast an enchanted light on the green lawn where the play was acted. 'It recalled', said one reporter, trying to do justice to the beauty of the scene, 'one of the most graphic chapters of Marie Corelli's great works.'

It was a triumph of friendliness and imagination. The play itself was of a rather simple kind, and it would be unkind to criticize it too severely. Its purpose was explained in the Prologue, of which one verse runs:

> Brave, proud Ultonia hither sends today
> Her gallant children here to act her play.
> In gentle bonds they would unite once more
> Ulster and Leinster, Lagan and the Nore.

In all this he had the support of Ellen, Lady Desart, his eldest brother's widow. She too joined the Gaelic League and told them that her own people, the Jews, had kept alive their language, Hebrew, as a bond of union between them. With her vast wealth, she helped him to start the Kilkenny Woodworkers, the woollen mills, a tobacco farm, a model village and hospital, a recreation hall, a public library and a theatre. There was no cultural or social activity in Kilkenny which they did not support.

It is fashionable now to deride 'uplift' and to suspect the wealthy or independent of being patronizing or to pity their innocence in being exploited. In fact, it was no naïve optimism that urged Cuffe on. He knew that the pleasant, not uncivilized life to which he had been born, rested on unstable foundations. A great effort of renunciation and adaptation would have to be made, if even a remnant of the old traditions was to survive.

O'Grady had written of the Irish gentry: 'Ireland and her destinies hang upon you, literally so. Either you will refashion her, moulding us anew after some human and heroic pattern, or we plunge downwards into roaring revolutionary anarchies, where no road or path is any longer visible at all.' Cuffe may have had some premonition of the smoking walls of Desart, of the tragic exile of his brother and the final negation of that influence which the Anglo-Irish still enjoyed. The need for haste perhaps stimulated them to more ventures than they could reasonably control, and very soon there were bruising disappointments.

You can reconstruct what happened from paragraphs in the Kilkenny press. Under the dust and the cheap varnish, you can see the fine grain of the wood, the careful, fastidious workmanship.

In June 1907 the model village of Talbot's Inch was being built and Ellen, Lady Desart's own house was ready, in which all the furniture, except the grandfather clock, had been made by the Kilkenny Woodworkers. One evening, in the words of a reporter, 'she entered into possession of her picturesque bijou residence' and the Corporation met her with swords and macebearers on the road from Sheestown. The fire brigade was there and pipe bands and an address was read by the Mayor and the town clerk.

Lady Desart said to them:

I dream of Talbot's Inch becoming the rallying-point for all Kilkenny, not only of industry (which I may surely say it has already become with our woodworkers and our tobacco and the woollen mills over the river, which we have linked to us with our little golden bridge), but for all also that makes for joy and harmony and the higher pleasures that refine the mind and elevate the spirit and the soul.

Give me the great happiness to know before I die that the name I bear, which is unspeakably dear to me, will go down to your children and your children's children, enshrined in your hearts as one who loved you and deserved your love.

Otway Cuffe seldom made speeches. He had none of Ellen Desart's warm Jewish readiness of tongue, her quick facility to interpret a mood and to strive to make it enduring with words and money. I can find only one of his speeches. It is, characteristically, to the Kilkenny YMCA and about the four orders of the Brahmins. He contrasts their organization with that of the ancient Irish society, a system that was patriarchal, regional, communal and yet aristocratic, where the 'individual personality counted and men felt a responsibility for each other's defence, a small and savage society, which yet contained in itself the germ of a society happier than our own'. The Christian young men were flattered and interested, and there was a grateful, flurried reply, before they passed on to subjects that were familiar to them, the 'Catch-my-pal Temperance Club' and the need of a new table for the Badminton Club. Cuffe was content to cast his ideas on the most unlikely soil, hoping that here and there a seed might one day germinate. Lady Desart's more commonplace emotionalism, her enthusiasms which were easier to understand, floated his ideas into regions which they would otherwise not have reached. The love she felt for her neighbourhood and its people she had derived from the Cuffes, but she expressed it with a robust sentimentality from which they would have recoiled.

When she was given the Freedom of the City, she said:

> I lost my heart to Kilkenny that May morning six and twenty years ago, when it opened its arms to me, a young and happy bride. My husband taught me to love every inch of Kilkenny and every living being within the four corners of this fair county. It is a real solace to me in these days of my widowhood to see that my love, which has deepened with the years, is so overwhelmingly returned. I cannot say thank you for such love. I can only cling to it and appreciate it. I can only hope it will live on and increase and give Kilkenny in the giving something approaching the happiness it has given and gives me to receive it.

Quite soon things began to go wrong. As related in *Escape from the Anthill* ('Anglo-Irish Twilight', p. 85), the Kilkenny Woodworkers struck when Cuffe took on a non-trade-union cabinetmaker from Glasgow; there was also a mysterious fire at the Woodworkers whose origins were never cleared up, and finally there was a series of embezzlements on the part of trusted officials. The blame for most of these things rested with outsiders and Kilkenny people remained strong partisans of Cuffe and Ellen Desart and never for a moment suspected the purity of their motives. Lady Desart refused to prosecute or to be discouraged. But after a time the factory had to close its doors.

Bad news also came from the woollen mills. At a meeting of the shareholders in 1911 they were told, 'After a few years working the great part of the original capital has been hopelessly lost.' But Lady Desart herself came to the rescue with £10,000. Today the woollen mills is one of the very few of their enterprises to survive.

The strikes cannot be blamed on Cuffe. They were the result of a collision between the routine politics of the Big World with its ready-made strategy and slogans and the subtle personal politics of the small community. As for the repeated evaporation of capital, explanations were not easy. Idealists, especially wealthy ones, are supposed to be easy to deceive and perhaps Cuffe and Lady Desart were too trusting, but they had seen the defeat of Standish O'Grady and must have known disillusionment long before. Possibly they were too arrogant in their refusal to take advice. They were trying to turn the dragon of industrialism into a harmless domestic animal, but by the beginning of the century almost everyone was directly or indirectly in the pay of the dragon. The Cuffes were obliged to depend on experts, thick-witted, lopsided men, who observed only that their employers lacked all interest in personal profit and decided that this deficiency must be due simply to wealth and inattention. They also noticed that the Cuffes were humane people. Delinquents expected and received indulgence.

Cuffe was not a young man. These disappointments wounded him deeply. They undermined his health and clouded his mind. He was advised to go for a long sea-voyage. In January 1912 the news came that he had died at Fremantle in Western Australia and had been carried to his grave by Kilkenny men, members of the Perth Hurling Club.

A provincial press can often be accused of insincerity, but on Cuffe's death the sense of bewilderment and loss which was recorded was unfeigned and not exaggerated. There were endless deputations, adjournments, condolences.

The day was in mourning for the loss of Kilkenny's great benefactor. Heavy clouds rolled across a leaden sky from early morning and the surrounding hills were enveloped in mist. In the city all the shops were closed and the flag on the Tholsel was at half-mast. . . .

A man of noble soul, who burst through the prejudices of his class and worked side by side with the humblest of the people . . . he was one of the greatest promoters of industry that Ireland has known for centuries. That work of his may well be the beginning of a period when the aristocrats of Ireland, so long estranged from the democracy, may come to the front to take the place which every well-wisher of Ireland would be glad to see them occupy.

To his widow, they said: 'We may be quick-tempered and impulsive but we are not an ungrateful people and to us that lonely grave in Western Australia will be as revered as any spot held sacred by our race.'

She answered that many times he had told her that his country was to him dearer than anything else in the world and that he had indeed given his life for his country.

It would be cynical and untrue to say that Cuffe was quickly forgotten but all his activities were centrifugal, towards the small and local, and the pull upon conventionally educated minds towards great remote events was, in 1912, almost irresistible. A few weeks later Corbett Wilson, who had flown the Channel, settled in Kilkenny and from there did flights of great importance. There was wild excitement and a flow of poetry and prose. The old era seemed to be closing.

He flew over Windgap in a clear atmosphere and over the cliffs known as 'The Fairy Steps', where Finvara the King of the Fairies and the White Woman entertained the ancient hunters. Downwards with the graceful sweep of a sea-bird, till the topmost pinnacle of St Canice's was the centre of a revolving circle and then a low gliding movement and the machine was running along the grass of the Show Ground.

Here was the theme for poetry, which Cuffe, that poetical yet somehow inhibited man, had failed to provide:

'Twas on the 23rd of May and in the afternoon
That Mr Corbett Wilson went up to see the moon.
He gradually ascended just like a big cuckoo
And flew for miles around us that day from Ardaloo.

Kilkenny always held her own with all that came her way
But now through Mr Wilson she proudly takes the sway!
You know he is the first great man, who o'er the channel flew
And landed down in Wexford town not far from Ardaloo!

Long life to Mr Wilson! May his courage never fail!
May a hundred years pass over ere his coffin needs a nail!
For None But Him Who Rules The Waves And Can The Storms Subdue
Could shake the nerve of that brave man that day at Ardaloo!

He was entertained by the Protestant Dean at the Club House Hotel and platitudes that differed from ordinary platitudes by being fantastically false as well as dull were uttered and printed. It was felt that a great new era was being ushered in when nationalism would no longer count. The countries of the earth would be so linked together by speed that all regional jealousies and differences would disappear. Elsewhere in the paper it was written that Lieut. Gregory, a Kilkennyman, had demonstrated at Weymouth that 'it is possible to release an object weighing 300 lbs without disturbing the flight of the air-craft' and that in the Reichstag, Herr Bernstein, a deputy, had declared that Germany should take the lead in banning the use of aerial bombs. All these loud noises from far away, ambiguous and contradictory, drowned the message of Otway Cuffe, though it was clear and concrete and from near at hand. He had failed to demonstrate that neighbourliness pays, while what Lieut. Gregory had proved was both dramatic and unanswerable.

After Cuffe's death Ellen Desart found herself no longer able to pick her way with confidence through the increasing complexities of the Gaelic movement. Like her sister-in-law, she came almost to think that 'buttons and teeth' were more urgent necessities than poetry and music. She relapsed into being a very intelligent, very philanthropic Countess, an excellent committee-woman for bee-keeping and cow-testing associations, always ready to give her money or advice for the prevention of disease or the spread of enlightenment, the patroness of public libraries and model hospitals. In fact, as those of the Anglo-Irish who hated the new Ireland left the country, she ceased, as did many others, to be a rebel. Like W. B. Yeats, she found herself latterly defending values that had once seemed so safe that they needed criticism rather than defence. In the senate she became a recognized spokesperson, as he did, against the narrowness of nationalism and all petty encroachments upon personal liberty.

She never gave way to the bitter cynicism and despair which devastated the greater part of the Irish ascendancy class in the twenties nor, like so many, did she treat as a personal grievance disasters whose origins were in Irish history. These came thick and fast. Early in 1923, with the departure of the British army, the Civil War reached a climax and many of the houses of those who had accepted office as senators from the new government were burnt, including Desart Court.

I think that these events gave satisfaction to those who were hostile to the new Ireland. Lady Sybil Lubbock says that her mother seemed almost to feel a sense of relief that with the calamity Lord Desart's Irish responsibilities might come to an end. Many of the Anglo-Irish had localized all their Irish loyalties on their estates, and when these disappeared it was like the loss of a septic limb, after which they could start again, crippled but healthy. But Lord Desart was more gravely shattered and wrote with the bitterness of despondency: 'I feel most deeply for all those who whether for business, honour or profession are tied to the miserable future of Ireland, and perhaps to some awful form of minor death. It is too appalling to think of.' His daughter relates how often when he was working at his small garden in Sussex a look of sadness and indifference came over him and she knew he was thinking 'of the long borders of Desart and the great flowery terrace at sunset'. Before he died he said, 'I cannot bear to think of Desart. All gone, all scattered, and we were so happy there. It is sadness itself!'

I quote Lord Desart not to raise regret or sympathy, but to give an idea of the thicket of passionately restricted loyalties from which Otway Cuffe extricated himself and tried to extricate others. Contrasted with the despair which overwhelmed and almost extinguished the rest of the Anglo-Irish, he came very near to success.

[1948]

2

THE AUCTION

I am not quite sure how soon after Otway Cuffe's death, in 1912, Mrs Cuffe gave up Sheestown and went to live in Kerry, but I was already a public schoolboy, a Carthusian, and ripe to be embarrassed when my relations made scenes publicly, and there had been just such a scene at the Sheestown auction to which I had gone with my mother in the pony-trap. Mr McCreery, the auctioneer, had offered for sale a large wooden hut and my mother, who needed a new hen-house, rather tremulously bid it up to £17. It was knocked down to her, and she was walking away, appalled at her own audacity, when someone remarked how kind the Cuffes had always been to the poor of Kilkenny. Not one tuberculous slum-child but several had passed successive summers in that hut in a leafy glade by the Nore. Tuberculosis! My mother for a couple of seconds was frozen with horror, and then she was gesticulating frantically across the crowd to Mr McCreery and to Aunt Harriet, who stood within reach of him. 'Tell him! Stop him!' I felt a *frisson* of sympathy and dismay. Tuberculosis! Tuberculous poultry! Tuberculous eggs! A quiver like an electric current ran through all the better-dressed bosoms in front of me, because Lady Aberdeen, the Lord Lieutenant's wife, had started a crusade against tuberculosis – it was a word that was on everybody's lips, particularly unionist lips. I must here permit myself a digression about tuberculosis.

It was one of those rare and blessed battle-cries, like co-operative creameries and village halls, which appeared to have no political or religious implications. Indeed it was better than either, for often a priest wanted to consecrate a village hall or put a crucifix instead of a clock above the rostrum, and there were rumours that the creameries were used for political agitation when the farmers' boys for miles around, having taken their milk-churns from their donkey-carts, had leisure for exchanging views. But nobody could say anything of the kind about tuberculosis. When my mother had started a branch of the Women's National Health Association in Bennettsbridge, Lady Aberdeen had come down and talked to the Association and driven round the neighbourhood. My sister had sat on one side of her and Miss Foley, the priest's sister, on the other, and Mrs Cuffe beside the chauffeur. It was an immensely amiable, non-political, non-religious occasion. Tuberculosis acted like a love-potion, and at the end of it we children had distinctly heard Miss Foley say, 'A thousand thanks, Countess, for my most delightful drive.' With the savage snobbery of children, learning for the first time the exciting art of speaking in inverted commas, we had pestered each other for months and months with poor Miss Foley's over-unctuous gratitude. So now tuberculosis, which had once seemed a sordid, almost shameful secret between the doctors and the dying, was invested with dignity and importance. Now that it was made everybody's business, it attracted to itself not only the tender and the charitable but also the ambitious and the interfering and the timid, who saw that sympathy for the sick might be interposed as a fluffy bolster between themselves and Home Rule which they saw irrevocably approaching. But because I found it all a bore when I was in my teens, I am likely to underestimate the self-denial and unrewarded service of those who like my mother spent endless hours with ledgers, petty-cash books, subscription lists, committees. My mother, unlike the Cuffes, had never been sustained by any golden dream of a new era in Ireland, but simply by a Victorian sense of duty to the poor and her own humorous curiosity about other people's lives.

For a moment or two I felt rather proud of the effect that my mother had caused in the large crowd with the magical word 'tuberculosis'. All the expected responses could be seen and even Aunt Harriet, who as a Christian Scientist considered tuberculosis 'a form of false thinking', had leant over loyally and, seizing Mr McCreery by the sleeve, had whispered some agitated remarks into his ear. But quickly the mystical moment passed, the auctioneer and the public began to get impatient, and at my elbow I heard the curate of St John's, Kilkenny, say sourly to his neighbour: 'I don't wonder she wants to get out of it. £17! Ridiculous! Why, I could knock it up myself for £7. As for tuberculosis, all that's needed is a little disinfectant.' I was greatly mortified on my mother's behalf and scarcely noticed how the episode ended. (I think she decided to write herself to Mrs Cuffe.)

I wriggled unhappily out of the crowd in the yard and walked down past Cuffe's Model Dairy to the river, which for a mile or two upstream above Sheestown weir flows under park trees through the small demesnes of Sheestown and Kilfera on its western banks. It is full of trout and salmon, and all the way from Durrow in Co. Laois to New Ross in Co. Wexford there are meadows of rich grass on each bank, the Scotch firs and larches grow straight and thick, and every now and then, south of Kilkenny town, beeches spread themselves out extravagantly over bluebells and wood sorrel. Through them you can see the hindquarters of a fat pony, the sparkle of a tomato-house, the corner of a tennis net and, less frequently, a real exotic like a contented Jersey cow or a disconsolate but still defiant cricket pavilion. Surely this valley had everything in the world that anyone could wish for, the raw material for every variety of happiness? Why is the manufactured article so rare? Why, at sixteen, were my parents convinced that I would never be able to live here? Has any river in the world carried so many cargoes of nostalgia and bitter-sweet memories to the sea, for one could cover an acre with faded newsprint about the Nore, sad simple verse composed in Tasmania or Bangkok or Pittsburgh, and sent home to Kilkenny? If the Nore ends one line you will know infallibly that a succeeding line will end with 'days of yore', 'distant shore', 'never more', 'long years before', 'memory's door', 'parting sore'. The answer to my last question is no doubt that all the rivers of Ireland are the same.

In fact, though, I don't want an answer, because the answer is obvious. I want an admission. Living in social harmony is a most difficult art; the most absolute concentration is required, and perfect equilibrium. Our island is dangerously tilted towards England and towards Rome, good places in themselves but best seen on the level. Everybody is rolling off it and those that remain, struggling hard for a foothold, drag each other down. But it is not necessary to argue, it is only necessary to look.

Sheestown is divided from Kilfera by a small rocky glen in which St Fiachra's Well is situated, and beyond it across smooth lawns, a tennis court and a high embankment built above the rapids of the Nore, you can see the Norman castle of the Forrestals now incorporated into Kilfera House. There is also the ruined church of Sheestown in which the Forrestals and Shees are buried, and the small cemetery of Kilfera where the roots of the beech trees have tilted or flattened half the tombs. A headless statue of a medieval ecclesiastic is propped against the railings of the Victorian table-tomb of Mr Kenny Purcell, 'One-time Clerk of the Peace Kilkenny' and a former owner of Kilfera. It is said locally to be St Fiachra himself, that much-travelled saint, who in Kilkenny gave his name to Kilfera, in Paris gave it to the 'fiacre', because there was a cabstand beneath his church; but the statue is a thousand years later than Fiachra's time and is probably an abbot from some dissolved medieval monastery, Jerpoint perhaps, or Kells. A small stone building, said to be his hermit cell, had to be removed when Mr Kenny Purcell went to his rest in 1869, but he too has been disrespectfully treated because the marble walls of his sepulchre are gaping apart. My toes were just small enough to get a foothold between the iron bars and I could see a couple of stones and a tin can, but no trace of the Clerk of the Peace.

You get all the confusion of Irish history in a few acres. First St Fiachra, then the Norman Forrestals, then, overshadowing them, the Shees, English you would suppose. But no, they are Irish Uí Seaghdha from Kerry, who anglicized their name and their habits with immense rapidity and success in Tudor times. Robert Shee had allied himself with Piers Butler, eighth Earl of Ormond, and had been killed in 1493 in Tipperary fighting against the O'Briens of Munster at the head of a hundred Kilkennymen. The Shees were one of the ten great merchant families of Kilkenny, the other nine all being English. Robert Shee's son, Richard, had become Sovereign of Kilkenny; his grandson, Sir Richard, had been educated at Gray's Inn, became legal adviser to Queen Elizabeth's friend Black Tom Butler, the tenth Earl of Ormond, and when Ormond became Lord Treasurer of Ireland, was made Deputy Treasurer. He and his family acquired great wealth and many houses in Kilkenny town and county and had built the Alms House in which Standish O'Grady had established his knitting industry and permanent craft exhibition. Sir Richard's son, Lucas, married the daughter of Lord Mountgarret, whose other daughter married the eleventh Earl of Ormond. Lucas's son, Robert, when the Civil War broke out, persuaded his uncle Mountgarret to accept the presidency of the Confederation. The royalist parliament was held in the Shee mansion in Parliament Street which till 1865 stood where the gates of the Market now are.

The Shees were an urbane and cultivated family who wrote for each other long epitaphs in elegiacs and hexameters, which are more pagan than Christian. '*Homo bulla* . . . (Man is a bubble) . . .':

> *Nec genus antiquum nec honesta opulentia rerum*
> *Nec necis imperium lingua diserta fugit*
> *Nec fidei fervor nec religionis avitae*
> *Cultus ab extremo liberat ense nihil.*
>
> (Neither ancient lineage, nor honourably amassed wealth nor eloquence can evade the stern summons of death, nor can fervent faith and the practice of the religion of our fathers reprieve us from the sword of doom.)

Then a prayer is asked for a speedy passage to Heaven, supposing, that is to say, heaven exists:

> *Si tamen haec mors est transitus ad superos* . . .

Elias Shee, from whose tomb in St Mary's, Kilkenny, I have taken these five lines, is described by Richard Stanyhurst as 'born in Kilkenny, sometime scholar of Oxford, a gentleman of passing good wit, a pleasing conceited companion, full of mirth without gall. He wrote in English divers sonnets.' I do not think the Shees or the nine other Kilkenny merchant families, all Catholics, all dispossessed by Cromwell, could be considered 'priest-ridden'. Had fate treated them more kindly, would they, like the wealthy Flemish burghers, have become patrons of the arts and sciences; would they have produced their own Erasmus and formed eventually the nucleus of a proud and independent Anglo-Irish civilization? Elias Shee was described by his sorrowing relatives as '*orbi Britannico lumen*', a light to the British world, because of his wit, his learning, his breeding, but his family remained conscious of their Irish descent, calling themselves after Cromwellian times O'Shee, when more prudent families were dropping their Os and Macs.

Yet I cannot feel very confident of any such Anglo-Irish development in the seventeenth century. Is there, perhaps, as AE (George Russell) suggested, 'some sorcery in the Irish mind' rebelling against any peaceful and prosperous fusion, some intense pride of race?

When I got back to Sheestown I found that my mother had bought me a bookcase full of Otway Cuffe's books. She was looking at them apprehensively, wondering whether she was not infecting me with something more virulent than tuberculosis, and, when we were driving home, she tried to counteract any possible bad effects by telling me how Cuffe's heart had been broken by ingratitude and that, when a couple of years before he had invited the Cave Hill Players from Belfast to act in a play of O'Grady's about Red Hugh O'Donnell at Sheestown, a couple of thousand spectators had streamed out from Kilkenny. They had trampled down some rare shrubs, and stolen and broken teacups. She also said that O'Grady's play was very bad, and that she had had to laugh at Otway Cuffe in a saffron kilt reciting a roistering rebel Irish ballad in a refined English voice. Manager after manager had cheated Cuffe at the woollen mills and woodworks. And she said that all the intelligent people had emigrated. Her own brothers, Etonians, Harrovians, Carthusians, had all gone, except Uncle Charlie at Graiguenoe, and were British officers or Indian civilians. Ireland was an exhausted country. 'Look how stupid X is!' and she mentioned one of my father's oldest friends.

Everything she said was true, yet I knew that she herself would never grudge her teacups or her shrubs where her own ideals and affections were involved, and that she was trying to inoculate me against the terrible virus of nationalism. My responses cannot have satisfied her, for a few days later I found that she had torn out from some of the books the blank page on which Cuffe had written his name, and had used upon the title-page the little machine for stamping notepaper with our address, Maidenhall, Bennettsbridge, Co. Kilkenny. I diverted some of the annoyance I felt with my mother to the little machine, which I ever afterwards regarded with abhorrence. I could remember our excitement when it had arrived ten years before and we had won countless pennies for 'The League of Pity' by stamping notepaper for my mother and father with it.

My mother bought a large red book called *Careers for Our Boys* and tried vainly to engage me in conversation about the British consular and diplomatic services. She suspected rightly that I was not merely indifferent but hostile: she trembled for me because the 1914-18 War was on and all the heresies which had seemed so venial a couple of years earlier now carried on them the mark of Cain. Our bishop, Dr d'Arcy, the successor of Dr Crozier, a mild and scholarly commentator on the Pauline Epistles, had himself a few years before, as Bishop of Down, consecrated Unionist machine-guns to be used against Home Rulers, and sometimes Kipling's poem on Ulster was quoted. I remember only one verse:

> We know the war declared
> On every peaceful home,
> We know the Hell prepared
> For those who serve not Rome.

It would have been social suicide to question that God and the Empire were indissolubly allied. My mother was not herself given to adamantine loyalties, there were few of them which she could not have adjusted in our interests. She was not a Roman matron like my grandmother, who would have sacrificed us all upon the altar of God or Empire, but she saw that we, unlike the Cuffes and Lady Desart, were not in the income group which could afford to be unorthodox. My father belonged to the minor Anglo-Irish gentry and, except for remote kinship of blood, had no link with the two or three noble Butler dynasties which still reigned nearby, and which we were to survive in Kilkenny. And if ever I made some heretical remark about the Easter Rebellion, she would look at me not with indignation but with loving anxiety, as though I had coughed up a spot of blood onto my handkerchief. There was no precedent for it in my upbringing or my heredity. Nothing like it had been seen in her own family; in my father's there had been Aunt Harriet, but when the Gaelic League had become 'political' Aunt Harriet had shut her Dinneen forever and become a disciple of Mrs Eddy. It could not, therefore, be a congenital disorder, it must have been acquired by contagion, and looking round in a wide sweep for possible 'carriers' she fixed on my distant cousin Theobald Fitzwalter Butler, who had been head boy at Charterhouse a term or two before I had gone there and who had visited us several times and had made contentious remarks at mealtimes. 'He's got it off Theo,' I often heard her murmur dismally, desperately to my father, after some evening of unprofitable disagreements.

Theo and his friend, Eric Dodds, had done relief work in Serbia before conscription had come and then, dissociating themselves from the war, had returned to their own country. Theo had taught at a school in Co. Down, Dodds at Kilkenny College. One day Dodds, a stocky independent fellow, walked out to tea from Kilkenny and inflamed my grandmother by his pacifism and his defence of Irish sedition. Theo told us that Dodds had won 'The Craven Scholarship'. Ritual Irish jokes, one part mirth, three parts gall, were later made about the Craven, though not by my grandmother, who was too deeply shocked and too fastidious, in the well-bred English way, for puns. Dodds did not come again. But nonetheless, almost as much as Theo (who was thought more insidious because he was more ingratiating), he was supposed to have corrupted me and perhaps, indeed, he did leave behind a stimulating breeze of heterodoxy for which I should be grateful, though it would have needed a hurricane to do more than ruffle our settled Anglo-Irish loyalties.

I wish I had seen more of them, since they could have helped me to a less inhibited introverted patriotism, with facts and external contacts; had I had more confidence and been less dependent on my family, I could have been pleasanter to them. I could have acknowledged, I think, that my mother's powerful intuitions were often right, even when they were irrelevant. Of Dodds and Theo she said: 'They're great Irish patriots now, but when the war is over they'll take jobs in England.' And so indeed it happened. They are both of them now, like Elias Shee, *'orbi Britannico lumina'*, since Dodds is Regius Professor of Greek at Oxford and Theo a legal luminary at the Inner Temple. Yet I cannot regard either of them as backsliders. Though it seems to me to be man's duty to work in and for the community which he acknowledges to be his own, we also have a duty to develop our faculties to their fullest extent. Often these two duties cannot be reconciled and we have to choose between spiritual and intellectual frustration. So long as we do not accept our mutilated destiny with levity or resignation, we cannot be condemned as dodgers.

My mother's intuition about Cuffe's books was also sound. Among those from which she removed Cuffe's name was Edward Martyn's *The Heather Field*. This now almost unreadable play, which George Moore declared to be 'the first play written in English inspired by the example of Ibsen', has not yet lost its magic for me, but forty years ago I found it overwhelming. Is it sentimental, morbid, is the dialogue forced and preposterous, are the characters overdrawn? I am still blind to all its defects; it seems to me the most poetic expression I know of the terrifying intellectual isolation of Ireland, its power to breed ideas, ideals and emotions in rich abundance, its incapacity to nourish them or defend them from the venomous dislike of the 'niddys' (I got that word from Standish O'Grady) and the professionally virtuous. It shows how that isolation, in time, breeds isolationism driving poetry into suicidal extravagance and generating in sane and sober people every variety of arrogance and eccentricity. Carden Tyrell, who tried to reclaim a heather field with grants from the Board of Works, is a tragic figure, a symbol of the incompatibility of poetry and practical life. The drainage of the heather field swamps the land below it and that necessitates more loans from the Board of Works and 'a vast ramification of drains' to carry the water away to the sea. Carden is hypnotized by the magnitude of the enterprise, the huge tract of luxuriant pasture which will take the place of swamp and heather. But it is the vast expenditure that appals his wife and her worldly friends, and she tries to get Carden certified as insane. Carden becomes more and more the slave of his dreams, till one day his little son comes in joyously with a posy of purple flowers. Then Carden does, in fact, enter the dream-world of the insane, a world of happy hallucination, in which reality is a passing nightmare and the rainbow fantasies of his boyhood alone are permanent. Everyone is bewildered with the wild and witless poetry of his remarks, till his friend Barry Ussher solves the mystery with the curtain-line: 'The wild heath has broken out again in the heather field.'

That line could almost act also as an epitaph on O'Grady's work in Kilkenny, on Cuffe's, on Lady Desart's, on the work of the scores of poetical social reformers who flourished in Ireland in the first quarter of the century. In every case the wild heath has broken out again in the heather field, and the memory of those who tried to eradicate it by 'modern' methods has failed. Yet the urbane nihilism of the Shees belongs to a more prosperous age. 'HOMO BULLA. *Vita quid est hominis gracilis nisi spuma, quid ipse? Nil nisi bulla.*'

I don't suppose anyone, for example, will write about old Albinia Broderick, the sister of Lord Midleton, the leader of the southern unionists, who conceived it her mission to atone for the sins of her ancestors, exacting landlords of the south-west; she dressed as an old Irish countrywoman and ran a village shop, while behind her on a stony Dunkerron promontory rose the shell of a large hospital which she had built for the sick poor of Kerry, but which, because of its unsuitable though romantic site, had remained empty and unused. There is a labyrinthine story of idealism, obstinacy, perversity, social conscience, medicine, family, behind this empty structure. The man who could unravel it would be diagnosing the spiritual sickness of Ireland, and diagnosis is the first step to a cure. It might be a more worthwhile task than the hospital, had it come into being, could ever have performed. But that task belongs to Kerry, not Kilkenny.

Here, I want to find out what happened to Otway Cuffe. This implies a rejection of that mystical interpretation of Irish dreaming which Shaw has expressed so memorably through the mouth of Larry Doyle:

> Here [in England], if the life is dull, you can be dull too, and no great harm done. But your wits can't thicken in that soft moist air, on those white springy roads, in those misty rushes and brown bogs, on those hillsides of granite rocks and magenta heather. You've no such colours in the sky, no such lure in the distances, no such sadness in the evenings. Oh, the dreaming! the dreaming! the torturing, heart-scalding, never satisfying dreaming, dreaming, dreaming, dreaming! No debauchery that ever coarsened and brutalized an Englishman can take the worth and usefulness out of him like that dreaming.

Shaw, the great realist, had nothing but a fatalistic philosophy of abdication to offer the Irish, 'Leave Ireland.' It was the same philosophy which my parents, rejecting it for themselves, offered to their children, and, rejecting it for myself, I have not yet anything better to offer mine. Yet malaria has not always existed in marshes and can now be expelled from them, and frustration and melancholy are not ineradicable in any corner of the world.

Looking at my own family history, I was unable to trace a single one of my paternal ancestors who had lived out of Ireland since the thirteenth century, when they came here: why should our island in my generation suddenly become uninhabitable for us? I could not and I cannot accept that there is anything inevitable about this, or that misty rushes and magenta heather inevitably debauch the intelligence.

Seen against the backcloth of a lunatic world, Irish lunacy is an ephemeral and contingent disorder. Sometimes cosmic lunacy dwarfs and counteracts the regional kind. Hitler's war stopped the importation of foreign timber and building materials to Ireland. They became costly rarities and Miss Broderick's chimerical hospital turned under demolition into a profitable business investment, I have been told. In a less crude way projects doomed to failure, like Carden Tyrell's, are not unprofitable if the apparent waste of energy and enthusiasm can be scrupulously recorded. Perhaps Cuffe would have been more of a Carden Tyrell than he was if O'Grady had not published two of Edward Martyn's other plays that were in the Nore Library in Kilkenny, and if *The Heather Field* had not been in that bookcase at Sheestown.

[1957]

Endnote This, and the piece that follows, 'Home-coming', is a draft section of uncompleted autobiography. Titles have been added. (*Ed.*)

3

HOME-COMING

I was over forty when my father died and we came to live permanently in Kilkenny, but though I had always been at odds with the environment in which I grew up, I had decided when I was a boy that I was going to live there. Since I was nine everybody had been trying to tug me up by the roots and it seemed to me that only the tap-root, which guarantees survival, still held to my native soil. The precious fibrous roots (I am a gardener and must be allowed this image) which bring one surface nourishment and help one to adapt and expand had all been badly bruised and shaken.

The disadvantages of being fixed, when most people like oneself are free, are obvious. If you belong to a small remote community and keep returning to it, you seldom achieve those climaxes which more mobile people enjoy. You are cut off from a huge choice of experiences and acquaintances or at least you are jerked back before they mature into adventures or friendships.

And you have to deceive yourself a good deal. For of course it is only a makeshift community. Today you might have to go to Africa before you found one that had more than a shadowy reality. The fragments of history or geography that once seemed to define a local community were never very firm and now are easily pushed on one side. Many people live in their communities accidentally like passengers at a railway junction and it would be absurd to expect from them more than the most transient solidarity of feeling.

Yet to me belief in a co-operative community is a substitute for religion and has had little to do with fulfilment or satisfaction, though I have continually hoped for these and sometimes had them. Does this sound portentous? I do not see why. If one were a Methodist or a Jew or a Roman Catholic one would not feel priggish in explaining that one's faith did not necessarily bring material contentment. I do not claim to be disinterested in any of these sectarian ways; I was baptized and reared a member of the Protestant Church of Ireland and do not wish to call myself anything else till I am expelled for heresy. Yet it is not my real religion. Everybody's religion is full of fantasy and symbolism and what to critical minds looks like pretence. Perhaps no creative idea would be able to germinate and sprout unless it were sheltered from too penetrating a scrutiny by some woolly blanket of absurdity. I do not claim that my Heaven, an earthly one, is yet very probable or practical. It is not so plausible or imminent that I would be justified in decrying the supernatural Heaven which is preached at our Protestant church of Ennisnag or the Catholic chapel in Bennettsbridge. Perhaps if we ever venture to strip off all these envelopes of foolishness, the fragile growth which they shelter will prove to be the same.

Oddly enough my religion too, because of Plunkett and AE, had its local shrine, though not much spiritual effulgence radiated from it. It was the Bennettsbridge Creamery. I got superphosphates there and sulphate of ammonia and muriate of potash for the orchard, cement for patching the outhouses, and when I gave up my cows I used to get skim milk for pigs, but nothing else. Our fresh milk now comes daily by lorry to the local grocer from the Slaney Valley thirty miles away, and the best local milk, from Jersey cows fed on Bennettsbridge grass, goes daily in big churns to Dublin. In fact the creamery after twenty years exercised only a fraction of the co-operative functions which the practical visionaries to whom it owes its existence, Horace Plunkett and AE, expected from it. They saw it as the nucleus of a harmonious social organism, concerned not only with buying and selling but also with communal living. And of course it was nothing of the kind and that goal has long been forgotten.

Yet their vision is still valid, despite its imperfect realization. Lately I was reading Martin Buber's *Paths in Utopia*, which was republished in Boston a couple of years ago. He is a famous Jewish theologian who believes in the full co-operative as 'the cell of the new society'. There must be a network of such cells 'territorially based and federatively constructed, without dogmatic rigidity, allowing the most diverse social forms to exist side by side, but always aiming at the new organic whole'. And he finds that AE expounded this notion with greater clarity than anyone else in his book *The National Being*. He quotes a passage from this book in which the specialization of co-operative societies is condemned on the grounds that they can develop only economic efficiency. 'The evolution of humanity beyond its present level depends absolutely on its power to unite and create true social organisms.'

I ought to say that I no longer believe that in any Western country such territorially based 'social organisms' can now be constructed out of existing communities. If, when George Russell bicycled round Ireland on his missionary work, the centripetal force of society, the magnetism of megalopolis, had been as great as it is today, possibly even the creamery at Bennettsbridge would not have lasted as long as it did.

Though full of butter and cement and artificial manure, it is for me empty but revered, rather like St Lachtan's Shrine, an arm-shaped reliquary of chased silver, which once, it is supposed, contained the bones of a Kilkenny saint. St Lachtan, I am convinced, no more existed than AE's social organism, and if there were ever bones in his silver arm, they belonged to someone else. All our ideals are composed equally of holiness and self-deception and sometimes downright fraud. We value them for some spark of illumination in them which has not been completely smothered. So, in revering the creamery for something that it is not, I am no more ridiculous than anyone else.

I read *The National Being* when I was eighteen or so and at Oxford and at about the same time I met AE himself and Sir Horace Plunkett, and this threefold experience, allied to my naturally centrifugal tastes, fatally disrupted the Oxford curriculum. I cannot say I regret this. I was very good at Latin verse composition, but I think there is no better way of stamping on Shelley and romance and spontaneity and rebellion, and everything else that I valued, than by translating the 'Adonais' into Lucretian hexameters. A silly vanity allowed me to do this but till twenty years later when I rooted up some box hedges at Maidenhall and re-laid the main drain, Latin verse, like Greek and Roman history, had only burdened me with useless accomplishments which I could not use yet did not like to throw away. I covered the cement kerbs with which I replaced the box with appropriate Latin elegiacs about drains and flowers and wartime gardening.* I would like to have been asked to compose a

Latin or a Greek epitaph for somebody's tombstone, but this has never happened. I do not believe that any other Anglo-Irishman has tried to unpack this extraordinary luggage which we shouldered as children, and, since, unlike our compatriots, we do not say prayers in Latin, we use it for nothing but clues for cross-word puzzles or, with discretion, a snappy tag in a letter to *The Irish Times*. Some people of course become teachers and transfer the luggage and the problem of what to do with it to younger shoulders, but most people, I believe, do not unpack it at all. These ancient rags of learning do not even impress the bystander; they just intimidate and annoy.

There is a great deal else in this vast cabin-trunk, which I took twelve years filling for a voyage on which I never wanted to go, and for which in any case all the sailings have been cancelled. What, for instance, can one do with that thick layer of Greek and Roman history? Classical scholars maintain that by making it a basis for a humanist education, it stimulates general curiosity and establishes the continuity of past and present. It does not, of course. Pisistratus and Hannibal and the Scipios had only a shadowy connection with the social, political and historical shaping of the community in which I live and was reared. All the links are there, of course, but to discover them is not a young man's task. Greeks and Romans stood like spectres blurring the immediate background of those turbulent, interesting years in Ireland. On such a scale our native history dwindled to illegibility and the most scholarly of us were in fact the most historically illiterate. If our education had had any organic relationship with our lives, it would have been back to front. Somewhere far behind Parnell and his agrarian wars one might have groped and found the Gracchi.** One might have learnt Latin, because many of the great figures at the Confederation of Kilkenny, which opposed Cromwell, had used it. Through Latin one might find one's way back to some prototype, hard to relate and interpret, of our own momentous clash of interests and ideals.

[1957]

* *Hic, incaute, tuam dejice furcam./ Fetida sub flores nostra cloaca fluit.* (Here, incautious one, throw away your fork./ Our stinking drain flows under the flowers.)

** Roman tribunes

4

THE BARRIERS

Out of over twenty small states in Europe now, only four, including Ireland, are free and at peace. It is hard, however, to make an Irishman's flesh creep with foreign analogies. Most of the defunct states were British protégés or part-creations, and it is through British channels that news of them comes; it is therefore regarded sceptically here. The Czechs had a far longer history of national independence than the Irish, they had a still living and vigorous language and a very distinctive culture, but their fate did not trouble Ireland deeply. 'It is all British propaganda,' said a prominent Republican at the time of the German Occupation. Still – it is quite possible that of all the small nations which after the war devoted themselves to self-sufficiency, Ireland alone will survive.

Just as our island is physically protected by the sea, there is an ocean of indifference and xenophobia to guard our insularity and to save us from foreign entanglements. Whatever its political value, culturally this self-sufficiency has been and will be a disaster to Ireland as to the other small states. It is a strange time to maintain the theory that a distinctive culture cannot exist without cultural intercourse, but since the mainspring of our freedom was not political theory but the claim that Ireland possessed and could develop a unique culture of her own, it is seasonable to examine this claim. It need not take us long, not longer than a walk down O'Connell Street past the bookshops, the cinemas, the stationers, the theatres, the hotels. By the time we are in Parnell Square we can have no doubt that after twenty years of effort, the culture of Ireland is still overwhelmingly Anglo-Saxon, nakedly or in word-for-word translation. The machinery of the national culture is of the approved (international) model, but the wheels have never once gone round.

If we cross to Europe or even England itself a surprise awaits us; everywhere in books and plays and even in temper of mind we find traces of Irish culture, if we can use that phrase for the influence of Irish exiles. To take the best known, there is not a culture in Europe that has not been radically influenced by Shaw's distinctively Irish habit of mind. I doubt if since Voltaire and the French ascendancy in Europe any national genius has had so wide a range as ours. On a later generation James Joyce has had a more selective but scarcely less widespread influence.

What is the significance of this contrast? It surely is that individual genius is the cement by which a nation is given shape and substance. A nation cannot be created negatively by elimination or strategic retreats into the past. It must crystallize round the contemporary genius that interprets it. The interpreters will be those who can see the national life as well as live it. To acquire this detachment, they will need to have access to other forms of society, so that they can see their own lives objectively and in totality from the threshold, and unless they can obtain from their own country this approach to other civilizations, by spiritual channels or by personal contact, their allegiance either to their country or to their interpretative mission will weaken.

It is not necessary to labour the point that self-sufficiency is in fact insufficient for a national culture. It is a fact, whether or not the explanation I have given is the right one. Great cultures have always risen from the interaction of diverse societies. And where that interaction has been varied, easy and reciprocated, as between the city-states of Greece, or during the Renaissance, national genius has expressed itself most freely. Its flowering period has been briefer and less abundant where it proceeds from a long interbreeding between two peoples, often involuntary and conditioned by geography rather than by mutual attraction.

In the eighteenth century French culture was as dominant in Germany as English culture in Ireland. In both cases the ultimate result was a bitter recoil to self-sufficiency, pedantry, mythology and linguistics.

The problem of a struggling national culture is thus an international one. It can preserve itself only if the spiritual channels by which it can communicate with foreign cultures are kept free and its intercourse is equal and reciprocal. In Ireland intercourse with England only was possible and that could not be on equal terms. Anglo-Irish culture, which should comprehend all literature from Swift to Edgar Wallace in translation, could never become the focus of a nation. The same might be said of the old Austrian civilization, on which the Succession States of Eastern Europe tried to base their new national cultures. It was too strong and powerful to be assimilated. As soon as this was apparent, they dedicated themselves, like Ireland and the new states of the Baltic, to cultural self-sufficiency. Their only contact with each other was through consuls and diplomats, tourists and bagmen, and always in the interests of politics or commerce. There was none of that easy social intercourse by means of which the cultural centres of the Middle Ages were nourished. These little states were formed to protect and foster small cultural units. They failed. Everything that was unique and spontaneous in their national life was smothered behind the barriers reared to protect it.

It is unlikely that these small units will ever be revived in a political shape. A total Anglo-Saxon victory will probably bring some federal solution; a total German victory, a still further disintegration of non-German peoples into small administrative blocs, Bretons, Marcomans, Ukrainians, etc. Whether these federal or linguistic units will possess sufficient unity and freedom to attract to themselves the genius of a national culture or whether that genius will emigrate once more, cannot be predicted. None the less a national culture, since it depends more on individuals than on governments, has a continuity that survives political changes.

It is a big leap from the Czar to Stalin; the passage from Chekhov and Gorki to Zoshchenko, Leonov and Romanov is gradual and easy. Accident, which plays such a large part in the political relations of peoples, where their genius is only lightly engaged, is far less prominent in their cultural intercourse, where the relatively permanent and fundamental is brought into contact.

It would be easier to influence the cultural than the political future of Europe. And if what I say about the necessity for intercourse is true, then it is not premature or absurd to ask where we are to look for the spiritual channels between the peoples.

In the last decade cultural intercourse has loomed very large in the political schemes of the great powers. Russia started with Voks and Intourist and the Society for Cultural Relations. Her example was followed by German Bunde and Kraft durch Freude cruises; by French Institutes and holiday courses; by British lecture tours and university exchanges. Lesser powers like Italy advertised themselves by exhibitions, cheap railway fares and presents to national museums. Was there any reciprocity or spontaneity about this? Scarcely. It was a one-way traffic. Culture was the jam by which the nasty taste of political penetration was disguised. The small states, which were most in need of foreign contacts, had to satisfy themselves with resisting political influence since they could not exert it. Intercourse with their neighbours had a purely commercial bias. It was often startlingly unpolitical. Some Yugoslav journalists who applied for facilities at the Irish Tourist Association are said to have been refused with the reminder that one English city like Liverpool was of more importance to Ireland than the whole continent of Europe.

It was in the most backward and improbable parts of Europe, where cultural isolation was most deeply felt, that lively efforts to combat it on the right lines were made. In Serbia, Croatia, Slovenia and parts of Romania and Bulgaria, life in the provinces is not unlike our own. People are lazy, sociable, individualistic, with a passion for gossip and a deep attachment to their land. They began to solve the problem of international intercourse by welcoming foreign visitors to the small provincial clubs, originally formed for the study of foreign languages. A plan was made to link up some of these clubs in each country in a single scheme, by which they entertained in succession travellers from outside. As their organization became recognized, it began to receive official favours in the form of railway tickets, wireless engagements, visa reductions, while remaining cautiously independent about official patronage. The audiences were small and intimate and the visit was sometimes more like a party than a lecture.

Once an Irish singer came and in the small clubs of Macedonia Irish songs alternated with Serbian ballads. That was not the only contact with Ireland, for the visit was returned some months later by a schoolteacher from Novi Sad, who lectured, travelled and broadcast in Ireland. It was curious how those who were attracted by the scheme, which had no money in it, were seldom mere travellers. Artists, writers, folklore students, professional men, they did not often lack talent or personality.

Soon the spontaneity of the plan was spoiled by the potential implications of English culture round which many of the clubs were built. Big halls were hired to hold big audiences gathered to listen to bigwigs with titles and other recommendations based on public services. The faint smell of power politics pervaded the atmosphere; reciprocity gave place to rivalry, personal exchange to diplomatic courtesies. The scheme changed beyond recognition under official patronage and international snobbery.

There is no reason why it could not be revived in its original form. The smaller peoples must take the lead once more and hold it tenaciously. Round the most ordinary British traveller there hangs an aura of wealth and Waterloo and the British navy, which either antagonizes or enthrals. The traveller from a lesser country, rich in traditions but politically weak, can meet and mix fruitfully on a reciprocal basis, as himself alone. Travellers like these in an unromantic age might take the place of the craftsmen, crusaders or minstrels, who by their wanderings kept alive the spiritual unity of Europe through the Middle Ages, and at the same time enriched the cultural diversity of its provinces.

It was in the eighth century, when she was most closely in touch with Europe, that Ireland enjoyed a native culture of her own. Irishmen had in Christianity a motive for exploring the world. They had a new message, freshness of fervour, a clear field. Ireland is not so fortunate today. Here contact with foreign culture must be organized on more artificial but not less personal lines.

Today we are cut off completely from the outer world, and between north and south, between cities and provinces, the barriers are rising. The war has forced on us a cultural self-sufficiency more complete than the most fervent separatist could have imposed by law. Now that we have seen its dangers, we can fight against them. We must create some social organism to overcome the barriers between ourselves, so that it can extend its scope outside our island when peace returns.

[1941]

5

THE TWO LANGUAGES

It is fortunate that men are as a rule well insulated from each other, that is to say they do not absorb more of each other's sorrows than they can conveniently exude in sympathy and assistance. Now and again, of course, we commit ourselves to a surfeit of fellow-feeling, and compassion that we are forced to inhibit turns to exasperation and dislike. Men protect themselves from such over-indulgence by withdrawing into groups, communities, states, for an aggregation of men exposes a smaller surface of sensibility to outer impressions than does a loose collection of individuals. It is the principle of the potato clamp.

In spite of that we go on expecting that states and governments should show the same susceptibilities as those who compose them. We expect them to be sensitive to appeals to pity and honour and, when they are unresponsive, to exhibit signs of shame. In fact it is only through the fissures in the fabric that such influences travel. A solidly built state will show only a surface reaction. Thucydides is still the best interpreter of the humours and idiosyncrasies of the small community. His chronicle of the Peloponnesian War should convince us that it was only those cities which were divided against themselves, in which there were Laconizing, Medizing or Philathenian parties, to which it was ever worth addressing appeals for help, reminders of past friendships and common causes.

Our Irish state has kept its course through the distractions of war with a composure which the warring peoples, forgetful of former phases of their own collective existence, find neither natural nor decent. Is it the indifference of the untroubled, undivided community? Hardly. I think it masks a deep suspense. Of the dozen states which were created from fragments of empires a score of years ago (Russian, German, British, Turkish, French, Dutch), ours alone is intact. The others were told that they had never existed, they had been amputated, not born. Those who sponsored their liberation could not save them from extinction. The same arguments have been heard in Ireland for centuries. Unuttered, they are no less formidable than before. We are deeply uncertain of ourselves, less frightened of what we might be made to suffer than of what we might be made to think. With one or two exceptions, those other states (Czechoslovakia, Yugoslavia, where there was a German minority) were destroyed more by schizophrenia than by violence. Therefore we welcome every sign of solidarity and are proud that the cleavages in our state have not gone so deep as to violate its integrity. Control has not passed from the body to its members. The sympathies of the citizens have been warmly dictated by those impersonal laws which regulate the intercourse of all small communities.

What proof have we that such laws exist? The small modern state is overgrown and artificial, and much further removed from the realities of human nature than were the city-states of Thucydides. All the same, as if in a discoloured mirror, it reflects something of the natural forms and phases of human association. In its struggles and factions and epic catastrophes, a recurrent, inevitable pattern is traceable. The evidence of such affinities is, however, unwelcome. Small modern states resent the imputation that their destiny is dominated by their social structure rather than by those distinctive racial qualities from which they derive their right to be free. Their claims to be unique have been recognized so that their behaviour, in time of war, has become the subject of moral judgments rather than of sociological analysis. They are credited with the same good and evil qualities which we distribute among their citizens. But surely, from the moment they were created, they were as different from the component individuals as is a crystal or a molecule from the atoms out of which, in elaborately formal arrangement, it is combined. Men do not pool their qualities in a community like flavours in a pudding. Association truly changes them, thaws the queer shapes into which the individual is cast, disperses the film of idiosyncrasy with which he protects himself. The whole is not the sum of the parts. The moral laws which develop out of the intercourse of persons have, therefore, no authority over the intercourse of communities.

Only an accident of geography preserved our state from the fate of the other eleven, and there is evidence enough that in our position they would not have acted differently. Men as individuals can be chivalrous, generous, impressionable, but a community of men can accept no obligation that threatens its existence. At the first sound of war we have seen the small modern state abjure all the enlightened sympathies of its citizens, contracting into a tight ball like a hedgehog at the bark of a dog, seeing nothing, hearing nothing, smelling nothing. At such a moment a hedgehog cannot think of other hedgehogs. It cannot permit itself a single twitch of curiosity or compassion.

How is it that, while the state is so circumspect in all its movements, many thousands of its citizens have been able to betray their sympathies in action? I think it is because we have always been realists about our state, however many delusions we have had about the Irish nation. We have grown up with it and never thought of it as transcending common experience or giving more than a vague and precarious expression to that corporate existence of which we believe ourselves capable. We have never made it the guardian of our social conscience or expected it to speak prematurely with the voice of the National Being.

In this we are unlike older countries and easily misunderstood by them. When someone says, 'Slums are a disgrace to England,' 'The loss of Alsace-Lorraine is a wound in the side of France,' even the most matter-of-fact can see for a moment a bowed monumental figure symbolizing a bad conscience, a sunk ship, an unflinching resolve. If free Ireland had been born at the same time as Belgium or even Norway, we should have some such substantial, rather domineering phantom to blush for us, grieve for us, expect us to do our duty, confuse us in fact into thinking that the solidarity we aim at is moral rather than biological. But there is none.

The Ireland for which men died, even when as Cathleen ni Houlihan she took a human shape for them, was aloof and indifferent, demanding but not preaching. She was a projection of their yearnings and frustrations, not of their designs for a social order. In the favourable air of the Victorian age, when social consciences were crystallizing, Ireland was not yet a sovereign state. So our internal affairs are very little influenced by abstract and humane ideas. Our politics are highly personal. We blame people and we praise people. Our slums are not a disgrace to Ireland but to Mr So-and-so who owns them, and he is made to feel this just in so far as pity for the poor, an elusive abstract thing, can overcome our concrete liking and respect for Mr So-and-so. That is how things work and it might be worse. The throne from which the National Being might speak is empty but at least it has never been profaned.

Because of that it is only as individuals, as free elements on the surface of our state, that we respond to the moral climate of the world. That this response is active enough few would deny. Not many small states have so deep a zone of free elements: people, that is to say, whose attachment to our state is so loose as to be precarious, who are at any moment more accessible to influences from outside than to those within. If these outer influences were to penetrate deeper, the nuclear solidarity of our state would be dissolved, as a state we should cease to exist. It does survive, because, as in all agricultural communities, there is an ultimate impermeable core of obtuseness and self-sufficiency, which is at once our shame and our salvation.

This is the explanation why many Irishmen feel profoundly and personally implicated in the moral problems of Europe and at the same time are passionate supporters of Irish neutrality. Wireless sets, newspapers, tell them of free nations like their own being destroyed, of men being bullied and tortured, of free minds being enslaved, but they feel that it is they themselves and not their nation who are being addressed. They do not wish their neighbour across the hill to be coerced into feeling this shame or into pretending to feel it. For such feelings are the price that is paid for a range of interest and sympathy wider than his. They stand on the periphery of their nation, he at the core. Their hearts are not warmer than his, merely the warmth ranges outwards and not inwards and is more widely diffused. When he goes to England for a job in the building trade and later dies in Cyrenaica, they feel that it was through the flaws, the wormholes in their state that the challenge to which he responded reached him. In such a way a Czech or a Croat peasant, released from the claims of his state by its disintegration, might easily enough be recruited for a remote crusade in Russia. By their natures such men are fitted to play a creative part only at the heart of their community; drawn outside it, they become passive elements, equally serviceable for good or evil ends. The community to which they belonged suffers by their defection, for all the warmth of their natures was needed to preserve its cohesion and integrity. It is only when its integrity is guaranteed that the community has a life of its own and, through the men of the periphery, radiates an influence greater than the sum of their individual contributions.

Modern states correspond only roughly to the natural organic community, and in them men seldom play the part for which they are fitted by nature. All the same, in any society which lays claim to organic unity, we must expect to find this impermeable core. Those who compose it are as a rule inarticulate or express themselves in reach-me-down language a size too big for their thoughts. If they could speak naturally, as the Greeks did, and censorship of thought played as small a part as at Athens, I think they would talk about the war as did the farmers and charcoal-burners of Aristophanes. The peasants of Attica had suffered unspeakably, their olive trees had been cut down, their farms and vineyards destroyed by the Spartans. They were not pacifists or anti-anybody or anything, for that suggests the power to think about the war abstractly. They just wanted peace. It is clear that you could not make idealists of such people any more than you could transplant carrots. Here is Trygaeus, the vine-dresser, appealing to the goddess Peace:

> We have been praying to you for thirteen years. Do now put away battles and tumults! Put a stop to our suspicions of each other and our tale-bearing! Blend us Greeks as before with the balsam of friendship and temper our minds with a milder fellow-feeling. Grant that our market be filled with all manner of good things, with garlic, early cucumbers, apples, pomegranates and little cloaks for slaves, and that we may see people bringing from the Boeotians geese, ducks, wood-pigeons and sandpipers and let baskets of eels come from Lake Copais!

The Peloponnesian War dragged on for twelve years, waged by men who saw far beyond the horizon of the peasants, men of high ideals and brilliant attainments, who expected far more of life than eels and sandpipers. Thucydides put speeches into their mouths in which they balanced remote probabilities, estimated the claims of honour, loyalty, friendship, justice. In contrast to Trygaeus, they were typical men of the periphery, pursuing remote sympathies so far that often they lost touch with their base – like Alcibiades and Themistocles, betraying their countries in the interests of oligarchy or pan-Hellenism or mere ambition, whose lofty scale robbed it of vulgarity. The war ended in total ruin and the ultimate subjection of Hellas to Macedon. Is the moral that the Trygaeuses should be the arbiters of war and peace? No, the moral is that there is an outer and an inner language talked in every state and if no one is coerced into talking a language other than his own, the life of a community will be preserved even when its material existence is threatened.

This, like all social generalizations, seems far too simple and also far too elaborate. But societies as they grow seek to fill out the patterns we suggest to them. The feudal system must have become more like a pyramid the more it was interpreted as a pyramid. Today society is dominated by a subtler, truer conception of itself as an organic system of separate parts which grow, contact, coalesce and disintegrate again according as some vital force ebbs and flows in one direction or another. Men associate in 'cells' or, in Russian, in 'little eggs'. We remind ourselves how we submerge our personalities in groups, reassert ourselves as individuals, claim for ourselves the qualified autonomy of the highly differentiated cell. We are struggling to use these ideas for our happiness and every time we apply them we have to act the part of creators as well as interpreters.

We must therefore apply, as well as accept, the idea that groups of men – states or nations or whatever association claims for itself a conscious solidarity – communicate with each other by means of their surface elements and that if the surface is too deeply penetrated the group's integrity is undermined. In time of war the natural social processes are reversed and the group contracts upon itself, the feelers with which it explored the world becoming bristles for repelling it, but war cannot last for ever and soon the natural processes are resumed. In the peace which follows the war the conditions will be as strange and difficult; the sudden relaxation of tension, the expansiveness and quick renewal of contacts, may be as fatal to the integrity of the small state as war itself. Racial affinities are rarely powerful enough to hold men together in the face of opportunities and enterprises which the convulsions of war make accessible. Many communities have been exterminated by violence, but more have perished by outgrowing their strength, responding too readily to the seductions of the world outside. Apart from smaller peoples, what became of the Normans, the Goths, the

Gauls, all of them conquerors or favoured by their conquerors?

In so far as a nation has developed an organic life of its own, the impact of the outside world will be met and answered upon the periphery. The energies of the greater part will not be deflected from their true function, which is to maintain the strength and solidarity of the nation. It is only when that solidarity exists that the men of the periphery will represent more than themselves and become in a true sense the interpreters of the National Being.

History, which respects above everything political unity, has done less than justice to that queer unpolitical cohesion which enabled the minor peoples of Europe to resist assimilation. For generations prudence has obliged them to avoid the overt mechanical forms of association and to develop an interdependence that is warm, personal and clandestine. One day men will move away from political combinations towards more organic forms of association. When that happens there will be more understanding for those who, like the Irish and the Czechs, learnt for long years to keep their communities alive without political sanctions.

Will our nation be dispersed before it is resurrected to organic life? The pious have collected the bones, the wise can reassemble them; but that process of nature which can clothe them with flesh is not yet at our command.

[1943]

Airton House,
Tallaght,
Co. Dublin.

November 27th, 1943.

Dear Hubert,

Sean sent me your TWO LANGUAGES article. It's probably too deep for me, and for any ordinary reader I'm sure it wants expanding. I'm afraid I have marked your MS in red pencil for my own convenience; I hope it will rub out, but I haven't got a rubber! I don't know if you want my opinion, but for what it is worth here it is.

The whole article stimulates my interest and imagination, but it does *not* illuminate my understanding. It's rather as the eye may be directed to an aspect of the landscape by a shadow falling on it! You doubtless know your stuff, but the uninstructed (like myself) need to be soothed with FACTS. Some of these you could give without adding much in the way of words – e.g. the names of the twelve states referred to at top of page 2 [p. 37], and the names of the two exceptions later on the same page. And you ought to have a foot-note to say that 'Students of Political History will not be perturbed by the apparent anomaly of such states as Switzerland, Belgium, and those of the Scandinavian and Iberian peninsulas'. I am not a Student of Political History, and I should need that much reassurance. On the same page [38], I don't understand the passage from 'Control' to 'communities'; it needs expanding and linking to its context. Further on you say 'What proof have we . . . ?' and you don't anywhere fulfil the implied promise. Again, one wants examples of *modern* states being removed from the realities of *human* nature (from the nature of the primitive 'state'?). At the top of page 3 [38] you speak as though morality were wrongly attributed to the State, but on page 4 [39] you speak of a 'social conscience'. At the bottom of that page you suggest that we are 'realists' about our state, but at the bottom of the previous page you have suggested that small states (with no hint of exception) tend to be 'romantic' about themselves. On page 3 [39] you suggest that we have been saved by 'geographical accident', but on page 2 [38] you suggest that we have been saved because certain 'cleavages' have not gone deep enough. These may be contingent facts, if so, they might be stated contiguously? Top of page 5 [40] – there seems to be some confusion between the 'individual' who is accessible to outside influences and the 'state' into which they might penetrate. Further down the page you seem to assume that your chap who is not open to these outside influences is the one who is most likely to get himself killed in Cyrenaica – but *is* he? Why? On page 6 [41], the opinions of the peasant Trygaeus seem to me identical with most informed Pacifist opinion of today – to be oddly enlightened, in fact. Page 7 [42], what is the difference between the 'life' of a community and its 'material *existence*'? Page 8 [42] – 'social consciousness' (like 'social conscience') implies a very advanced organism. Something of the sort, having a 'race-memory', seems to be needed by Freud and Jung, but it's pure myth, surely? Your thesis rather depends on this, but you don't demonstrate it, and if there is a 'social organism' (other than those of the Hymenoptera) it has only been demonstrated as something at a very low level – certainly not as having reached consciousness? Further down the page you talk of war and peace conditions in a confusing way (to me). On page 9 [43] you say 'only when solidarity exists, etc.', implying that it does not yet exist (here?), but on page 5 [40] you have attributed to us an 'impermeable core of self-sufficiency'.

My criticisms may be due to my stupidity, but they could be got over by expansion and FACTS – at least I hope so!

Love,
Geoffrey.

Maiden Hall,
Bennettsbridge.

December 8.

Dear Geoffrey,
I was awfully pleased that you took so much trouble with my article. It is easier to be vaguely polite and non-committal when no contact is made, so I was very grateful for your extremely intelligent comments and even disposed to accept the truth of about 15 per cent of them. With your knowledge of writers you'll admit that is pretty handsome of me.

It's difficult, without a better technique than I possess at present, to put an idea across and to work on it at the same time, and in the article I sent I was thinking mostly of putting it across. Though you'll be sceptical of this, I *am* able to pick my way through all those confusing synonyms, and they didn't confuse *me*. In fact as I felt fairly certain where I wanted to get, and there wasn't much space, my idea was to hustle the reader (for his own good) past all the forks and turns and *not* picnic at each cross-roads and take him into my confidence. That would have been a different kind of a journey. I was quite ready to make it, but not in that article. I think you are the wrong sort of reader for me as obviously before one submits to be hustled by someone else and agrees to suspend a certain kind of criticism (some sort of suspension accompanies all reading), one must want to arrive at the same place as the writer does, and you probably don't. I have a picture of the sort of society I would like, so have you; if either of us could describe it we should be almighty geniuses. As it is we can only poke about hopefully among analogies and parallels and be rather pleased when the same one takes our fancy. Because of this I didn't feel reproached by your suggestion that I was indicating a point on the landscape by casting a shadow on it. Better that way than none. I usually find indirect methods the best and have sympathy with the man who gave his son a good slap so that he would remember having seen a salamander.

Inevitably the terms one uses are fluid. To take an example of possible confusion which you did not mention, I have used words like 'group', 'community', 'society', etc., with very little effort to distinguish between them. In fact I avoided too much precision as I feel it is premature to be precise about sociology. Inevitably all the terms one uses have a different aura for all of us. What, for instance, is an Irishman or a Czech? Clearly what is written in his passport (and that is what would chiefly concern many sociologists) has nothing to do with it. I myself made several Irishmen like that out of Viennese Jews.

I don't know whether you are right in wanting more 'facts'. Historical facts have that gritty, substantial feel about them only in the examination schools and their too-extensive purlieus. I discard them as building material because they are really too plastic to use except as ornament. For example, in a small state like Yugoslavia you could get a purely factual account of its creation from a dozen representative citizens, Croat, Bosnian, Slovene, Macedonian, etc., or from representatives of the various economic and religious cross-sections, and each would give a different but quite truthful picture. When Yugoslavia comes to be reorganized, facts will be so cogent and clamorous and innumerable that they will be used just as seasonings to the theoretic puddings made by the powers. Subjective considerations will weigh the most, shaped by the views of society current at the time. In 1918 the pundits of the moment, Seton-Watson, Pares, Miss Durham and others, felt queer atavistic attractions towards primitive forms of society, and were able to ignore the irresistibly dominant Austrian culture. I feel the same attraction and so have only sympathy for this astounding *tour de force*, but it is due to mental gymnastics and has nothing to do with the facts. Ireland, as a state, is the same sort of intellectual concoction, emanating probably in part, like Yugoslavia, from Anglo-Saxon brains. There are such things as real human societies, in *posse* if not in *esse*, but they are masked by these political figments, not revealed.

I left out Belgium, Holland, Spain, etc., quite deliberately. I ought to have explained that I was collating only those Succession States which were formed at the same time (1918-21), and under the influence of much the same ideas. I don't think it is remembered now to what an extent they were created in the brains or the bile of Professor So-and-so. I counted a dozen because I felt that committed me less to precision than eleven, but I can, if forced, count a dozen, with many tedious qualifications, e.g. Finland was less a creation than Lithuania.

The gist of my article was the extraordinary similarity of their reactions to similar stresses, which could not be explained *only* by their birthdays, their common origins in the professors' brain-pans and other contingent facts. I believe there must be some constant factors in all human associations, some rules of growth in the human community similar to those in our bodies. If they existed once in the primitive community, what became of them? Herbert Spencer ran the organic analogy to death for his contemporaries, but I believe it could profitably be restated for ours. If I groped, it was not for facts. In fact I conscientiously sieved out a page or two as I feared it would make the article still more indigestible.

Your comments were really helpful and showed me why I failed to explain myself. What was nicer was that I felt the defects you found were fairly remediable.

Love,
Hubert.

P.S. I ought to take one of the passages you complain of and see if I can prove that I had a meaning which can be conveyed. Peggy, too, finds my views on Trygaeus obscure so I shall take him.

Trygaeus is a normal element in most states. He likes peace but defended himself bravely against the Spartans, who interrupted the routine of his life. He isn't in the least, as you say, an 'enlightened pacifist'. He has no philosophy (an enlightened pacifist surely believes in pacifying, not just in being peaceful). In fact he only starts to function when and where there is discord. Otherwise he would be a quietist or something of that kind, if, as Trygaeus doesn't, he *wanted* an 'ism'.

Put such a Trygaeus in an average small state, say Czechoslovakia. Though he is a pious Catholic, it is most improbable that while that state is intact he would ever have had the inclination, apart from the opportunity, of going on a crusade against the Bolshevik Antichrist. A few enlightened Catholics might, and did, but not he. But later on the whole state collapsed and these influences penetrated quite easily to him. They started to take effect on him. Even if they had always filtered through to him in the form of newspaper propaganda, his faith in his immediate surroundings and the demands they made on him gave him a kind of immunity to them. But now he is recruited without difficulty for this religious crusade. Thousands like him have gone off not too reluctantly to the eastern front. I expect he thinks it rather fine and perfectly in line with what he has always been taught. All the same the fact that he is accessible to such a stimulating idea proved that something had gone wrong with the state. Similarly, I said that when our Trygaeuses in Ireland respond, as they do, to the 'appeal of the allied nations etc.', something is wrong with *their* state. The section of the community to which they belong would not show any strong reaction to such external stimulus if the fabric of the community was in perfect condition. It's like an orange: the weather only ripens it when it meets the outside alone, but rots it when it gets inside through a crack.

I am constantly struck by the way that many ordinary Irishmen with strong healthy roots here can say about foreign events, 'Oh, how bad! Oh, how sad!' and be receptive to newspaper propaganda about the war, but yet feel emotionally quite uninvolved. This seems to me, for their type, normal, and quite *abnormal* when the propaganda really strikes home. This in my experience happens first with those Trygaeuses who, for one reason or another, already stand in a bad relation to the community.

Probably I tried to telescope this up far too much. If I was to improve the article as an article (I mean make it readable for the ordinary reader) I could only afford to expand it there, if I eliminated here.

You are probably confused by my habit of not explaining when I am referring to a 'social organism' that really exists, and when it is a purely imaginary ideal of perfection. I don't see why one can't use the idea fairly loosely. After all one says that somebody has a triangular table or even face, and yet one knows there is no such thing as a triangle and never could be, since by definition it is composed of lines without breadth. In a short article one wishes to escape stating all one's axioms. Maybe one can't.

Endnote This unpublished essay is accompanied by the intellectual exchanges of magazine editor (Geoffrey Taylor, literary editor of Sean O'Faolain's *The Bell*) and author – the one pleading for clarification, the other giving a brilliant and sustained defence of his ideas and their expression, refusing to 'picnic at each cross-roads'. In sum, they form a fascinating commentary on the original (matter in parenthesis has been added in concession to Taylor's queries) as well as giving an insight to the thought processes of a writer-at-work as he seeks to articulate the moral and communal notion of self, or the identity of that creature called man – or Irishman, or German, etc. – in the midst of a world war in which Ireland played no formal part. (*Ed.*)

THE COUNTY LIBRARIES: SEX, RELIGION, AND CENSORSHIP

In 1948 the old controversy about censorship revived in *The Irish Times*. The majority of the writers disapproved but there was a sharp difference as to who was to blame for it. Sean O'Faolain traced it to the obscurantism and philistinism of the government, an anonymous writer traced it to the Church.

Almost at the same time I read a letter in a local paper, signed 'Harassed Librarian'. He complained that there was not half enough censorship and that 15 per cent of the books he circulated were what he called 'questionable vintage'. He suggested that it would be a fine task for a band of young idealists to get together and form a voluntary censorship group. I found this a horrifying letter, yet I have some sympathy with 'Harassed Librarian' for I was a County Librarian in Ireland myself twenty years before. I can guess who is harassing him and how little help he is getting in dealing with them. The pressure towards censorship does not principally come, as Sean O'Faolain and his adversaries think, from either Church or State. It is entirely democratic and comes from the people. It is closely connected with education and book distribution and social organization, and till the cause has been accurately diagnosed the cure cannot be found.

I believe that it is largely the spread of free libraries that has made the censorship important. The private purchaser can always elude the censor, his pride may be humbled by what many feel to be an insult to his intelligence and good sense, but his reading matter is not seriously curtailed. It is round the libraries that the conflict rages hottest. Therefore it is worth taking a look at the libraries.

The County Library which I was organizing was in Northern

Ireland. I am not by birth or inclination a townsman and this seemed to me at the time the most congenial and useful work which I could do in my own country. I did not have the fashionable horror of 'uplift' and though I knew that a great many Irishmen considered Sir Horace Plunkett a Big Bore with his manifold schemes for raising the cultural level of the countryside, I revered him. Plunkett and AE and their associates were at the centre of this movement to bring self-education within reach of those who were too poor or too far away to reach it in the normal way. The library was to be the intellectual centre of the village, as the creamery was to be its economic centre. By means of books the animosities that arose from race and religion and class were to be dissolved.

It wasn't until 1946 that I realized that none of this was going to happen. That in fact something almost precisely opposite has happened is revealed by 'Harassed Librarian's' letter. What went wrong? The plan seemed reasonable enough. In each county there were to be two thousand carefully chosen books, a young man or woman who liked books, a select committee and a money grant. From all this in two years time (that was the period of incubation allowed by the Carnegie Trust), a new and independent organism would develop, acting like yeast upon our stodgy provincial society. A good idea, but in Ireland it was unfamiliar and no one was ready for it. Except in a favourable environment, books are not automatically active like yeast or even serviceable like tools. They are just books and books in Ireland are popularly regarded as mere commodities. The librarian found himself looked on as a tradesman retailing groceries and depending on the goodwill of his customers. Horace Plunkett was to recognize this himself, when he finally decided to transfer the magnificent co-operative library from Dublin to Doughty Street, London; in Ireland he found it was chiefly used by some Japanese students who happened to be studying at Trinity.

In the country the first librarians tried to be something more than the mere distributors of printed matter. Some organized literary competitions through the schools, some arranged lectures. Robert Wilson in Sligo took gramophone records round the country districts and gathered small groups of music-lovers. Yet these efforts got very little encouragement from the committees and the Central Organizing Council became involved in a squabble reminiscent of the censorship squabbles of today.

Here is the story as it is told in Lady Gregory's diary, which was edited (rather magnanimously because she disliked him) by Lennox Robinson. Calamity befell us because of sex and religion. In 1924 Lennox Robinson published a story called 'The Madonna of Slieve Dun' in *To-morrow*, a new periodical edited by a fine Irish novelist, Francis Stuart. It was about a peasant girl who had been raped and who thought she would give birth to another Saviour. It seems a familiar theme, and surely after tragedy girls have often dreamt of supernatural compensations. But it shocked Father Finlay and he sent in his resignation to the Advisory Committee, and Cosgrave, the head of the government, even thought of suppressing *To-morrow* because the rumour went about that Robinson was trying to pervert the nation to a new conception of the origin of Christianity.

Lady Gregory had not seen *To-morrow* or the story, but she thought them 'mischievous and unnecessary' and likely to damage both the Abbey Theatre and the County Libraries. She told Yeats that Lennox Robinson was setting fire to his neighbour's house in order to roast his own pig. Yeats himself had written a poem called 'Leda and the Swan' for *To-morrow*, which some might have thought offensive, and told Lady Gregory that it would be scandalous if Robinson were forced to resign. There were many private discussions before the committee meeting. The President of the Hibernian Academy pacifically suggested that Robinson, who had much else to do, might be ready to resign from pressure of work and that would be a wonderful idea. But Mrs Yeats repudiated this notion. The Provost of Trinity College, Dublin, it was learnt, was outraged by Robinson's story and also by Yeats's poem and even more by a story which proved to have been written by the wife of the professor of history at Trinity: 'One must speak plainly – it is about the intercourse of white women with black men.'* As for AE, he was torn with doubt and misgivings. He was the least sexy of writers, and Lennox's story and also *To-morrow* itself had offended him deeply. If he was to have a fight with the Protestant and the Catholic Churches, which would no doubt stand behind Dr Bernard and Father Finlay, he would prefer that it should be on some better grounds. Yeats and McGreevy approached him

* 'Colour' by Margaret Barrington; married to Edmund Curtis at the time, in 1926 she married Liam O'Flaherty.

urging him to stand firm against the Jesuit and the Provost; angry words were exchanged and Yeats came back to Lady Gregory dispirited and rather ashamed.

The following day Lady Gregory went to the Carnegie meeting with AE and listened to the Provost reading aloud Father Finlay's letter of resignation. (It was so astonishing that she asked for a copy.) With some surprise the Committee learnt that the Provost had written without consultation to the Carnegie Trust in Dunfermline and that the Trust replied that it would take no action till the Committee had given its views. Lady Gregory took her stand for Robinson, but only Thomas O'Donnell, an Irish-speaking Catholic from Kerry, defended the story. He said he had read it aloud to his two pious sisters 'and they thought it a beautiful story'. The Provost listened to this with polite surprise. Finally, with AE horribly confused and wavering, they agreed to send a letter to Father Finlay begging him to reconsider his resignation and deploring the article. It was passed by one vote. 'Let us amend it to "deploring the publication of the article",' suggested Lady Gregory. 'After all it is no concern of ours what our secretary writes.' The amendment was carried with AE still in an anguish of indecision.

In the meantime Cosgrave was anxious to have *To-morrow* prosecuted but the Minister of Justice, Kevin O'Higgins, a man of striking intelligence, refused, saying: 'The prosecution would merely represent the moral attitude of certain people, at a certain place and a certain time.'

The apologists for *To-morrow* explained that the next issue of the paper was to contain an article in favour of handing over all the Protestant cathedrals to the Catholics. 'That will puzzle them!' commented Lady Gregory.

A month later another Carnegie meeting was held to consider a letter from the Provost, for he too had now resigned. He had privately told a member of the Committee that when a clergyman of the Christian Church took the view Father Finlay had done he felt he must 'go with him and see eye to eye with him'. 'If the Provost intends to see eye to eye with the Catholic Church,' said Lady Gregory, 'he is not a Protestant,' and the Committee burst out laughing.

Then Mr Wilkinson, the librarian from Cork, said, 'It doesn't matter if both the clerics leave the board . . . the people want the books and will have them.' To prove his point he showed her the statistics from Cork. But Lady Gregory found them very depressing, for Cork read mainly bad silly novels. 'Why', she asked, 'should we supply them with Ethel Dell? They can always buy that kind of thing in the little cheap editions and do so. They read history too, and that is what we should encourage.'

That was the last meeting of the Committee. By their disputes about sex and their competitive pieties and purities and their irrelevant arguments, they abolished themselves and destroyed the bright hopes of the libraries. A month later a letter came from Lennox Robinson:

> The Carnegie situation has resolved itself into the suspension of the Committee and my dismissal. It's a complete victory for the obscurantists but only a temporary one, I think, as even within the last ten days the County Councils of Clare, Cork and Monaghan have passed resolutions asking for county schemes so the work will go on. I am awfully sorry that all your work at that horrible meeting in October has resulted only in this. I blame people like Dermod O'Brien, who were for placating the Church at any price – as Tom O'Donnell says, 'the most priest-ridden people in Ireland are the ex-Unionists'.

Actually the victory of the obscurantists and ignoramuses was final, though the libraries did go on. But Lennox Robinson, rereading his remarks twenty years later, was pleased that he had said so courageously 'the libraries will go on', and justified himself thus: 'In 1935, the last year I have figures for, the number of books issued in country places was two million nine hundred and twenty-four thousand.'

The first County Library Committees were in most cases better than their successors, yet they were a handicap rather than an assistance to the librarian. They recognized that books were more like tools than groceries but they still regarded them as dangerous tools. The crisis in Dublin confirmed them in this attitude: libraries were doubtful blessings. At the end of the two years' probation, many County Councils agreed to continue the library only by a minute majority.

The committee members in Coleraine, the northern town where I was County Librarian, paid occasional visits of inspection. I only remember one of them getting a book out himself. From the beginning they plainly thought it was their mission to supervise reading rather than to read themselves. My impression is that some, to whom the idea of 'free books' was still a novel one, felt that they would lose caste by borrowing them. It was not only the more illiterate committee members who felt like that; I remember an imperious Mr Ingram who prowled round our library, snapping the books in and out of the shelves and fluttering through them suspiciously. I knew he was searching for some kind of contamination but was puzzled why he examined the general rather than the fiction. At last his eye caught the long green row of the Irish Texts Society. He snorted angrily and said that he strongly objected as a ratepayer to supporting political propaganda from Dublin. I learnt later that his father, John Kells Ingram, had written 'Who fears to speak of Ninety-eight?' Then there was a Mr and Mrs McWhitty, a Presbyterian farmer and his wife, who used to come to the library on fair-days, bearing books which they wanted withdrawn immediately from circulation and looking at us reproachfully. My colleague had a special way of dealing with them. He used to keep ready for them three or four books of doubtful propriety, which he asked them to report on. They went away flattered and self-important. In the North at that time the most censorious in regard to morals as well as politics in literature were Presbyterians, but I believe the wish to decide what other people should read is a matter of temperament rather than denomination. How pleasant it was when once in a while – but how rarely! – somebody came in who saw the possibilities of building up a play-library for the local dramatic company or of assisting local history or natural science, who looked at the library not as a dangerous ammunition dump or a way of escape from his surroundings, but as an instrument for interpreting them and enlivening them.

It was a misfortune too, perhaps, that these first literary librarians looked at books from the standpoint of the creative writer rather than the scholar. The imaginative writer, particularly when he is young, is individualist to the point of anarchy. Books can be a stimulus to his creative work, but they are not essential to it. Perhaps as a legacy from their school-days, where the imaginative writer usually comes off second-best, they retained a slight horror of serried ranks of informative books. Lennox Robinson, our chief organizing librarian, was in the habit of saying to us: 'I loathe a lot of books all in a row.' I found this understandable but I wondered why he had mixed himself up with the libraries. His scepticism was shared by some of his colleagues, and those of us who believed in the County Libraries began to feel we must be rather naïve priggish people.

At least, however, the organizers had their eyes open for talent and were not interested in those fantastic things 'Library Certificates'. (The technical business of running a County Library is simple and any educated person can quickly master it.) As a result, several gifted Irishmen, who would otherwise have looked for work abroad, found it for a few years at home. They were mostly 'writers' rather than scholars. Scholars, those who read books for knowledge rather than inspiration, would have made better librarians perhaps. Yet scholars are usually urged on inexorably by examinations to a career. It is not easy for them to take on work merely because it is interesting, full of promise and appears to need doing. A 'writer' is not so securely lashed to the conventions. Five or six of those early librarians were of outstanding ability, but their enthusiasm was soon quenched by the indifference of the Committee and the preoccupation of the Central Body. Irish writers have often acquired a warped, rather cynical disposition and I think some came to take a malicious pleasure in dispatching to the countryside the bales of bunkum which were asked for.

Only a strong lead from Dublin could have mended matters, but it never came. As a result of the squabble about the story, the Central Committee in Dublin was abolished and the headquarters of the Irish County Libraries transferred to Dunfermline. This was a characteristically cowardly retreat. From then on each librarian had to battle on his own with his committee and no help or encouragement came from outside. Worse than that, when the Dublin Central Body went, the last cultural bridge between the Twenty-six Counties and the Six was broken down. There had never been much traffic on that bridge, but at least it had existed. At the worst those twelve volumes of the Irish Texts has passed across it to the northern libraries. The first collection of two thousand books with which each library North and South was equipped had been admirably selected. The hope that a central co-ordinating administration might watch over further growth had now to be abandoned. Each library grew haphazard on its own.

The fact that the cause of the dispute had been a story by a well-known writer seemed to throw the whole writing fraternity under a cloud. But possibly there has always been a deep distrust of the writer in the library profession. Books, like the children of fallen women, should in the opinion of many be removed from the control of their author as soon as possible. The ideal librarian is a sterile and conscientious professional with a library certificate. Only very rarely does a writer find his way nowadays even onto a library committee.

The first committees were chosen with great striving for impartiality. There were Protestant clergy, Catholic clergy, Presbyterian clergy and representatives of various regions and professions. In fact they represented every conceivable sectional interest, except an interest in books for their own sake. The idea prevailed that books were very dangerous indeed and might be used for political or religious proselytism and the committee members at first attended regularly in order to watch and checkmate each other. The sectarian and political section in our northern library was scrutinized suspiciously by the committee members but scarcely anyone took books from it. It would be nice to be able to say that there was a run on the Irish Texts, which Mr Ingram considered political literature, but he was almost the last visitor to handle them with interest, and I expect that today the volumes of the Ulster Saga are as bright and clean in that Ulster town as when I left them in the mid-twenties. The committee members successfully stymied each other. In their heart they probably believed that no thinking was better than wrong thinking. When the proposal that the library should be taken over from the Carnegie Trust was brought up before the County Council the leading committee members, who were on it, wired their regrets. It was passed in their absence, but they continued to attend committee meetings till they had assured themselves that the County Libraries were not likely to stimulate thought of any kind. Then they gave up. I do not remember a single interested or helpful suggestion from one of them.

In the South the Anglo-Irish soon lost interest in the libraries. The Civil War had reduced their numbers but I think that their withdrawal from cultural activities in the countryside had other causes too. The First World War had drawn their interests further from Ireland which seemed to most of them small and unimportant as well as unwelcoming. They had come to think that a larger stage was necessary for their talents and only a discerning minority was aware that the world in which the individual could play an effective part was contracting rather than expanding. Such influence as they still retained in Ireland, they lacked the patience or the courage to exert.

What have the Anglo-Irish to do with censorship and libraries? A good deal. We have reached in Ireland the nadir of Anglo-Saxon civilization and, whereas the majority has dissociated itself, in theory at least, from that civilization and cannot logically deplore its decline, the Anglo-Irish cannot be indifferent. What they see is not a displacement of Anglo-Saxon culture – it was never so strong and irresistible as now – but a progressive and appalling vulgarization.

The fate that has overtaken the County Libraries is symbolic, a shelf of untouched Irish Texts and several tons of what 'Harassed Librarian' calls 'doubtful vintage' from England. English literature in Ireland is shameless and furtive like a neglected child. Nobody will take responsibility for it and as a result it keeps bad company. Our County Libraries have facilitated rather than impeded the commercial exploitation of literature. They are doing for the arts of knowledge and literary craftsmanship just what the commercial cinema is doing for the visual arts and the holiday camps are doing for the social arts, though these last are not heavily subsidized by the community. A flood of imported Anglo-Saxon vulgarity is pouring irresistibly into a vacuum. This vacuum is one of the least creditable achievements of the Irish Revival. No doubt some resistance had to be made to the encroachments of English civilization if a native one were to struggle into being. But the most effective resistance has always come from those who respected English civilization sufficiently to criticize it, who could detect the shoddy because they loved the good. We owe our libraries with their 'questionable vintage' and also indirectly our censorship, not to these discriminating critics of English literature, but to the fanatics to whom all modern English literature, from E. M. Forster to E. M. Hull, is equally reprehensible.

I have found an old County Library catalogue from the library to which 'Harassed Librarian' succeeded. Its date is 1936 and no present librarian or library committee can be blamed for it. It must be typical of many. I cannot decide how the nasty thing happened. Does it reflect the brainlessness of the library committee, the taste of the country districts or the indifference of the librarian? I believe my simile of the vacuum is the right one. The Irish attitude to the libraries has always been negative. Committees and censors, readers and librarians, have all set to, purging and sweeping, and have produced a mental emptiness by which more cynical people have profited. Only the bookseller has had a positive attitude, and who can blame him if he dumps all the ephemeral rubbish on the libraries.

In the library catalogue of 1936 I looked up the statistics of books issued in an average year. Ninety-four per cent were fiction. Therefore one must suppose that it is the fiction-readers who are now harassing the librarians hardest. Yet among the novels I found no book, banned or unbanned, by Mr O'Faolain or Mr O'Connor, whereas there are nineteen by Edgar Wallace and fifty-one by two ladies called Charlotte M. Brame and Effie A. Rowlands. These write about the sins of English peeresses. For example, to quote four consecutive entries from the catalogue, we have *Lady Brazil's Ordeal*, *Lady Damer's Secret*, *Lady Ethel's Whim*, *Lady Evelyn's Folly*.

The books are old-fashioned and I expect that these follies and whims are described with some restraint. On the other hand their successors from the bookseller's dump were probably more sexy and the readers who had endured untruthfulness and vulgarity without complaint then began to harass the librarian. Who would blame them? But they should have started harassing years ago. And if they had directed their grumbles in the first place against fatuity, the need for censorship would never have arisen. Mr O'Connor and Mr O'Faolain are deeply serious writers with whose errors of taste or wisdom other writers and critics would, in an educated society, be perfectly competent to deal. Yet they are being pilloried because of the whims, follies and ordeals of Lady Evelyn's daughter. Only a negligible amount of public money has been spent on the support of serious Irish writers, hardly sufficient to pay for the administrative machinery of the Boards which sit in judgment on them. They are right in resenting bitterly that the public authorities should take notice of them only to persecute them, while public money is spent on drivelling English fiction.

There are not many cultural organizations in Ireland to assist voluntary self-education. Of them all, the County Libraries demand and receive the most lavish government subsidy. The abuse of that subsidy is, therefore, of some importance. To make a few comparisons, the Cork County Library in 1947 presented an estimate of £13,757 (as it happened the County Council cut this by half); contrast this with the budget for the National

Gallery of £8010 or that of the Institute of Advanced Studies of £53,810. Who would grudge £13,000 on raising the cultural level of a large Irish county? But, in view of the facts, we are forced to ask, is it right that public money should be lavished on bogus cultural enterprises while the National Library and Gallery are understaffed and starved of funds and it is difficult for a serious scholar, artist or writer to obtain a livelihood in Ireland?

There is no answer to this question and only a drastic reform of the County Libraries can prevent its being asked. It should not be impossible to raise our educational level by means of libraries, bookshops, lectures. I do not like exploiting 'The Red Menace' or arguing that we should do from panic what ought to be done from good sense. All the same I cannot resist comparing the splendid, well-equipped bookshops which I have seen rising from the ruins of Communist towns with our down-at-heel repositories of trash. In their educational policy some Communist governments pay something more than lip service to the maxim 'Know thy enemy!' so that in the same street as these state bookshops, I saw, in the larger towns, the crowded reading rooms and libraries of the British Council and the cultural institutes of other Western democracies. It is strange too that here in Kilkenny, where Dean Swift was educated, the bicentenary of his death passed almost unnoticed, whereas in Russia there were many meetings and lectures in honour of this Irish clergyman. His works have been brought out in huge editions and translated into many languages of the Soviets. Will we not be punished some day, and terribly, for our extraordinary apathy?

Yet in most Irish towns there is a good enough cultural tradition on which an intelligent library system could be built. Only because it is associated, often wrongly, with the Protestant ascendancy, has this tradition been interrupted. There must be some way of repairing the breach of continuity. Some months ago I spent a few hours in the old Evans Library in Kilkenny, which might serve as a suitable mausoleum for Anglo-Irish civilization. It was founded in the eighteenth century and endowed with a small income by a Protestant squire called Evans. Its members were Kilkenny townspeople of all denominations. It was for about fifty years the centre and focus of the most varied activities, historical, scientific and literary societies. From the group which ran it the Kilkenny Archaeological Society, Museum and Library took shape. It also performed some of the functions of the RDS today, organizing lecturers from Dublin. On one occasion, for instance, a celebrated physicist gave a course of ten lectures on 'The Theory of Light'. Its decay was gradual, and though the spirit had long fled the body, the Library itself survived till in 1922 the County Libraries were looking for accommodation for their books. The Evans Library was put out in packing-cases in an open courtyard, and only a damp and plundered remnant returned to the shelves. Three times since, the Nore has risen and flooded the Library, now reduced to little more than a thousand books. Some of the books were unique and the Director of the National Library once thought he might rescue a few, of which there were no good exemplars in Dublin. He found the big manuscript volumes for which he was looking piled up as a barricade to keep out the waters from the new fiction library of the county scheme. That was many years ago, but the Evans Library is still there with an inch of blue fungus growing out of the cracks in the bindings. Nobody is sure whose is the responsibility for these books and I think that subconsciously it is hoped that if the decision is postponed long enough, the books will be valueless and no decision will be necessary. The County Library has not been able to assimilate them, but last year it managed to digest the still quite considerable yearly grant which Joseph Evans left for their maintenance. Twenty years ago some pleasant volumes of Berkeley, Hume and Sterne were stolen, but as the thieves are looking after them well and have told me that they will return them if ever the Library is re-established, who can blame them? The thieves are Anglo-Irish Protestants and their attitude seems to me inevitable. So long as the Protestant and Anglo-Irish heritage is regarded with contempt, those who loot it will feel no shame.

Because of all this, I do not think that my fear for the County Libraries is exaggerated. They have, like Frankenstein's monster, taken on a life of their own, stupid and tyrannical, which would appal their first champions and creators. They are the original begetters of censorship and also of the need for censorship and in that way they strike at the creators of serious literature. Instead of encouraging originality and independent thinking and local initiative in arts and sciences, they are suppressing it, for bad money drives out good. If you can get the second-best without any effort, then there is less incentive to strive for the best.

What is to be done? I think if we went back to first principles and asked for what purpose free libraries were originally started, the right course to be followed would quickly become apparent. Davis, O'Grady, Lister and AE have all answered this question in Ireland.

It has often been held that the state should provide small pleasures for the old, the blind, the crippled, free of charge: wireless sets and braille books for example. But it has seldom been expected to provide entertainment for the able-bodied; there are many commercial bookshops and libraries which would gladly do that and were there no County Libraries there would probably be more. The government does not compete with the cinemas in the sphere of entertainment; why should it compete with the private fiction libraries and bookshops?

I can hear some 'broad-minded' person saying, 'I don't see why poor old Mrs X shouldn't enjoy her Annie S. Swan. Why should you deny her her little pleasures? Don't be high-brow, priggish, totalitarian.' But this is typical middle-brow escapism. It is poor old Mrs X, multiplied by a million, who is today the totalitarian monster, gorging herself with those fifty-one novels of erring peeresses, imposing her will on the divided and ineffectual minority who do not think Annie S. Swan touching or P. G. Wodehouse very funny. They are the Irish counterparts of that negligible group in Germany which did not think *Mein Kampf* the masterpiece of the century. Let Mrs X pay for her silly books, just as she pays for her silly films! Or let her neighbours look after her just as they did in the days before entertainment was canned. Or if they are too proud for that let them form a Benefit Society for her. It is not the ratepayer's job.

If books are not to be groceries, librarians, it is clear, should not be grocers. They should understand how books can be used to foster the creative arts in country districts. Two or three Irish librarians are working on those lines but the bulk of their time has to be spent manoeuvring bales of print, in which they take no interest and from which they draw no hopes, around the Irish countryside. It is only as a side-show that they can run a museum or an art gallery or a play-library.

Though the control of a County Library should ultimately be regional and democratic, we must draw back a bit before we can leap. Till there are regional committees capable of selecting books intelligently, the choice should be made, as it was for the first two thousand, by a central Dublin committee, which should also appoint the librarians.

The first Irish county librarians were writers and scholars in embryo or achievement. They had many faults and so had their libraries, but those faults were mostly curable, if anybody had been interested in curing them. The librarians were, for the most part, wisely chosen. They belonged rightly to that class by whom and for whom libraries were originally created.

At present we are exporting or starving the vast majority of our young men and women with literary gifts and tastes. Those who get drawn into the BBC and the British Council are more than merely lost to Ireland, for inevitably they are used – we all know many such – to foster among strangers a view of Ireland's place in the Commonwealth, which is that of the *émigré* rather than of the resident and subtly wrong, even when it is kind. At present we have scarcely any inducements to offer the young men and women to stay at home. The County Libraries would not attract them today as they did twenty-five years ago, yet if Irish country life is to be resurrected from the slough into which it has fallen they should be asked to play a part, they should be made welcome and given a living wage.

The appointments should be made with realism. It is obvious that there is no resistance whatever to Anglo-Saxon ways of thought but the most grovelling capitulation. Therefore, when appointments are made, those who love Ireland and who also love the English language and have no inhibitions about it ought not to stand back or be overlooked because they are Anglo-Irish.

I doubt whether a detailed consideration of library reform is at present so necessary as a correct diagnosis of the disease of the library system. Flexibility is probably its chief need. Good books with a librarian in control who loves them and believes in them, those are the first essentials, as Plunkett and AE once prescribed. But the librarian must feel that he has the support of his colleagues, of a central co-ordinating committee and of the various cultural organizations in the capital, whose interests he can forward in the countryside. In this way the libraries might soon begin to realize the high hopes that were once held for them.

Endnote This essay, first published in *Irish Writing* No. 8, July 1949, as 'The County Libraries and The Censorship', has been amended and augmented by an account of the collapse in 1924 of the initial County Library scheme, from which the present system evolved. (*Ed.*)

7

CROSSING THE BORDER*

The Bridge is thrown across the border because something of the kind is needed. It is manufactured in southern Ireland, assembled for publisher's reasons in the North. It is quite a small bridge and cannot take much traffic, but all who sincerely want to see the other side are invited to use it. It is a movable bridge and when we have had some experience with the border we'll try it across some other chasms and obstacles as well.

At present the border is more of an obsession than it need be. Those small sheds which extend from Pettigo to Ravensdale are not, in fact, supposed to stop ideas, but only cattle, clocks, silk stockings and so on. Yet they have an inhibiting effect on the writer. We have been hypnotized into thinking that there is a real barrier there, and, like those neurotic hens which can be kept from straying by drawing a chalk ring round them, we do not venture across. The editors of *The Bridge* intend to ignore the border till they bruise their noses against it. They intend to bring as many and varied ideas backwards and forwards as they dare, because they believe that, in that respect, demand and supply are complementary.

Political union when it is enforced has never of itself brought happiness, and ours is not, in the political sense, an anti-partition paper. We believe that free and friendly intercourse is an essential preliminary to happy union. Without that a united Ireland might prove a disappointing place when we reached it, a

*This unpublished text forms a draft editorial for a projected new literary magazine to be called *The Bridge*, written after the closure of *The Bell* in December 1954 (see '*The Bell*: An Anglo-Irish View', *Escape from the Anthill*, pp. 147ff). Geoffrey Taylor was interested in the scheme and the piece was shown to Peadar O'Donnell, who suggested that £2000 would be needed to float the new venture. It never appeared. (*Ed.*)

mere atomic cushion whose unity results from the decay of regional loyalties and the displacement of small rivalries by large ones. A pessimistic Ulsterman once told me that there were not enough borders and that in his opinion we should make a few more down South. A period of appalling cosmic boredom was ahead of us and the only hope was to diversify it a bit by interposing frontiers. They might delay the passage of the mass-produced standardized ideas and emotions with which we are being overwhelmed.

I think he was wrong. Borders do not keep out vulgarity and stupidity. The only way of holding them at bay is to have an intelligent and vigorous public opinion. At present there is, south and north of the border, an almost unbelievable spiritual stagnation. A dumb, stupid antagonism breaks into an occasional muffled snarl or jeer. Where there is disagreement, there should, at least, be the stimulus of conflict. It is from challenge and response that civilizations have arisen in the past. Why are our differences so unfruitful?

Here is one reason. Too many people would sooner be silent or untruthful than disloyal to their side. From cowardice they keep their private opinions suppressed till they have a chance of becoming public ones. Then they burst out with the force of an explosion. What should be said is blurted. There are clarion calls and crusades and political landslides and united fronts, but the art of free controversy was never so neglected.

Timid or stupid people often enjoy times of crisis. They can suspend, for the country or the cause, those careful discriminations, which tire the brain and do no good to the career. 'Now', they cry, 'is not time for academic straw-splitting and parlour-theorizing. Close the ranks! He that is not with me is against me!' And so there is always a drift towards crisis, a gentle, persistent pressure towards some simple alignment of Good and Evil, Friend and Enemy. Even the Churches are drifting slothfully towards a crude Manichaeism of Darkness and Light and away from Christ, who said so inscrutably that we should love our enemies.

Some think we can solve all our problems by saying there is only one problem, Communism, and only one border, that which runs from Stettin to Trieste. Destiny, at first, often plays unfairly into the hands of such people and appears to justify their cynicism. Arguments like theirs once seemed to unite and invigorate Italy and Germany. A crusade against Bolshevism was proclaimed and, as if by a miracle, we saw harmony and industry and uniformity instead of chaos, and all by suppressing 'destructive thought'. Now Italy and Germany are spiritually prostrate. Bolshevism, more triumphant than ever before, has started a counter-crusade in Eastern and Central Europe and produced there a semblance of uniformity, federation and strength, again by suppressing 'destructive thought'.

No, you cannot exorcise the lesser bogies by conjuring up a larger bogey to scare them away. There is nothing so flattering and encouraging to a bogey as to fear him. Moreover the solidarity, which is based on hate and fear, when it cracks, cracks irreparably.

What effort is being made here to resist totalitarian thinking? Our newspapers and clergy and public men should always be ruffling the surface of unanimity, stirring it round to keep it from boiling over. Too often they are doing exactly the opposite, lending their sanction to easy sweeping statements and collective damnations. Instead, we ought always to be looking for evidence of the variety and complexity of men and labelling them with caution. A label may give the clue to one man's whole personality, of another it may describe only a vague tendency or passing impulse. Think how hard it is to say what an Irishman is! Some say it depends on his passport and domicile. At other times there is talk of Faith and Fatherland and it is said that an Irishman must be a Catholic. But nationalism is not always in vogue among Irish Catholics and often, as today, you will read in Catholic papers that the idea of an Irish nation is a Protestant one and a bad one at that, the product of humanitarian liberalism and the hatred of Catholic universalism. Grattan and his colleagues would probably have agreed to much of this and it is worth arguing that those who have accepted the Irish label with fewest reservations have been Protestants. In fact, we cannot refuse it to anyone who feels a concern for this country and is ready to put its interests first.

We shall aim at being serious without being self-important, and we shall not be in the least afraid of being thought provincial. We live in a small country but its problems are complex and interesting enough for the most ambitious intelligence. We all know those weighty sentences which begin: 'The fate of Europe for the next two generations may well depend on the decision which is made at X— next Tuesday week.' We shall try to avoid them because I do not think our fate depends on these things. For example, God made Mr Trueman an unimportant person and, therefore, whatever he decides is unimportant or decided already or soon to be reversed. The important events are those which result from our own energy or enthusiasm.

All the same we are Europeans, and England does not now stand between us and Europe. Other small nations have been crushed and planted and half obliterated. They have had minority and ascendancy problems. They have had partitions and language revivals. It is possible to trace a general human pattern. Those who deny that there are laws of social development are usually most enslaved by them and here in Ireland we seem innocently to be falling into traps from which others have just laboriously extricated themselves. We are stupidly, snobbishly uninterested in other small nations, yet we have more to learn from them than from the large ones. For example, the culture of the United States of America is now something which we absorb with our mother's milk. It is so ubiquitous that we swallow it without even recognizing it. Even less does it stimulate us to creation.

As for England, she is no longer, as she used to be, the oppressor of Irish culture. She is more subtly dangerous. She is like one of those rich kind aunties who undermines the family by indulging and then adopting the pretty nieces and the clever nephews. The old parents are left behind with the plain, stupid ones and home life is poisoned with envy, loneliness and a sense of inferiority.

Perhaps Ulster suffers more than we do from the kind aunty, because she has been more dearly loved and has sacrificed more clever nephews. Surely even the most loyal subjects of King George must be aware of what is happening. They must have guessed that the more formidable of Ulster's enemies are those who keep quiet. 'Time is on our side,' they are saying. 'We breed faster than they do, and Ulstermen with imperial responsibilities are leaving Ulster or neglecting it. The Province has the artificial vitality of the garrison town and no organic life. If ever the pipeline were cut, it would perish. Fermoy is ours today, Enniskillen will be ours tomorrow.' That, no doubt, is how the Britons exulted when, after the Romans left and for a few short years before the Saxons came, they surged back into Verulam and Caerleon. It is an argument as sound as it is hateful. Yet few southern Irishmen would wish to absorb Ulster like greenfly invading a neglected tree, like Poles pouring into German Silesia or Czechs into the Sudetenland. Ulster would no longer be of value to Ireland if she were robbed of her rich history, her varied traditions. If she gives up these, which link her to the rest of Ireland, and becomes a mere imperial outpost, she will deserve the fate of Breslau and Fiume and Königsberg, arrogant and alien towns ultimately overwhelmed by the unsophisticated countryside which they had dominated. On the other hand, if she keeps her Irish character the border will slowly cease to be a menace and an anxiety. Either it will become meaningless and will drop off painlessly like a strip of sticking-plaster from a wound that has healed, or else it will survive in some modified form as a definition which distinguishes but does not divide. It will not be the policy of *The Bridge* to minimize or deny any distinctions of culture or history or traditions that are real, but sometimes fictitious distinctions have been introduced irrelevantly and maliciously where they do not belong. I do not think that Ulstermen will say we are violating their frontiers if we choose to ignore them.

[1955]

8

ABORTION

The 1956 trial of an abortionist in Dublin was reported in only one newspaper. I imagine that the reticence of the greater part of the press is to be explained by the plausible theory that reading about other people's sins, even when they have been chastised, is a doubtful incentive to virtue, and that, if a sinner has been adequately punished, he should be spared the extra humiliation of publicity.

The Irish Times took a contrary view, justifying its publication of the facts on the grounds of public morals. Society must be made aware of its frailties before it can correct them. There may have been a further motive which was not avowed lest it be misconstrued as sympathy for the criminals. The interpreters of the law are, in a democratic country, responsible to the people and the people have a right to judge for themselves how this trust is fulfilled.

This sharp distinction of policy does not depend on editorial caprice, it runs through our whole social existence and particularly the insufficiently explored danger zone of sexual morals. Even when we condemn the same thing, we condemn it from such different standpoints that the unanimity of our wrath seems precarious and accidental. The angel that stands at the gate of the garden is attentive to Catholic doctrine but his sword, the law, came from a noted Protestant workshop. Time has blunted it a little and he wields it with more ferocity than skill.

Unanimity, even of disapproval, is so rare and valuable that it is necessary to examine carefully the points at which it is threatened.

Abortion is in Ireland universally condemned. Even those who believe most in the Protestant private judgment would not wish the laws against it repealed. Private judgment on moral problems has in their eyes had too little training here to be trusted with so heavy a responsibility. Reflection, therefore, may lead us to rebel against the application of the law but not against the law itself.

The impact of the law has not seldom been diverted by such reflection and justice has not suffered. When men commit offences against themselves, they are often liable to be punished as though it were against others they had offended; yet embarrassment is usually shown in imposing the penalty. The man who attempts to take his own life is often treated with pity and comprehension. Excuses are sought for him in mental or physical breakdown, or if he be a hunger-striker or a defeated general, in patriotism or principle. The convicted abortionist who tried to kill himself was not therefore considered to have aggravated his guilt.

There are other unnatural offences which the law has always been disinclined to punish. Origen, putting a strange interpretation on an utterance of Christ's (Matt.19: 12), deprived himself of the hope of posterity. Such an act was a breach of the civil law of Rome, but his contemporaries recognized the purity as well as the perversity of his intention. It was not till many years later that a jealous rival sought to have him condemned for a 'monstrous act'. He failed.

In Romania there is a sect of Christians of high moral character whose men have for generations, from mistaken piety, committed the sin of Origen. As far as I know, the Romanian government has not taken proceedings against them.

Suicide and self-mutilation lie within the same range of unnatural acts as contraception or abortion, and raise the same moral problems as state sterilization and euthanasia. Non-Roman Catholics can discuss them from the standpoint of social expediency without disrespect to the moral order. In their interpretation of natural law and its adjustments to society they are more sensitive to humanitarian than to doctrinal considerations, and their principles are as likely to carry them to extremes of ruthlessness as of indulgence. For example, Bernard Shaw, who was brought up an Irish Protestant, in a letter to *The Irish Times*, advocated 'involuntary euthanasia' but was himself opposed, on principle, to imprisonment and punishment. Very few Irish Protestants would follow him far in either direction along this road, but it is one on which our thoughts, if they move at all, travel easily, while Catholic thinking has long diverged from it. Shaw is not, I believe, further away from contemporary Protestant orthodoxy than was John Milton when *Areopagitica,* the gospel of free speech, and the *Doctrine of Divorce* were written. The *Doctrine* was more than two centuries ahead of its time; *Areopagitica* is, in Ireland at least, still poignantly topical. Two fortresses of Protestant opinion, captured with difficulty, have been abandoned with hardly a struggle. Only Yeats, like Milton the greatest poet of his age, defended them with passion.

The Protestant toleration of contraception is often treated as a symptom of newfangled self-indulgence and degeneration. In fact it is in line with the Great Puritan's distrust of that

> fugitive and cloistered virtue . . . whose whiteness is but an excremental whiteness. There would be little work left for preaching [he declared] if law and contemplation should grow so fast upon these things which heretofore were governed only by exhortation.

Abortion, on the other hand, is in most Protestant, as well as Catholic, countries still strongly condemned. Liberal thinking has not yet discovered for it a place in that sphere of exhortation to which the prophets of science will soon, in all likelihood, relegate it. Yet already the law can only grasp it by the tail. The bird escapes the table and grace is solemnly pronounced over a handful of dirty feathers. The recent trials reveal with what hypocrisy and confusion of thought the topic is inevitably attended.

Abortion often comes within reach of the law solely because in a number of cases it still cannot be achieved without a skilled accomplice, who charges black market prices. This person can be caught and punished.

Yet is not this accomplice, who is made to bear the full weight of the punishment and retribution for the unnatural act, a mere incident in its achievement? The will to withhold life or to destroy it unborn will already have expressed itself in action before, as a last and terrible resort, the technician's aid is invoked. The originators of the unwanted life will first have exhausted all the resources of the drugstores and their own invention. By Roman Catholic teaching, that will is evil from the moment it enters the heart, but except for the ban on the import and sale of contraceptives, no attempt has been made to incorporate this doctrine in our country's laws. First, it would be impossible; secondly, in the eyes of the law and in actual fact, we are not all of us Roman Catholics. It is only the last phase of this destructive endeavour which the law can recognize, and blackmail or bribery or professional jealousy or incompetence and physical suffering are the unvarying routes by which detection travels.

The Roman Catholic has been trained to respect as sacrosanct our natural reverence for the body and the fruits of the body. It would be impertinent for a non-Roman Catholic to guess how far the sanctions of such a faith, unsupported by the law, can govern behaviour. But outside the Roman Catholic Church this powerful instinct is, for the most part, allowed to take its own course, a congenital revulsion against all that impairs the body or its functions. It is not without the blessings of religion, but there are few anathemas to guarantee it. It admits, therefore, a strong counterpoise in an equally potent inhibition, deriving from nature but refined by civilization. I mean that strong revulsion against encroachment upon the physical intimacies of others, or the secrecies of passion. Only prurience or deep moral indignation can override it.

The power of imaginative withdrawal from the privacies of other men's lives is surely an important element in morality which the moralist too often disregards or disposes of with a glib quotation: 'To the pure all things are pure.' He asks us to infer that this aloofness is a rare privilege of holiness. On the contrary, it is one of the mind's most precious resources, an aspect not of acquired saintliness, but of uncorrupted human nature, reflected daily in our lives and in our legislation and in our complex and incalculable reaction to moral problems.

The repugnance which the abortion trials inspired sprang, I believe, not only from the nature of the offence but also from the manner of its exposure. Two taboos, not one, had been violated. An unnatural act had been committed, and a more than unnatural searchlight focused on it. We revolted against looking in the direction in which the searchlight pointed. It was as if we feared that, if we explored those recesses of the erring soul, we might find more than we bargained for: faithfulness, perhaps, or tender forethought; anyway a confusion of tortured but normal emotions, from which it would be hard and hateful to disentangle the guilty impulse. We turned with relief to the outer fringe of light, where abortionists and procurers were momentarily illuminated. No taboo protected them. Some advertised, most took money, all courted a moderate publicity. Other offences seemed likely. In such a setting the dingiest sin looked scarlet. Here were the obvious *corpora vilia* for the moral demonstration.

Since taboos are often in conflict, it is sometimes impossible without the selectiveness of faith to regard them as inviolable. A taboo can be brought under the control of reason and yet survive undiminished. The dissection of corpses was condemned by the Church in the Middle Ages (as was inoculation in the eighteenth and anaesthetics at childbirth in the nineteenth centuries). The abortionist, to the common man, for long remained as evil a figure as his parasite, the body-snatcher. Today the dissection of the dead is as repulsive to our senses as it was to our ancestors; yet we accept it with our intellects, which have power to control our senses.

The arguments by which taboos are manipulated are not always as good as the humanitarian arguments of medicine. Two, at least, in common use at abortion trials seem crude and disingenuous.

It is assumed that the desire of gain is the only motive which can induce a man to assist at these illegal operations. If he tried to palliate his offence by asserting that he believes, as Protestants believe of contraception, that it is a matter for private judgment, he would not be credited with sincerity. Therefore, he seldom does. Even when his charges for a delicate and often risky operation are less than a third of his defending counsel's it is still he who is the bloodsucker, drawing his wages from the panic and distress of his client. Is this true? I am not thinking of Dublin personalities; I am merely recalling that almost all European countries where the laws against abortion exist have free and open debate about the consideration and modification of that law. In some countries these modifications have been adopted by the state. I am not qualified to say whether the state was right in so doing, but I refuse to believe that all these would-be reformers were influenced by the profits to be drawn from abortion or would indeed have tolerated them. Clearly, in fact, the baser type of abortionist and his ally, the blackmailer, will thrive and do the best business where his trade is regarded as most dangerous and nefarious, and tariffs can, in consequence, be highest.

There is a second argument. With constant use, the element of truth in it has been worn down like the surface of a matchbox. Roughly the thesis is that private moral practices have far-reaching social effects. To challenge it seems to be condoning immorality, so it has escaped the analysis it deserves. I can do no more here than suggest grounds for supposing that it is firstly highly dangerous, secondly untrue.

To associate the welfare of the state with private morals is only to open the door to a materialistic eugenics equally repugnant to Protestant and to Roman Catholic. It was through that door that state-licensed abortion came in Russia, and in Germany the laws for the sterilization of the unfit and the annulment of the *Misch-Ehe*. It is useless to deny that these innovations occurred at a time of social invigoration or that moral purges are seldom effected without the aid of some corrupt fanaticism, racial, political, religious. Except with a stupid or a servile people is there any point in employing such a clumsy and two-edged instrument of control? It can be used as easily to attack the domestic virtues as to defend them. Personal morality must be built upon the natural impulses of loyalty, love and disinterested affection, without appeal to that general well-being of the state around which controversy will always rage.

Secondly, there is evidence enough that men are, like certain other mammals, by nature monogamous, philoprogenitive, child-loving, and that contrary impulses either depend on congenital idiosyncrasy or are the symptoms not the causes of social decline. Rationalist historians argued that the decay of Roman civilization was accelerated by the withdrawal of the best and most intelligent to monasticism and celibacy. Christian propagandists are constantly guilty of a similar inversion of the facts. We were used, for instance, to hearing that the decline of France in the political world was due to the overthrow of moral standards. If that is so, what is the explanation of the fabulous growth of Russian power and influence? At a time when the marriage laws were so loose that divorce could be achieved in a few hours and abortion clinics were distributed over the whole country, the population was expanding rapidly. Though five great states had been carved out of imperial Russia, in a very few years Lenin had as many subjects as the Czar. When the time comes for a nation to expand, the abortionist cannot stop it; in a time of decay or uncertainty his popularity has the significance of a symptom, not a cause.

There is little connection between morality and the birth rate, and even less between the birth rate and national pre-eminence. Do nations make their chief contribution to civilization at the time of their greatest fertility and expansion? Jews, Greeks and Southern Slavs increased enormously in numbers but not in repute after they had suffered defeat and degradation. Negroes and Red Indians multiplied like cattle when they were treated like cattle. Our own period of greatest expansion was in the ignoble decades before the Famine. When Ireland was Christianizing Europe our population would have fitted into one of our great cities. If there is any connection between spiritual superiority and birth rate it would be as easy and as profitless to say it was an inverse one. The more conscious we are of our responsibilities to those who come after us (and such consciousness must be one of the tests of civilization), the more attentive we shall be to the conditions of their birth, the less ready to give nature her head. These misgivings are not proof of health and wisdom, but they most often assail those who lack the armour of ignorance or apathy. They may lead men to neurotic thoughts and acts and yet be neither base nor self-indulgent.

Finally, does any doctor seriously believe that science, which is every hour perfecting new ways of destroying life swiftly and anonymously, which has succeeded in reproducing animal life without intercourse, will be for long baffled by the problems of destroying unborn life? It is possible that before our abortionists have served their sentence, inventions will be accessible to all which will throw the professional out of business. In that case the law would abdicate a control it could no longer exercise and bequeath it to the sanctions of the Roman Catholic faith, the Protestant private judgment, and, if he could help, the customs officer.

In the meantime the law stands and must be enforced and the abortionist is the obvious scapegoat for the public abhorrence of abortion. If he acts in accordance with principles, he must be prepared to suffer for them; if he is a mere blackmailer few will regret his condition. Sometimes the same man doubles the part of blackmailer and abortionist, and blackmail is seen as a secondary attribute of his crime. In fact, blackmail is bred not of abortion but of the law against abortion, and it is necessary that the law should take rigorous and public measures to disavow it. This does not always happen.

The sentence pronounced on the offender should be in accordance with enlightened opinion, not with popular sentiment which is readily misinterpreted or exploited. Men gladly 'compound for sins they have a mind to by damning those they're not inclined to'. Moral indignation can be stimulated by loose or foolish words, but it is today too precious a commodity to be abused or squandered.

The offence was likened to murder which is thereby belittled, and the savage penalty accorded with this interpretation. The analogy is false and cannot be defended without callousness or casuistry. We live at a time when widespread homicide is organized by states and condoned by Churches. Inside the state itself, society, mobilized for war, can exert upon its incompatibles a pressure for which there is no precedent. Thousands have chosen unsanctified modes of escape for themselves and their progeny.

The names of only the more eminent of these criminals are known. About them all the moralist is forced to be as reticent as the statistician. We have not the data either to count or to condemn. One thing, however, is sure. Only the very inexperienced can now maintain that every attack upon the living or the about to live which the state has not authorized is necessarily occasioned by murderous impulses. Our vehement and implacable feelings about the taking of unborn life, if they are genuine, may derive as easily from ignorance and good fortune as from morality.

But are they genuine? There is a simple test which we can practise upon ourselves. Let us suppose that behind that flamboyant doorway in Merrion Square we knew that children were being not prevented but ill treated. How would we have reacted? Would we not have burst through it ourselves, had the law delayed intervention? Instead, for years we have passed it by, laymen and professionals, with at most a disapproving shrug, a cynical observation. True feeling expresses itself otherwise.

[1956]

THE REFERENDUM

AN ADDRESS TO THE ANTI-AMENDMENT MEETING AT THE CLUB HOUSE HOTEL, KILKENNY, 18 MAY 1983

I believe the proposed Amendment to be religiously divisive but, if all these discussions help us to understand each other, these months of complicated argument won't have been spent uselessly.

There are many Protestant sects, but most of them attach weight to private judgment and we hesitate to force our own convictions on others, especially when we do not fully understand the other person's world.

Yet I am speaking for myself alone when I say that we have no right, as outsiders, to put pressure on others to bear children against their will, against their judgment and maybe against their consciences. Abortion is always an evil but best seen as a symptom of a far greater evil, the total uncaringness of our society. The child belongs to its father as much as to its mother and he, no less than she, may be unwilling to launch into the world a child which for some reason he cannot acknowledge and to which he cannot give a father's love and care.

What happens to these unwanted children that are born to a single parent? I suspect that a great many of them find their way into institutions, or are advertised around for adoption. Many of them never lack the sense of being unloved and deprived, and few parents will ever lack a sense of guilt towards them. It is a human dilemma which the Amendment will in no way help us to solve. It will merely give to those who vote for it a totally barren and unjustified sense of a duty accomplished.

For it is not just a moral issue but a practical one as well. If through our easy, unreflecting votes an increased number of unwanted children are brought into the world, are we going to shoulder our responsibility towards them? We may persuade ourselves we will be able for it – but stop and think! What have we done in the past year for an unmarried mother or an unwanted child? Answering for myself I should say 'precious little'. What are we likely to do in the future? Ask yourselves about that too. And indeed what can you do? The world in which the unwanted child is born today is a very cruel one. It is no longer one of settled families, settled neighbourhoods, long-standing, hereditary friendships and obligations. Each man has to fend for himself much more than ever before.

For us to talk passionately about the killing of the unborn is sanctimonious and hypocritical. Who gives unqualified respect now to the commandment 'Thou shalt not kill'? In every country in time of war or civil disturbance such as exist today all over the world, killing is regarded not only as venial but even as heroic, though it leaves behind broken families and fatherless children. What are armies and navies for, except for killing? What else is the object of our stupendous armaments? Let us not add hypocrisy to callousness. When we go in a few weeks' time to vote, let us in full confidence vote against the Amendment.

Endnote The background to this hitherto unpublished essay and address is as follows.

Nurse Mary Ann Cadden was arrested on 28 April 1956 at 17 Hume Street, Dublin, and charged with the murder of Helen O'Reilly, a young married woman from Ballyragget, Co. Kilkenny. At her trial, which opened at the Four Courts on 22 October 1956, ninety-four witnesses were called, eighty-eight for the prosecution and six for defence. Although evidence was largely circumstantial, on 1 November (at the time of the Suez Crisis) she was found guilty and sentenced to death by hanging three weeks after the trial. As the judge pronounced sentence, bidding the Lord to have mercy on the defendant's soul, Nurse Cadden interrupted him saying, 'I'm not a Catholic – take that!' Her sentence was commuted to life imprisonment and she later died at Mountjoy, aged fifty-seven.

The referendum for the 'Pro-Life' Amendment to the Constitution (Article 40.3.3: 'The State acknowledges the right to life of the unborn and, with due regard to the equal right to life of the mother, guarantees in its laws to respect, and, as far as practicable, by its laws to defend and vindicate that right.'), which aimed to copper-fasten an existing law against abortion, took place on 7 September 1983: 66.45 per cent voted Yes, 32.8 per cent voted No. There was a turn-out of 53.67 per cent. Those in the majority represented 35.66 per cent of the overall electorate.

Between 1926 and 1987 Gardaí in the Irish Republic investigated some sixty cases involving abortion. (*Ed.*)

9

THE DECAY OF ARCHAEOLOGY

AN ADDRESS TO A MEETING OF THE CLERGY OF THE DIOCESE OF OSSORY READ AT KELLS RECTORY, 15 NOVEMBER 1963

Kilkenny has a claim to be considered one of the earliest and greatest centres of archaeology not only in Ireland but in the British Isles, and the man who set it going was James Graves of Ennisnag Rectory in our parish. It is exhilarating to speak of that period, the middle years of the last century, and I shall do so later, but I am going to start with the reflection that provincial archaeology, which I consider to be the most important branch of it, is at a low ebb and has to contend with forces that seem almost insuperable.

Some weeks ago I was at Kilfane which, for a variety of reasons, is one of the focal points of this story. In the 1840s three young Kilkennymen, John Prim, who was later editor of *The Kilkenny Moderator*, James Lecky, a poet and a relation of the great historian, and a novelist called Paris Anderson, wandered together around the county, exploring the ruins of the past and later writing novels, poems and essays in the romantic mood of the time about local history and traditions. On one of these expeditions they came to Kilfane and found Cantwell Fada, the crusader, covered in rubble and ruins which they carefully removed. It had been a Protestant schoolhouse before and Long Cantwell had lain in one corner of it, and naughty children used to be told to kiss him on the lips as a horrifying form of punishment. Then the roof had fallen in and nettles had grown up, and by the time the three romantics arrived he was completely submerged. They put the crusader on end and leant him against the rear wall where till a few years ago he remained, a majestic figure, the most beautiful stone effigy in Ireland; far more impressive confronting the visitor at the end of the long roofless church than he now is in profile as the Office of Public Works have set him half-way up the church.

Developments followed quickly; in the 1840s the same enthusiasm that had caused John Prim to help in the resurrection of the crusader caused him to collaborate with James Graves in the establishment of The Kilkenny Archaeological Society, and in connection with it they published a poem about Cantwell Fada by James Lecky. It is not a very good poem but it is important because it recalls the mood and motives of those who were responsible for this great intellectual renaissance in the Irish provinces. It was expressed in sentimental terms that are unfashionable today but it was hugely dynamic. Lecky's sonnet on Cantwell Fada, written before they had cleaned him up, ends:

> 'Ah me!' said I, 'men's hearts are hard and cold;
> Else would they move the rubbish gathered round;
> And cherish this the piety of old.'

After Cantwell Fada had been cleaned up, four plaster casts of him were made. Two were sent to Cork and Dublin, one was sent to the Irish Exhibition of 1853, another was housed in the Kilkenny Museum. A period of enormous bustle and intellectual activity ensued in Kilkenny, but it all emerged from the challenge to men's hearts more than to their heads, and the first archaeologists were clergymen, poets, novelists, editors, amateurs, a word that comes from 'amo', I love.

But I must leave this cheerful period of dog-carts and strong boots and come back to an autumn afternoon in 1963 when I took three Dublin friends to see Cantwell Fada. Our first surprise came at the entrance gate, for he is to be found in the old fortified church in the back avenue of Kilfane House. Till the trees were cut and nettles grew over the stumps it had been a beautiful place and remained accessible. But we found the entrance gate and the side gate both securely locked and made unclimbable with thick coils of barbed wire; or almost unclimbable, I should say, for we put our coats over the spikes and the barbs and after a considerable struggle and only a few tears in our trousers we got across. The crusader and the old church are vested in the Office of Public Works which has put up threatening notices about defacement of their property, but it was plain that though middle-aged antiquarians might be deterred by the barbed wire, it had acted as a challenge to the small boys of the neighbourhood. Not only had the threatening notice about defacement itself been defaced. That goes without saying; they always are and perhaps they deserve to be. The old Kilkenny Archaeological Society sought to 'cherish this the piety of old' by trying to arouse interest and affection around the countryside and not by fines and intimidation. No, the defacement that mattered came from stones thrown at the crusader himself; the expression of his face had altered because minute chips had been knocked off from his eyelids and elsewhere.

And I had confirmation of this from an odd source the following week. Two antique-dealers from Manchester turned up, two pleasant and highly educated vultures who were attracted across the sea by the smell of social decay. They said they had just been visiting Cantwell Fada and that they were appalled at the deterioration he had suffered. Why had he not been put under shelter? Did we not realize how easily Kilkenny limestone weathers? But it was what one of them said next that really appalled me. 'Oh, I had one of the bitterest disappointments of my life when I was here last. I came to buy the crusader and I was prepared to offer as much as £5000 for it, but I found that the old lady, would you believe it, had given it to the Office of Public Works just a fortnight before. Oh, wasn't that bad luck!'

This story shows how official archaeology has had to fill the gap left by the old voluntary society, and how, try as it might, it is an impossible task. The metropolitan experts are hardly to be blamed, because about a generation ago the amateurs created the experts rather as Frankenstein created his monster, by endowing chairs and agitating for laws and state control; then they themselves became fewer and feebler and more faint-hearted, and finally abdicated to their salaried creatures all the control they had once freely exercised over their own neighbourhood.

In the days of Prim and Graves no one would ever have dared contemplate selling Cantwell Fada to Manchester, nor would the expert have ventured to change his position without consulting those in Kilkenny who were interested.

My father could just remember Mr Graves of Ennisnag, a hideous old man with a sallow complexion, a bothered expression and buck teeth. He grew elaborate ferns on the river bank at the rectory and tried to scare small boys away from his orchard with a notice-board: BEWARE! SCOLOPENDRIA SET HERE! He was a true amateur archaeologist: polymathic, independent, touchy and truculent. (He was a kinsman of Robert Graves, who has something of the same temperament.) He was far more widely educated, as were the other amateurs of the time, than the average archaeological specialist is today. I use amateur here and throughout in the old-fashioned sense of unpaid. He was a dedicated man and when offered his travelling expenses for an archaeological outing to Truro, he refused almost huffily. Nobody offered him a chair or lectureship – there were not any – and his zeal if anything hindered his promotion. The government regarded the study of Ireland's past with some mistrust. A survey of Irish antiquities, parish by parish, had been initiated by the state and entrusted to Petrie, O'Donovan and O'Curry, but after a parish in Co. Derry had been completed, it was abruptly suspended. It was feared that by stirring up memories of ancient history the work might cause disaffection.

Yet the amateurs were pugnacious and confident and the Kilkenny Archaeological Society grew famous. Its aims were quite different to those of present-day official archaeology. They were expressed best in the sentence from Camden's *Britannia* with which all the early issues of the *Journal* began: 'If any there be which are desirous to be strangers in their owne soile, and forrainers in their owne citie, they may so continue, and therein flatter themselves. For such like I have not written these lines nor taken these paines.' They really believed that the wounds of history might be staunched by accurate knowledge properly applied. Local history was the core of the matter, the centre from which one worked outwards, and for a very long time expert knowledge was thought of as something to be used in the interests of the community and not as metropolitan knowledge was to become, an end in itself. This was widely understood and the membership of the Society grew; in its first years, for example, while it was still the local Society of the south-east of Ireland, it had as many as 106 clergy, Protestant and Catholic, as members. After the focus of the Society had shifted to Dublin and it became the Royal Society of Antiquaries, this membership rapidly declined, and when I revived the Society locally in 1945 the total Kilkenny membership was three or four.

The first journal of the Society, that of 1848-52, is now almost impossible to obtain and I once asked the secretary of the RSAI to help us with a reissue which at that time could have been cheaply edited. He said he saw no point since there was nothing that was of any consequence in these early journals. As a matter of fact they are in every way more important and interesting than the current ones since they show the sudden upsurge of the scholarly, enquiring spirit in a more or less dead country area. Graves and Prim and their colleagues were pioneers, throwing out new ideas in every direction; since then there have been individual scholars, but never a whole movement which infected masses of people and not just some select students. The editor of *The Kilkenny Moderator* himself reported the exploration of Dunbell rath in 1848. (See 'Lament for Archaeology', *Escape from the Anthill*, pp. 237-8). Defective as it was, it remained until 1928 one of the best and most serious archaeological investigations of its kind in the country. There were no further excavations in Kilkenny until a highly professional one was undertaken on Freestone Hill on the Dublin Road by my friend Professor Bersu of Frankfurt, when I was secretary of the revived Society. This excavation was financed through the Irish government, but Professor Bersu had been brought to Kilkenny by myself (he was a Jew and life had been made impossible for him in the Institute of Archaeology at Frankfurt), and the site had been found for him by members of our Society. He had given us lectures both at Dunbell rath and elsewhere, for which we paid him small sums. Nonetheless we felt that the Dublin authorities were rather surprised, perhaps even annoyed – so low had the prestige of the regional societies sunk – when this very distinguished scholar published the results of his excavations in our local journal. We were regarded as very parochial. The fact that the whole archaeology of Ireland had been shaped by the enlightened parochialism of James Graves, and that this was something basic, was soon forgotten when the Society moved to Dublin.

But I must go back to the 1850s, when Kilkenny was still a great centre of Irish and British archaeology. A museum and library was opened in Butler House, the Ormond dower house in Patrick Street, and later sited in an archway across the same. Many donations came from the Ormond family, the castle and its muniments room was always at the disposal of local scholars, and several papers were written from the Ormond Deeds. In these early journals a clear picture of medieval Kilkenny and its slow change into modern times can be constructed. Lord Ormond himself, the second marquis, was President of the

Society and a great enthusiast. He edited the *Life of St Canice* (from whom Kilkenny took its name) from the Salamanca Codex and made a gift of a free copy to all the Society members.

In 1856 the Society acquired a remarkable new member, M. Boucher de Perthes of Abbeville in France, who is known as the Father of Prehistory (see *The Children of Drancy*, pp. 95-106). He never came to Kilkenny, but until his death his name was annexed at the end of the Society's membership lists as the Honorary Foreign Corresponding Member. In this way our Society, without realizing what it was doing, became the first archaeological society in the British Isles to give an honorary membership to one of the great figures of European archaeology.

It was actually the material success of the Kilkenny Archaeological Society that at last ruined it. They wove their own splendid winding-sheet. As more and more members poured in from all over Ireland, it was inevitable that they should begin to think on a national scale and not on a purely provincial one. On the proposal of Graves, the committee forwarded a petition to the Board of Education that the Irish language be introduced as an optional subject in all Irish schools. It was curtly refused. They were right, of course, in most of their national projects but slowly and perhaps inevitably the centre of gravity of the Society shifted to Dublin, local interest waned and local membership fell off. A project of Graves's for sending questionnaires about local antiquities to all the clergy, teachers and scholars of the county was abandoned, the subscriptions were raised to metropolitan standards, and the whole character of the Society changed. Very soon it became tiresome for the widely scattered members to go down to Kilkenny for their meetings, so instead the quarterly meetings were held in Kilkenny, Cork, Dublin and Belfast. Finally this too became annoying to the Dublin people, so for the past generation council meetings have all been held in Dublin. The library was transferred to Dublin and housed in Merrion Square, and the museum was moved up in 1910 and loaned to the National Museum. There was a strong case for doing this, of course, because the library and museum were constantly being pilfered and neglected. In the old journals you will find long lists of books and periodicals stolen and lost. It is said that one day, a large and celebrated ogham stone, accompanied by smaller antiquities, walked out of the door and has never been seen since. Kilkenny people were of course blamed, but I don't think that was wholly fair. The life-blood of the Society had been drawn away from the town and it was inevitable that both museum and library should die of inanition.

The Kilkenny period of the Society lasted almost to the turn of the century, when the original motives of the founders were still understood, when it was still a voluntary body, and when the salaried expert was considered the assistant of the disinterested enthusiasts. He was their representative and not their indulgent mentor, as he later became. Of course the process was not specifically Irish but universal. It developed out of the world-wide acquiescence in specialization, but its results were more disastrous in Ireland than elsewhere.

As mentioned, I revived the Society in 1945; it still survives and is, I believe, the largest and most prosperous provincial society in Ireland. I had to sever my connection with it in 1952 (I have explained how this came about in 'The Sub-Prefect Should Have Held His Tongue', *Escape from the Anthill*, p. 274), but I still wish it well and am delighted and proud that it is still there. But I want you to understand how much circumstances have altered since the days of James Graves, and how much all these local ventures need the disinterested integrity and unpaid enthusiasm which the 106 clergy of those early journals afforded to those pioneers.

In October, for instance, an extraordinary thing happened, which will probably go unrecorded in our Kilkenny papers and excite not a ripple of interest in the county. As you know the Society has at last, with the aid of the Office of Public Works, got under way a project for which we were long working, that is to say, the restoration of the Rothe House in Parliament Street. They have ideas of forming a museum there and in the meantime they wrote to the RSAI, the former Kilkenny Archaeological Society (I don't know whether it should be called a parent society or a daughter society) asking that they should be allowed some Rothe relics belonging to the old Society to put in their restored house. The RSAI is now dominated by officials from the various Dublin institutes, including the National Museum. They have no confidence in provincial societies, believing that they will quickly dissolve and their collections disappear. So the council of the RSAI, moved to action by the letter from the

Kilkenny Society, summoned a meeting and unanimously handed over as a gift to the National Museum the contents of the Kilkenny Museum which had been loaned to it in 1910. An official of the museum then wrote that the Rothe House could have what it wanted but strictly as a loan.

The Rothe Stone, which the KAS had asked for, had been lying in the vaults of the museum for fifty years, and if you examine the original constitution of the Society you will see that the RSAI's hasty vote, at which none of the council members understood the issue, was totally illegal.

You will see in the Reports of the years 1850 and 1851 concerning the museum collection: 'All such objects are, by the Constitution of the Society, merely held as deposits entrusted to its care' (by their owners). You will also see that by Rule 21 of the Revised Rules (1911) the council has no right to dispose of the collection without prior sanction being obtained from the Society.

Yet we are all now so dependent on state institutions for our cultural ventures that nobody will dare question the legality of this move. And I understood why it happened. The contents of the old Kilkenny Museum had been dumped in the National Museum and partially incorporated, and even when the objects had not been lost the labels had; it would be now almost impossible to identify what belongs to us were we to make a row and claim them back. So we are to get back our own property as a loan. Remember these things had been given to the Kilkenny Society largely by Kilkenny people such as the Ormonds and Graves and Prim, without any idea that they would one day be permanently alienated from the town. I don't question that we have in the country districts become immensely careless of our property, but this carelessness comes from the feeling that to look after these things is now a public not a private responsibility as it appeared to Graves – but the answer to our problems is very definitely not to hand them over to Dublin.

There are two principal reasons for this: first, the hazards of fire and violence make it wise that our antiquities should be dispersed rather than concentrated in a capital. A generation or two ago (you will know these facts better than I) it was felt that the local parishes were not taking proper care of their ancient records so they were moved to the Four Courts. Then the Four Courts was burnt when it was seized by the Republicans in the

Civil War after the Treaty and in a few hours Ireland, which had been one of the countries richest in local history, became one of the poorest. So my view is that on the whole it is safer for something to be neglected in the place of its origin, where there is a faint hope that it may excite the interest of some native, as Cantwell Fada in his decay roused the interest of Prim and Lecky and Graves and inspired the old Society. For in our day capital cities and bureaucratic institutions can offer only a precarious asylum for these valuables. And often things that mean much to us here mean little in the capital, where there is a superfluity of records of every kind. So they are lost or jumbled like the contents of the Kilkenny Museum when it was housed in the National Museum.

My second reason may shock you. It may sound ungenerous to say so, but the salaried expert cannot afford to be as strenuous a defender of our antiquities and our right to free speculation as the amateurs of a hundred years ago. Archaeology, by becoming a profession out of which you support a family and/or an academic reputation, often becomes very timorous and self-important. Also the paid expert does not have to try to convert others to his enthusiasms – an ardent enquirer, if he is not a pupil, may seem just another ingenuous bore. Graves and Prim had to try to communicate their enthusiasm to others because at the lowest they wanted the subscriptions in order to publish their journals, at the highest they were trying to educate a whole neighbourhood and perhaps change its view of the past and the present.

I noticed this particularly when the Irish government gave one of our Kilkenny treasures to President Kennedy on his recent visit. It was a fourteenth-century treaty between James, Earl of Ormond, and the O'Kennedys of north Tipperary, one of the many Irish branches of the Kennedys (to which there is no evidence that President Kennedy's family belonged). It no more concerned the family of the President, of whom we are rightly proud, than it concerned about a million other Kennedys and Butlers throughout America and the British empire, and the gift was an example of the way in which archaeology has to capitulate to political sentiment when it accepts state support and state control. The history of these O'Kennedys was discussed in the first issue of the *Kilkenny Archaeological Journal* (that one which is unobtainable because the RSAI did not consider it worth reissuing) and the document was recognized as one of the great treasures of the muniments room in the castle, where it stayed secure for six centuries. Now this document is launched into the void. It will, of course, be carefully treasured by the Kennedys. But what will happen when their heirs are no longer millionaires and the American equivalents of those two gentlemen from Manchester approach them? Where will it end up?

I found the sequel to the donation of this document very interesting. When I wrote to *The Irish Times* in protest I got a great deal of support, public and private, and no official scholar defended the government action, but no official scholar attacked it either. All the more formidable attacks in *The Irish Times* came from retired scholars with pensions; from Galway University, a retired speaker of the senate, a retired comptroller and auditor-general for Northern Ireland, and so on. Nobody wrote officially from any of the universities, academies, libraries or museums, though they contacted me privately. No one wrote even from the Society of Antiquaries, which had owed so much in its early days in Kilkenny to the Ormond Deeds. One of the letters I received was from an old friend who is a principal librarian in Trinity. He explained that he had written to *The Irish Times* in my support, urging that the whole transaction was quite illegal, and, in the words of the Auditor-General, 'a misappropriation of public assets', which could only be legalized by a bill in the Dáil. But he said: 'I wrote from my private address, as a private person, and I suppose that is why they did not print my letter. But I couldn't very well write as a librarian of Trinity because we're expecting £400,000 from the government for the new Trinity Library and we couldn't risk offending them too much.' Now I hope you'll understand why James Graves of Ennisnag would not accept his expenses for that archaeological trip to Truro.

Through an accident of history the Communists in Russia have preserved the record of the Czarist days, both the ascendancy of rank and of intellect, more carefully than we have preserved the records of the eight centuries of Anglo-Irish domination here. The reason for this is, I think, that after the peasants had murdered the landlords in Russia they looted only the things that were useful to them; and the government, when it came round to confiscating what remained, often found all the most valuable things, the documents, the pictures, the books, more or less intact, and from them vast collections have been formed. In the freer atmosphere of Ireland the Anglo-Irish owners survived to sell many of our records. The same applies to buildings; whereas Kilkenny Castle fell into ruin after 1934 and is being laboriously restored, there are many great palaces in Russia like the Jusupov Palace in Leningrad, still surviving as museums with the furniture of the period, or else converted to old people's homes or schools.

This also applies in a more marked degree to the way we have treated the memory of our great writers of Anglo-Irish stock. Contrast the fate of Edgeworthstown and Coole Park and Moore Hall with that of the houses of Tolstoy and Chekhov and many other non-Communist writers. Tolstoy's country house near Tula and his town house in Moscow survive almost as he left them. The same applies to Chekhov's house in Moscow, his villa at Yalta, his little farm at Melihovo south of Moscow, and, I think, his birthplace at Taganrog. In the early period of the Revolution an attempt was made to do propaganda through these survivals from the past, and the guides sometimes still do a little, but in general these places are allowed to speak for themselves and they do so very dramatically. The Russians of the future, whether they are Communist or something different, will have an opportunity of observing this evidence of historical continuity which our children may lack. In 1956 I visited in the same year Tolstoy's home, Yasnaya Polyana, in Russia, and what is left of Edgeworthstown House in Longford, and afterwards I gave a talk on the Russian service of the BBC in which I compared these two famous houses as centres of enlightenment in their day. I felt too ashamed to say how much better Yasnaya Polyana had fared, or to recall that when some forty years ago Edgeworthstown House had been put up for sale, no effort had been made to preserve it or its contents as a record of Maria and her famous father and the great influence they had exercised from there.

In 1945, to commemorate the bicentenary of Jonathan Swift's death, the Russians printed 100,000 copies of *Gulliver's Travels*. The Irish did nothing at all. I don't believe the Russian way of preserving the records of the past is the best one. That would mean evicting Major Briggs-Swifte, confiscating his property, Swifte's Heath, for the state and installing an expert Swift scholar comparable to the learned Tolstoyan they have at Yasnaya Polyana. I am convinced that James Graves's way of ensuring that we are not 'strangers in our owne soile' is a far better way, which has to be applied with vigour.

To begin with, state-paid scholars should be delegated to voluntary societies. With a little experience we would come to do this better because we know our own neighbourhood, its needs and traditions. The case of Cantwell Fada is typical: without consulting us he has been moved from the position where James Graves set him, but he has been left more inaccessible to us than he ever was before. When the same thing happened after the Office of Public Works had done some restoration work at Kells and Kilree some sixteen years ago, they left both places equally inaccessible. There was a locked gate with a bull behind to deter visitors from Kells priory, and an impassable barrier of thorns and barbed wire at the Kilree round tower. I discovered that the County Council had power to co-opt a Monuments Committee and was authorized to carry out its decisions. We formed a committee of three members from the KAS and I persuaded them to set aside £25 to build the present gateways and stiles at Kilree and Kells. I also got the County Council to unearth the thirteenth-century effigy of Johannes filius Galfridi at Ennisnag. In 1952 the County Council held a special meeting to turn me off the Monuments Committee (see *Escape from the Anthill*, p. 273), which died soon after, but the point is that we have power through the County Councils to do a great deal for our antiquities, even in our churchyards, without applying to Dublin. And I found the County Council, when I worked with it, generous and efficient.

The work done by the Board of Public Works at Kells and Kilree came about in rather an odd way. Mr O. G. S. Crawford was staying with me. He was an original man, as you can tell from his autobiography, one of the principal archaeologists in Britain and the first to make use of air-photography for the discovery of ancient sites. He founded and edited *Antiquity*, which was the leading archaeological journal in England, and as an official in the Ordnance Survey at Southampton did much valuable mapping of English, British and Roman antiquities. He was a self-sufficient old bachelor, not at all officially minded but not society-minded either, and I totally failed to interest him in the KAS. His first reason for visiting me was to put an order with a Kilkenny butcher for a weekly supply of meat, as, after the war, he did not consider the meat he got in Southampton adequate.

While he wandered up High Street and Rose Inn Street pinching meat and comparing prices he was struck by the beauty of Kilkenny, and he said he would come back later and make a photographic survey. In the meantime I took him to a couple of our archaeological outings; at the first one he looked hugely bored and irritated, at the second one he fell asleep. Then he went to Dublin for a few days and he found the meetings of the Society of Antiquaries equally dreary and soporific. He regarded all our efforts as moribund and our societies dead beyond hope of revival. When he returned I took him to Kells. It was at that time covered with ivy and some of the walls were in danger of collapsing, so on his advice we reported the matter to the Board of Works. Mr Crawford's name had a magical effect and the next summer very extensive work was done on both Kells and Kilree. They spent £1000 and made an admirable job of it, but something happened which revealed to me what an impassable gulf yawned between the ideals of James Graves and the archaeologists of our century. One of the officials from the Board who came to visit me was a learned and charming man. He found my efforts to revive the KAS vaguely commendable but not necessary. After all it had been superseded by the RSAI. Why multiply societies? I found it difficult to explain to him that local interest was now almost stone-dead and that we were trying to revive it. We had had several meetings of our Society at Kells. We had sent out invitations to the local people and asked the teacher to bring his pupils. They had responded, taken part in our discussions and obviously been interested.

So when the work at Kells was nearly completed, I was astounded when one day he said to me at lunch: 'Oh, I've told the workmen that just three days before we clear out they are to pull down the handball court in the chancel. If they do it quickly enough there'll be no trouble.'

Now the handball court should never have been built on the property of the Office of Public Works, but it had been there for many years and Dublin had connived at it. Very recently £800 had been collected round Kells and spent on it. The surest way to alienate the Kells people was to destroy their handball court. I suggested, therefore, that we collect a fund to build a handball court somewhere else, but we were still a young Society and did not move with sufficient confidence. The matter ended in the worst possible way. The demolition plan leaked out, probably through the workmen, before we got the fund under way. The

Kells people immediately sent a deputation to the Ministry and the Minister intervened and stopped the plan. We were suspected of letting the cat out of the bag and both in Dublin and in Kells our Society suffered a set-back. And for many succeeding years the happy feet of the handball players trod down the noses of the abbots on the thirteenth-century slabs.

All this is very small beer, but we live in a small community in which such small things are deeply important. I hope I have not suggested that we were constantly at war with Dublin. We were not. The representatives of the museums and libraries and Office of Public Works and the RSAI were very generous to us. For example, when I organized a Kilkenny exhibition in the Tholsel, the National Library gave us photostats of a huge number of Kilkenny documents and pictures which I located and we have always had help when we asked for it. Our problem was how to resist the centralizing tendencies of the day and recover something of the originality and independence of the old Society. It was difficult and unfair to expect help from the highly centralized organizations of Dublin in doing this. Yet every year I became more conscious that this decentralization was urgently necessary and that only we ourselves could bring it about.

At this time a very pleasant and satisfactory thing happened. Mr Crawford did return to Kilkenny, as he had promised me, to make his Kilkenny Survey. He lodged in the Club House Hotel and got up between six and seven o'clock every morning, because he said that it was at that hour that the light was right for photographing certain buildings. They had often to be photographed from the top windows of the building opposite and, as he believed that everyone should share his disinterested admiration of Georgian fanlights, a great many people in Kilkenny had reluctantly to get up early too in order to show him into their attics. He is the only person I know who penetrated that small wooden or plaster pepper-pot which used to stand on top of the Monster House. The view which he took from it of the turret on the Tholsel I used for the cover of our first bound copy of *The Old Kilkenny Review*. In a couple of years this photograph became unique. The eighteenth-century turret was replaced by a copper one and the whole roof of the Tholsel altered at the time when the interior was gutted and the horrible winding butterscotch staircase was put in to replace the broad and dignified old one. Crawford took about two hundred photographs and as Kilkenny was soon after to recover from the shortages of the war and the shopkeepers were able to put up smart chromium fronts to replace the Georgian ones, Crawford's two volumes are already a valuable record of a period of Kilkenny that is slowly disappearing. Crawford did all this work freely. He charged only for the printing of the photographs which he insisted must be done by the only capable man in England, who lived in Wiltshire. So I sold the negatives to the National Library for £34, deducted the printing costs and lodged the balance to the Kilkenny Archaeological Society. And we sent him in return the largest Christmas turkey we could find in the Kilkenny shops.

With Crawford's agreement, I held on to the two volumes myself. I felt doubt arising about the Society and Crawford had never believed in it at all. He had all the disinterested love of learning that Graves had and he was just as cantankerous and individualistic, but he was typical of the modern expert in that he could not be bothered with people who were not as sophisticated as himself. And the members of our Society were mostly very innocent and some of them had complacency added to innocence, which, as you know, converts it into ignorance. Graves and his colleagues never despised innocence, but often went out of their way to meet ignorance and deflate it or chastise it.

I have said that official archaeology has turned its back on its own origins and betrayed them. Now I am going to suggest, on the basis of my own experience in Kilkenny, that this divorce from its original *raison d'être* has at times made it something dangerous and politically evil. I read recently an archaeological book in which our Irish government was commended because in its first years it had abandoned the narrow parochialism of the past and in 1934 had appointed an eminent Austrian archaeologist as the Director of our National Museum. Well, I met Dr Adolph Mahr once or twice, and possibly the rumour was untrue that he was to be our cultural gauleiter if Hitler occupied Ireland. But he certainly scorned the Irish as much as he scorned the Czechs (it was at the time of Hitler's victory over the Czechs that I first met him). He was a good Nazi and just before the war broke out he went back to Vienna, but the Irish government, I suppose to emphasize our neutrality, kept his place open for him and, till the war ended, sent him his salary to Vienna.

Towards the end of the war a very detailed collection of information about Ireland, *Militargeographische Angaben Uber Irland,* was discovered in Brussels and it was reported that the principal contributor was Dr Adolf Mahr.

I have had confirmation of this from Dublin scholars. It appears that our government was determined to be rid of him before 1939, but dared not risk offending the Germans by a direct dismissal. Therefore an Irish agent in Austria sent him a bogus official message summoning him home. It was learnt that on reaching Vienna he was very coolly received by the authorities, who wished him to remain at his observation post in Ireland through the war, protected by the prestige and the immunity that is claimed by salaried archaeology.

It was said that the assistant to him as cultural gauleiter in Ireland was to have been a scholar called Hartmann, working on Irish folklore. He was a well-liked person who went home of his own accord before the war broke out, but there is no reason to suppose that he would have refused the important post to be assigned to him.

I need not stress how difficult this prostitution of learning would have been if archaeology had been, as it used to be, decentralized and without an official or professional character, and if even a small attempt had been made to revive in the provinces the pugnacious integrity of the old Kilkenny Archaeological Society.

While he was in Ireland, Mahr was in charge of James Graves's collection, so you can judge how far archaeology had travelled from Ennisnag when it became a science. James Graves had believed that its object was to prevent a man becoming 'a stranger in his owne soile, a forrainer in his owne citie', and that it was a duty for which no man should accept payment (remember that trip to Truro), and here we were paying a 'forrainer' a salary in the name of archaeology when he was no longer even on our 'soile' but intriguing with those who despised us in order to take it away from us.

Another thing happened in the succeeding years which convinced me that the state-supported science of archaeology was a far inferior branch of learning to that championed by James Graves and Boucher de Perthes. It concerns Dr Bersu, the celebrated German-Jewish prehistorian, who, as I mentioned, came to Kilkenny first in about 1950. He was the Director of the

Institute of Archaeology at Frankfurt-on-Main and at the outbreak of the war had been excavating in the south of England. His reason for staying on was the same as Dr Mahr's for returning to Austria, only upside-down. Dr Mahr was a Nazi and Dr Bersu was a Jew. Though Bersu and his wife are very old friends of ours, I cannot tell you this story without saying things about him that he would prefer to have suppressed. Yet I can never speak unkindly of a German Jew, for we none of us know how we would react if we were told that our race was inferior and should be exterminated. An Irish republican told me lately that in his opinion the Irish had never recovered psychologically from being told for centuries that they were inferior and, of course, for the Jews it has been far worse. Dr Bersu never liked to admit he was a Jew and I never once heard him express any solidarity with Jews. And since none of his friends wished to wound him, we never mentioned it.

It was the extra-special torment of many German Jews that they had given up their Jewish faith and traditions and immersed themselves so deeply in German life that they could not face the fact that they were anything but German. It was, of course, in part the absence of this sense of solidarity among themselves that made them such an easy prey to Hitler. So since Dr Bersu had left Germany before the war of his own accord he did not consider himself a refugee; he found that the archaeologists of other countries, such as Mr Crawford, accepted him into the fellowship of international archaeology, and this fellowship was a sort of temporary substitute for his German citizenship. But he did not want to abandon being a German and therefore preferred to be interned on the Isle of Man with other German nationals. But since he was of known eminence he was allowed, with his fellow internees, to direct excavations in the raths and ringforts of the Isle of Man. He was a very meticulous excavator and his wife did the mapping and charting for him. He discovered that in many of the Manx forts traces could be found of concentric rings of post-holes, and he deduced from this that our raths had once been roofed over.

At the end of the war things were difficult for him. His position in Frankfurt had been filled and he was not sure he could recover it. Crawford suggested to me that he come to Kilkenny while he explored possibilities in Ireland, and that is how he came to be associated with our Society. De Valera proved very sympathetic and personally secured him a salary, and we found him a site to excavate, the Iron Age fort of Freestone Hill near Gowran.

I had hoped that he would encourage some of our members to help with the dig so that ultimately they would learn how to do it with modern methods. Dr Bersu was extraordinarily friendly and sympathetic and demonstrated to us several times the progress of the work. While Dr Bersu and his helpers, his workpeople and students, were in Freestone Hill, and reporting progress to us, we all felt things were moving and that we had assisted in a small way in the uncovering of our past. He was still working there in the summer of 1948 when the centenary of the foundation of the Kilkenny Archaeological Society was celebrated. For this occasion the RSAI had invited twelve leading archaeologists from Europe, England and America. They were to spend three days in Dublin and then they were to come to Kilkenny for another three days. With Lord Ormond's permission we invited them and the accompanying members of the RSAI to a party in the Picture Gallery of Kilkenny Castle, where the old Society had been entertained so often before by the Ormonds when it was still inhabited.

Some of our members were asked by the RSAI to put up the visiting scholars in our homes and my guests were to be Professor Sprockhoff, a leading German prehistorian, and a Spanish professor whose name I've forgotten. I was very pleased because we do not often see such eminent people in Kilkenny and I thought it would be stimulating to us all, so I gladly agreed and I told Bersu.

His reaction was astonishing. I had never seen him so moved. In tones of the deepest resentment he said: 'No! No! You cannot have Sprockhoff. Oh, if you have Sprockhoff, I can never come here again. It was he who prevented me from even reading in the archaeological library' (even then I don't think Bersu mentioned the word 'Jew'). 'Himmler, who was, as you know, a great patron of archaeology, sent him to Norway and he worked on excavations under Vidkun Quisling. They liked his excavations, because Himmler linked them up with his theories of the Aryan origins of the Germanic people. I don't mind about the Spaniard being a Fascist and Francoite. After all, the Reds killed his sister and he has some excuse – but Sprockhoff, no, no!!'

So I wrote straight off to the RSAI saying that I had to change my mind and would like to have the Spaniard but that I could not have Sprockhoff, and I explained why.

And the RSAI secretary wrote back in a friendly way. He understood my objections and said that the English scholars who had been invited had refused to come for the same reason. One of them was, I think, Sir Cyril Fox. And in fact no English scholar attended the centenary celebrations, though there were delegates from America (a McCarthyite archaeologist), Spain, Belgium, Germany, Norway and several other European countries. This struck me as very astonishing. Had all the Anglo-Irish, whose forebears had built the Society and formed 80 per cent of its membership, lost interest or influence, or had they become Naziphile? I've never discovered.

After my refusal no further hospitality was sought for Sprockhoff and he was put up at the Club House Hotel. The Spaniard was sent to keep him company, so, to my disappointment, I had nobody.

The RSAI was of course aware that there was a difficulty about Sprockhoff and Bersu. To settle it they used the smooth tactics that officially organized bodies invariably adopt. There was to be a special lunch for the visitors and the Kilkenny natives at the Club House Hotel; Professor Boe, the great folklore expert from Norway, was put in the chair and a list of the officials of the KAS to whom he was to express gratitude in his after-dinner speech was given to him. But anyone who had been tiresome about Sprockhoff, including myself, the secretary and founder, was omitted from the list. Bersu, the distinguished Jew, who had shown such kindness to our Kilkenny Society, was not invited at all. He was very wounded about this and urged me not on any account to mention it to his wife Maria: 'She will be so upset.' But I was annoyed at what had happened and, though I was secretary, boycotted all the country meetings that took place afterwards. Because of this it was from Bersu that I learnt what occurred on Freestone Hill. The RSAI had taken the whole party, Sprockhoff included, to see the excavations, and Sprockhoff had walked out into the middle of the ringfort and complimented Bersu on the excellence of his excavations and the interesting nature of his discoveries. This was important to Bersu, for the Irish archaeologists had all belittled the significance of his post-holes. 'It is all right about Sprockhoff,' Bersu told me afterwards, 'he was very nice.'

There was so much to say about this that I said nothing at all, though I have often met Bersu since. I was aware that something sad and wicked and all too human had happened, and that Bersu and Sprockhoff and the RSAI and, in our ignorance, our Society too had become implicated in it. It seemed to me that prehistory, by becoming a science, had lost the dignity and integrity with which it had been born at Abbeville. A trade union of professionals had taken it over, agreeing that even crime which conduced to the 'Advancement of Learning' was excusable. Bersu had had a legitimate grievance against Sprockhoff because he had made him feel that, as a German Jew, he was 'a stranger in his owne soile and a forrainer in his owne citie' and because he had worked for Quisling and Himmler. But all this was forgiven when Sprockhoff had been pleasant about the post-holes.

Yet the reputed post-holes which our ancestors made maybe three thousand years ago are merely a nuisance if, in order to investigate them, we must blur the record of what happened twenty years ago. Nearly a thousand German Jews who had escaped to Norway had been rounded up while Sprockhoff was excavating Aryans for Quisling, and if Bersu had escaped to Norway neither Boe nor Sprockhoff would have been able to prevent him and Maria from being burnt at Auschwitz.

I looked up Sprockhoff's works in the British Museum to find out if he was as wicked a man as Bersu said. Unfortunately they had not the book on Norway which he wrote when he was working for Quisling, but from the other works I saw he appeared to be a gifted and conscientious scholar, and probably quite a kindly one. He had simply felt he owed allegiance to the government which sponsored his researches.

Among the Sprockhoff books in the British Museum one that interested me most was a Festschrift compiled by scholars in Europe to congratulate him on his sixtieth birthday in 1952. Four years earlier no English archaeologist would attend the Kilkenny meeting because of Sprockhoff. Now they all contributed eulogistic articles or signed their names to the foreword, whether they were Communist or Tory, German or Jew. And Bersu's name was there too.

It seems to me that the archaeology of James Graves and Prim is a far finer thing than that of Sprockhoff and, if it is to survive, the RSAI must be restored to its old country basis and turned into a federation of county societies, all proud and tenacious of their amateur status.

For the implementation of such schemes we must depend on the old voluntary spirit. Only amateurs can build up vigorous and independent societies, holding to the old principles of free speculation and to the conviction that the purpose of archaeology is to prevent us from becoming 'strangers in our owne soile, forrainers in our owne citie' and not just to add one more science to the dangerous superabundance of sciences. These were the ideas that were born a couple of miles from here over a century ago, and I don't believe they are yet obsolete.

POSTSCRIPT 1989

This was compiled and read twenty-six years ago. Many of those I spoke of or spoke to are dead; personalities, places, institutions have changed or lost their significance; I was middle-aged and now am old. Yet I think it is worth reproducing for I still believe that archaeology should be treated not as a science or profession but as a voluntary pursuit. It is far better to return to the largely extinct county archaeological societies of the last century and to know your country far and wide, as few people do now, and to be able to decipher the traces that history has left upon it.

In this decade science has thrown the metal-detector into the hands of the amateur and that is how the Derrynaflan hoard of eighth-century altar vessels became the greatest discovery of recent times. The hoard was discovered on 17 February 1980 by an Englishman, Mr Webb, and his son, using metal-detectors, and caused a great sensation that rippled through the newspapers for a year or two before it was forgotten. It was said to be worth over £5 million and as no specific legislation about treasure trove had been introduced since the founding of the state, in 1986 a High Court Dublin judge pronounced that it was the property of Mr Webb.

This was, of course, disputed, and in 1987 a Supreme Court ruling declared the vessels to be objects of national heritage and they passed into state ownership. They are now on view in the National Museum where Mr Webb had originally brought them. Except for Derrynaflan Church being in the custody of the Board of Works and governed by the law of trespass, and the use of metal-detectors being forbidden, those are restrictions that are impossible to enforce. Mr Webb behaved honestly, reporting the find as soon as it was made.

For the future it has been suggested that a Monuments Inspector should be appointed for every three or four counties to watch over their antiquities. This seems to me a characteristically expert opinion. How could one person control the use of metal-detectors in three or four counties? Some years back, my grandson as a small boy camped with a friend in a wood a couple of hundred yards from my house and found a large grove of cannabis, with bags of fertilizer and gardening tools. A dozen treasure-hunters with metal-detectors could have wandered through it unobserved, and if they chose their time judiciously there is scarcely a spot in the hills and fields and woods of Ireland that they could not explore.

People like responsibility, and I believe many societies would spring into existence if they could be given the exclusive right of authority over the use of metal-detectors on a known project. A county committee is usually drawn from a wide area and a network of close observation would form itself automatically. With thirty-two related county societies and museums (or thirty-three to cover Tipperary north and south), the Derrynaflan Chalice would belong to the North Tipperary Museum and would have been found long ago if someone authorized by the local society had explored the old churches of Tipperary with a metal-detector. I suggest that the revival of the old county archaeological societies would be the best method of controlling and containing the threat and potential of mechanized archaeology.

10

MIDLAND PERSPECTIVES

I. THE DESERTED SUN-PALACE

The empty but still imposing shell of Desart Court stands at a crossroads a few miles from Callan in the County Kilkenny. This noble Georgian house was burnt in 1923, rebuilt and finally dismantled a few years ago. The Land Commission is prepared to make the shell safe and sound if any established society will take charge of it. The guardianship would be for many years to come a negligible responsibility, yet at present there is no association, either local or metropolitan, able to undertake it. A century ago the old Kilkenny Archaeological Society took abbeys and castles under its protection with the most matter-of-fact assurance, but nowadays we who live in the country, partly from modesty, partly from habit, look to Dublin for guidance and Dublin societies mostly have their hands full and can help us little. There is a danger that this fine fabric will disappear into road material.

Desart Court in its present form covers only a small plot of land and harms no one. Its avenues have been turned into roads which cross beside the house, and the huge brick-walled garden which faces it has reverted painlessly into an enclosed field and orchard. Its woods have been thinned but not devastated and are still lovely. The whole scene might be allowed to stay as it is for a few generations at least, like a rather dim but adequate illustration in a textbook of local history, recent as well as remote, for the Cuffes of Desart, who are now all gone, were active till the last.

They had been in Ireland before Cromwell, but one Joseph

Cuffe distinguished himself in the service of the Protector and obtained lands that had previously belonged to the Norman family of Comerford, which had backed the royalist and Catholic side. The Cuffe history for a generation was true to pattern. They were successful opportunists, turning from republicans to monarchists, from Stuarts to Hanoverians, when the suitable moment arrived. The Comerfords, who had been more consistent, were never allowed to interfere with them. Their only rivals were the Flood family of Farmley, from whom Henry Flood the orator was descended. With them they had a feud, which led to duels and lawsuits and even murders about the political representation of the borough of Callan.

Yet very early on the Cuffes showed signs of a generous, independent outlook and within the narrow limits of class loyalty they did their best. When the refugees from a tyrannical government in Geneva decided to build a town on the Waterford coast which was to become a centre of liberty, industry and enlightenment, a Cuffe was one of the principal Irish promoters of the scheme. But on second thoughts the British government of the time suddenly decided that it would be unwise to introduce rebellious and republican Genevans into this disaffected region. After Cuffe had superintended the laying of the foundation stone, the plan was shelved and the Genevans stayed at home. (See 'New Geneva in Waterford', *Escape from the Anthill*, pp. 25 ff)

There is much about the life of the Cuffes in the late eighteenth century in Dorothea Herbert's fascinating reminiscences. Her visits from Carrick to her uncle and aunt at Desart brought her into touch with the lively society which existed for some twenty years in Kilkenny during and before the Napoleonic Wars. The Desarts were highly temperamental. You can read how Lord Desart's daughter, Mrs Cooke, mourning for her husband, painted all the flowerpots black, reupholstered the furniture in sable and tarred the stables, turning an elderly visitor's white horse piebald for which he flogged the yard-boy. I wonder if the ill-omened portrait of John, Lord Desart was burnt in 1923? According to Miss Herbert it was painted with poisonous paint and the artist lost his sight, and Lord Desart and the three pets who were portrayed with him all succumbed to different diseases. His lordship died of a violent fever, the two dogs also perished and his fine horse was never any good after this fatal picture was painted. Lord Desart's end was so sudden and so much deplored that his funeral procession lasted for three miles.

They went in for high-spirited and rather callous practical jokes in those days.

> One day at Desart Mr Hamilton Cuffe, who was teazingly nice dressed, took the Parson's Nose of a Duck for himself and she, my cousin Lucy, knowing his foible, laid her finger on it. A fit of romping took place, which ended in a serious Quarrel and violent Hystericks on her part. This was no sooner over than my Uncles affronted me by recommending Mrs Jephson as a Stepmother, if anything happened my Mother. This threw Mama and her daughter into Hystericks and all the Servants in the House were dispatched for remedies before our Sobs could be abated. Many freaks passed at Desart that time which I now forget.

There is or was in Desart woods a famous oak claiming, like many others, to be the oldest in Ireland and it may well have been part of the ancient Irish forests. The woods have never been better described than by Humphrey O'Sullivan, the Callan schoolmaster, who wrote a diary in Irish twenty years after Dorothea's time, when Desart woods were being replanted.

> I went to Desart by the same roads which I took on Easter Friday. We walked through dark evergreen pinewoods, through fine lane-ways, now crooked, now straight, shaded from the face of the sun, listening to the fluting of the lark in the way-side meadows. We went through Derrymore, through the Lord's Plantations, skipping like goats through Derreen to the fish-ponds of Desart. The landscape from this beautiful sun-palace is exquisite: a gaseous exhalation came from the sun, the mountains to the south were dark blue. Ballykeefe Hill near us to the north was newly planted and so was Knocknarah and all around us sheltering oak and ash and meadows smooth as silk and green as corn grass. . . . The sky was cloudless save for one cloudlet adding to its beauty as a dimple to a damsel's chin. . . . Slieve na man cloudless, Mount Leinster and the other mountains to the east reclining on a couch of fog, raising their heads and nodding to the sun like a gentle young bride to her husband. It is in the heart of this valley that the head-mound and capital city of Ireland ought to be.

There seems to have been an unbridgeable gulf between the accomplished and benevolent Cuffes and the people of whom Humphrey O'Sullivan was the informative and sensitive interpreter. He is a remarkable figure with his home-made education and his passionate loyalty to the last remnants of the Irish traditions and language which he knew to be dying. Much of O'Sullivan's huge diary is uninteresting and repetitive, yet it is easy to believe that he had in him some seed of truth, some zest for life, which in a less unhappy and divided society would have flowered into poetry and prose of a high order.

Yet a deep pessimism undermined and discoloured all his thoughts. Everything he wrote was perishable for the language in which he wrote it was rapidly being outlawed. Little by little he had to renounce that dim hope which sustains the solitary writer, of being understood at least by posterity. It is not unnatural that he should often break into bitter railing, finding his sole consolation in the thought that rich and poor, oppressor and oppressed, are all equally doomed.

He may have been thinking of Desart Court, 'that beautiful sun-palace', when he wrote:

> What is the good of repining? The bright walled castles will disappear and the glittering sun-palaces, the earth form elemental, the entire universe like a wisp-blaze. Will it be long till this Irish language in which I am writing goes too? Fine big school houses are daily being built to teach in them this new language, the Saxon tongue. But, alas, no attention is being paid to the fine smooth Irish tongue, except by wretched Swaddlers, who are trying to see whether they can wheedle away the children of the Gael to their accursed new religion.*

The Swaddlers to whom he refers were a group of earnest Evangelicals who appeared in Kilkenny at this time and made war simultaneously on what they considered the frivolity of the Protestants and the idolatry of the Catholics. They learnt the Irish language and to propagate their views they tried to interrupt the Kilkenny theatre season and were denounced by the Protestant bishop.

O'Sullivan would certainly have been surprised if he had known that when the fate which he foresaw had overtaken the Irish language in Kilkenny, it would be one of the Cuffes of Desart who would try to revive it. The story of Otway Cuffe and his sister-in-law ought to be told because of its interest as well as its sadness. Though it happened for the most part only a generation ago, it already seems to be of another age. Yet it belongs,

* Some have compared this to Prospero's monologue in *The Tempest*:
'Our revels now are ended, . . ./The cloud-capped towers, the gorgeous palaces,/The solemn temples, the great globe itself,/Yea, all which it inherit, shall dissolve/And, like this insubstantial pageant faded,/Leave not a rack behind. We are such stuff/As dreams are made on, and our little life/Is rounded with a sleep.'

like the shell of Desart Court, to the shifting pattern of Irish history, and should not be forgotten. (See 'Otway Cuffe', pp. 3ff above; also 'Anglo-Irish Twilight', *Escape from the Anthill*, pp. 75ff.)

II. DANGAN REVISITED

A short distance on the Summerhill road out of Trim, Co. Meath, there is a gaunt ruin on a very bare hill. It is surrounded by a devastated park where stumps of trees and traces of avenues can still be seen. The name on the map is Dangan. It looks like a house that was destroyed in the bad times but in fact its decline and fall happened many years, perhaps even a hundred, earlier. Its owners felt called to a more illustrious destiny than that of an Irish landowner and the house passed to a Mr Roger O'Connor, who cut down all the trees that he could sell and skinned the rooms of every saleable fitting. Finally, after it had been well insured, the house burst into flames. No great effort was made to quench them.

I had always known that Dangan was the family home of the Duke of Wellington, but it was not till I was reading Mrs Delany's letters that I learnt any more about it. Mrs Delany was that agreeable, fashionable and gossiping lady who was the wife of the Dean of Down and the friend of Swift and many other notabilities. Mrs Delany made the acquaintance of a certain Mr Wesley while she was still in England. His real name had been Colley, but on inheriting the estate of Dangan from a cousin he had taken the name of Wesley, which later on his son changed to Wellesley. It is possible that he disliked the middle-class associations which came to the family name through his kinsman, John Wesley. Mrs Delany had been instantly attracted to Richard Wesley. He was very sociable, very rich and very cultivated; he had rather a peevish wife but charming daughters. For long there was no male heir, a great grief to the Wesleys, for the heir to their estates was someone they disliked. However, their luck improved. Mr Wesley acquired a peerage and also a boy, Garret, who was to be Mrs Delany's godson and the father of the future Duke of Wellington.

One of Mrs Delany's first visits in Ireland was to the Wesleys at Dangan. They were extremely gay; they ate prodigiously; even to a picnic they took cold fowl, lamb, pigeon pie, Dutch beef, tongue and cockles. Mrs Delany describes a typical visit: 'We meet at breakfast at about ten; chocolate, tea, coffee, toast and butter and caudle are devoured without mercy. The hall is so large that often breakfast, battledore and shuttlecock and the harpsichord go on at the same time.' Mr Wesley, in a fanciful mood, gave each of his visitors a white walking-stick, on which was inscribed the name of an appropriate Olympian deity, and when they promenaded with their sticks they looked so strange and impressive that Mrs Delany could only compare them to a sheriff's men at the Assizes.

The family into which the Duke of Wellington was to be born had two major enthusiasms: music, and the arts of war and navigation. There were three canals in the park at Dangan and Mr Wesley had built on them a model of the King's yacht, *Caroline*, a big barge on which his guests went picnicking with flags and a band, a number of sailing-ships and a complete man-of-war. He decorated his artificial waters with islands, groves, obelisks, and statues of Neptune and Apollo. Yet Mrs Delany loyally denied that he was ostentatious: 'He values his riches only as a means of making all about happy.'

When Mrs Delany paid a later visit to Dangan, everything was more opulent still. Mr Wesley was now Earl of Mornington and had made a park of 900 acres; her godson, the thirteen-year-old Master Wesley, had an elaborate fort on the lake. He was Lord High Admiral of the man-of-war; he hoisted the flag for his godmother and wished to fire her a salute of guns. 'Master Wesley', she said dotingly, 'is the most extraordinary boy. Whatever he studies he masters it surprisingly. He began with the fiddle last year, he now plays everything at sight; he understands fortifications and the building of ships.'

Ten years later young Master Wesley, who had succeeded his father, was indulging the first family passion; he had founded a music academy in Dublin. He himself was leader of the orchestra. It was amateur and fashionable and the proceeds were devoted to charity – and it introduced Italian music to Dublin. As the years went by Mrs Delany writes less cordially of her godson. She found him 'ill-educated', yet, she adds tepidly, 'he is a good young man on the whole, but where is the perfect creature?' His bride, the mother of the Great Duke, a Miss Hill from Ulster, she found as ignorant as himself.

The Duke was Member for Trim in 1790, but I don't know what memories he had of Dangan – or if he regretted its passing. I don't expect he wasted much time on such unprofitable sentiments. Family history of any kind bored him. When the Kilkenny Archaeological Society was founded the secretary reminded the Duke with unwise unction that the Duke's family, the Colleys or Cowleys, came from Kilkenny and suggested that he should honour their Society by becoming its most illustrious member. In dealing with such correspondence the Duke was always punctilious even when he was snubbing. He replied tersely that he was unaware of any family association with Kilkenny, he was much occupied and there would be little point in joining a society in a town he was never likely to visit.

All the same, the lakes of Dangan, the canals with their forts and men-of-war, may have played some part in shaping the Duke's ambition. He may seldom have wasted his time in thinking of Trim, but Trim must often think of him, with pride or indifference, for the victor of Waterloo still dominates the town from a lofty stone column.

III. SLIEVE BLOOM

The Slieve Bloom mountains are a low, demure-looking range of hills, very suitable for middle-aged, unadventurous mountaineers with children and picnic-baskets. Approaching from Mountrath in Laois, a good road trimmed with the plantations of the Forestry Department takes you almost to the summit and down the other side into Clonaslee. It is an admirable bit of engineering, sloping so gradually upwards that a considerable height is reached without much grinding of gears or hairpin bends. From above you look down on dozens of sheltered valleys. In one of them the Barrow, the mildest of rivers, makes its first modest appearance. In most of them silvery Sitkas and grass-green Norway spruces are slowly crowding out the heather and encroach farther and farther upon the spongy plateaus above. If you decide to advance to what is marked on the map as the summit, there is no question of leaping from crag to crag like a chamois till at last a wind-swept cairn is reached.

That happens on other Irish hills but not in the Slieve Bloom. In the early spring, anyway, it is a matter of hopping from tussock to tussock and squelching through the sphagnum moss. If you have not several pairs of socks, a good sense of direction and a mackintosh with which to drape the occasional strand of Forestry barbed wire, it is better not to go too far. An honourable retreat is possible because on these gentle gradients it is hard to distinguish altitude from perspective, and after a very short spell of tussock-hopping and puddle-dodging it is easy to persuade oneself that 'the summit' has been reached and one may return to the woods. These, I suspect, show as wide a variety of softwood trees as you could find anywhere else in Ireland. Even the cypresses, which with their wind-scorched lower branches look as bedraggled and alien as solitary trees in cemeteries and suburbs, have acclimatized themselves in the Slieve Bloom. Massed in thick ranks along the roads, they have a fine exotic dignity.

The Slieve Bloom, sprawling along the edges of three counties, Laois, Offaly and Tipperary, made the deepest impression on an earlier age. The foothills were crowded with monasteries and endless tall stories were told about the first inhabitants. One poet said the mountain got its name 'Sliabh Bladma' in Irish from a man called Blad, the son of Cu, but in the middle of Blad's unremarkable life even the author got bored, and, deciding he could do better, broke off. The mountain, he corrected himself, was called after 'bled', a whale, because the hills had once been infested with amphibious monsters from the sea, who had ravaged the whole countryside and torn branches from the trees.

He was a layman but the monastic scribes who wrote about the Slieve Bloom and its saints and villains did not lag behind in inventiveness. For generations quills must have been scratching in every valley here, copying, editing, revising, embellishing, the lives of founders, sometimes in Latin, sometimes in Irish. These saints are almost uncountable and many of their 'Lives' survive. Going round Slieve Bloom clockwise from Mountrath, you can trace St Fintan at Clonenagh, St Coemhan at Anatrim, St Manchin at Mundrehid, St Finan Cam at Kinnitty. Lengthen the radius a couple of miles and you will take in St Canice at Aghaboe, St Cronan of Roscrea, St Molua of Kyle, St Kieran of Saigir and his mother St Liadan at Killyon, and scores of others.

There are still some traces of these foundations. At Clonenagh, which is said to mean 'the ivy meadow', there is a ruin which lives up to its name by being three parts ivy to one part stone. At Aghaboe, where once lived a famous Protestant rector, Ledwich, who entertained his contemporaries but scandalized posterity with a sceptical book about the Irish saints, there is a fine array of medieval buildings. At Roscrea a broad street runs between the charming Romanesque gateway, the last remnant of St Cronan's church, and its old companion the round tower, which has almost been swallowed up by a garage. At Saigir, a delightful spot, there are the remnants of a vast wall said to have been built by Saive, Queen of Ireland, in the tenth century. While the wall was being built the funeral of her father, the King of Ossory, came to the church followed by nine evil men with blackened faces, who chanted a dirge over the body. They had come up from Hell, declared the clergy of Saigir, to claim the soul of the King, but Masses were said and holy water sprinkled and the demons flew away frustrated in the shape of ink-black birds. This sinister band was called the Crossans, a name which they passed on to a local family of Irish descent now called Crosbie.

St Fintan of Clonenagh is reputed to have been the most ascetic of Irish saints. He endured endless mortifications of the flesh and great pains were taken so that his food was as disagreeable as possible. Of him the poet monk has written:

> Generous Fintan never ate
> but the bread of blighted barley
> and strained muddy water.

There used to be a celebrated holy well of Fintan near Clonenagh but it is said that a century ago the landlord objected to the crowd of pilgrims trampling his crops and leaving his gates open and he tried to divert the water to the public road. But St Fintan, outraged by this desecration, swept the well away three miles to Cremogue. Wherever drops of water fell from it in its passage a sacred spring arose. Some drops fell in the hollows of an old sycamore and high up in its branches an inexhaustible pool of healing water was found and constantly visited. I expect this old tree which used to be decorated with rags and ribbons has crumbled away by now, but I think it must have left an heir between Clonaslee and Kinnitty, for at one point the metalled road suddenly divides and flows in two narrow lanes round an old thorn tree on a little island of grass. This tree too was covered with rags and ribbons. It was pleasant to see that now and again the road-makers can't have it all their own way, and we began to speculate whether they could not be frustrated at Durrow too. Has not beauty its claims as well as piety? The old bridge at Durrow in south Laois is now due to be demolished, and I could find nothing said against it except that it was not necessary when the new bridge and road are built to the east of it. But cannot it be allowed to survive as a foot-bridge? By the precedent of Durrow maybe the fate of a dozen other bridges across the Nore will be decided. They are all of them high-backed and sooner or later someone will say they are inconvenient or dangerous. But when that time comes, why must they be demolished? Why can they not just be retired from active service. They are fine structures, all of them, built I believe after the great flood of 1763 which swept away the bridges on the Nore and drowned a number of citizens standing on them gaping at the waters in Kilkenny city.

To come back to north Laois, there used to be an ancient Book of Clonenagh, the companion of the Books of Durrow and Kells. A few generations ago some said that the Protestant rector had left it to his son who went to farm sheep in Melbourne, others had seen it at Sir Charles Coote's library in Ballyfin House. But one of his neighbours, General Dunne of Brittas, engaged in the search and declared that neither the rector nor the Cootes ever had it. The search is still on.

The shell of General Dunne's large Victorian Gothic house still stands near Clonaslee. It was burnt by accident in the thirties, but I never saw art (or should one say artifice?) hold nature at bay for so long, and lawns and shrubberies put up so gallant, if hopeless, a fight for survival. In early April vast mountains of scarlet rhododendra were in bloom, one exceptionally beautiful with white and purple flowers. There were forests of flowering currants and mahonia, berberis and laurustinus waving long flowery arms despairingly above the brambles.

We ended the circuit of the mountains at Leap Castle near Roscrea. It was once the most famous haunted house in Ireland but now, like Brittas, it is a shell, and I believe that none of its innumerable ghosts survived the burning of the twenties. Any lingering mystery has been well exorcised, for on every scrap of bare plaster on the crumbling walls visitors from Birr and

Roscrea have pencilled their reassuring names and unmagical drawings. St Finan Cam is said to have left Kinnitty because there were too many devoted pilgrims and the spectres may have left Leap for the same reason. As we climbed the dark winding stairs to the roof, no clammy hand was laid on our shoulders, though clammy hands were once a vital part of the supernatural programme. Grisliest of all was the Hand that crept from under the spare-room bed and remorselessly gripped the hand of the unsuspecting sleeper; mad with fear, he would tug and tug and just before he fainted with fright the hand used to come off in his grip. Apparitions and psychic adventures alike were heralded by an overpowering smell of goat.

It was from the terrace on the east front of Leap that we got our last view of the Slieve Bloom. Girdled round with gorse and blackthorn, and with all their angularities smoothed out by conifer plantations, they are the homeliest, least awe-inspiring of mountains. You would need the imperious imagination of a Dark Age poet to picture whales tearing at the Department barbed wire to get at the Sitkas, or coveys of black-faced demons hovering above them and searching for souls to snatch. Even an ordinary Victorian ghost with clammy hands seemed inconceivable on that mild April evening.

Postscript There were two sequels to my story of Slieve Bloom. Firstly, Paul Hamilton of Moyne near Durrow wrote to *The Irish Times* supporting my appeal that the old bridge at Durrow should not be destroyed. Possibly what we wrote had some influence, because the old bridge is still there with the brand-new bridge jutting out from it at an acute angle.

The second consequence was an angry letter from the owner of Leap Castle accusing me of trespassing and of lowering the value of his property by repeating 'silly stories about ghosts'.

IV. IN COUNTY CAVAN

If one is to judge by emigration figures, there is no county in Ireland which its natives leave so precipitately as Cavan. Yet to an outsider, who has not to struggle with its bogs and rushes, it has an immense appeal. There are regions of west Cavan so full of lakes that sometimes the cartographers have decided it is all one lake, interrupted by scores of islands and peninsulas. The river Erne shambles undecidedly through this ambiguous land, through Lough Gowan and Lough Oughter to the thousand islands of Upper Lough Erne. It hesitates at every bog and makes a lake, it winds round every small hill and makes an island. Because of all these hills and lakes, communities are isolated, there are letter-boxes on trees, lonely petrol-pumps, and small shops in boreens where you can buy bootlaces, aspirins, doses for bullocks and long-bladed Cavan spades. You used to get fine cheap rush hats for haymaking, and potato baskets and clogs made from the local willows and alders, but I have not seen them there lately, and more exotic commodities like chocolate creams are soft and blotchy with age and long waiting.

The fact is that the social machinery which made living in a small community possible is breaking down, and science, which by 'annihilating distances' should have made geographical isolation meaningless, has on the contrary made it rather less tolerable. If you can walk to Cavan or Killeshandra and see Grace Kelly's wedding at Monte Carlo (for in these Ulster counties of the Republic televisions can be smuggled as easily as cattle), all the traditional patterns fade away in the glare of this distant radiance. A generation ago Irish was still talked in Glangevlin, the wild pass under Guilcagh which the Smith's Green Cow tunnelled out with her swinging udders. But even the memory that it was once spoken there seems to have gone now. And how would you possibly want to be a shanachie or a hero like Patrick Sarsfield or even like the raiders a few miles off at Rosslea, when every Monday afternoon, under slate roofs and thatched roofs, Mrs Dale can be heard confidently, comfortably, preaching the English middle-class gospel of common sense and material well-being. Her voice is more seductive than the song of the sirens for she tells of a lotus land where everybody has a refrigerator and a car and nobody has to struggle with rushes. The English Sunday papers, with which the newsagents of Cavan and Belturbet are stuffed, take up the tale. No wonder all the young men and women in Cavan are bewitched.

Something has been done to head off their stampede to the sea. We met a contented farmer near the source of the Shannon who showed us his Aberdeen Angus bull which the government had secured for him at a quarter the market price, and its calves which were earning him twice the normal Leinster price. He praised our agricultural experts who had judged correctly the aptitudes of the Cavan soil. But the problem is not primarily financial. Many Cavan Protestants, it is true, are trying to better themselves by slipping across the border into Northern Ireland. Looking at the northern rather than the southern slopes of Slieve Rushen, they collect their increased family allowances and pensions, their free dentures, without much psychological or geographical upheaval. But the majority, when they leave Cavan, also leave Ireland.

There is little or no tourist traffic. The lakes are not sufficiently big and blue, the mountains are not romantically craggy. There is only one round tower, Drumlane, and that has lost most of its top. There are plenty of stone circles and alignments, but hedges and bogs and barbed wire protect them from all but the curious. You must walk along the railway line to reach the Killycluggin stone and the hilltop where Cavan antiquaries believe that St Patrick destroyed Cromm Cruach and his twelve attendant gods. They say that the vast prostrate stones which crown a little hill are the fallen idols; hawthorn trees preserve the outline of the circle and create a scented numinous seclusion appropriate to a sacred grove. The Killycluggin stone is in two halves forty yards apart. The upper half is scored with a criss-cross La Tène pattern, the lower half is partly ploughed into the sod and its pattern is indistinguishable. A little to the south is Garadice Lough, the biggest of the west Cavan lakes. It is said to take its name from Guth Ard, 'loud voice', since St Patrick bawled his denunciations of Cromm Cruach from its farther shore. Local report says that not long ago it was far larger, comprising a chain of little lakes to the east of it. On the question of the source of the Shannon, cartography has been vanquished by legend, because plainly the Owenmore river is the upper course of the Shannon and the little trickle that flows down from the sacred pool on the slopes of Guilcagh is a mere tributary. Is it in that pool that the Salmon of Knowledge dispensed wisdom, or did it live at the source of the Boyne? To be on the safe side, the most learned of us took a muddy draught. (I went on my trip round Cavan with Professor Myles Dillon and Major-General Dorman Smith, a Cavanman and subject of a recent biography.)

Cavan is a land of wide vistas. From Seantemon, where six or seven vast pillar-stones mark the site of the inauguration of the O'Reillys, the chieftains of east Cavan, you can see to north and west the mountains of Fermanagh and Sligo, while southwards the pattern of small hills extends itself for miles without a break. The little hills hide the lakes and from high up you get no impression of the immense wateriness of Cavan. Wherever there are trees planted the country changes its character. There are forest lakes which recall the lakes of East Prussia, secret meres, where the shadows and strong scent of the pine trees reach far out into the water. But in sophistication what a difference! In East Prussia the lakes were linked by canals and small steamers voyaged up and down them heavily laden with schoolchildren spitting out cherry-stones into the waters. Between the lakes there were little towns with bandstands, cafés, coloured awnings; white-coated waiters raced up and down with glasses of Himbeer Saft and a stodgy sponge cake called Königs Kuchen.

And now they have all gone, waiters, schoolchildren, everyone, two million of them, a total evacuation which makes the slow depopulation of Cavan seem a much more remediable disaster. All that Cavan needs, I think, is a small inflow of money and civilization to balance the exodus. This exodus was of course in part political, and here and there in Cavan you still meet the traces of the post-Treaty withdrawal. There used to be an abandoned Eden at Castle Sanderson near Belturbet. The owner, Colonel Sanderson, had been one of the leaders of the Ulster Volunteers and the house was long derelict after the Treaty, but acres of bog-garden survived. Bridges of log and turf spanned the bog-pools, there were rhododendrons, which singly covered five times the space of a suburban garden, and azaleas had to be hacked down with axes so as not to smother more Gothic shrubs. There were many houses and gardens like this. Whether they were good Irishmen or not, the owners could not avoid spilling around a little of the leaven of their own prosperity, privilege, stability. Good books on Ireland, like Shirley's *Monaghan*, were written in these houses. And I think there is a case for regarding any man who lives and works in Ireland as a better Irishman (even if he has not a drop of Celtic blood in his veins) than those who leave it simply to better themselves.

The position is very grim, for what will happen if England can no longer employ the 800,000 Irishmen who now live there? Lately a very uncompromising Cavan anti-partitionist suggested in *The Irish Times* that money and leisure should once more be attracted to Cavan by reducing the income tax in the depopulated north-western counties to the Jersey level. Coming from such a source this unromantic remedy deserves respect. Maybe it would bring the Irish home, but even if it brought only aliens could not Cavan assimilate them? What if it brought Mrs Dale herself, attracted by the little lakes for Bob's children to fish in, and the hope that the income the doctor left her would go further in a taxless land, would it matter? Mrs Dale is here already in spirit; if she came in the flesh too she could at least pay her bills and help to keep five or six Cavan men and women at home. This is a rather disillusioned logic but it is logic all the same.

I have always wanted to see Templeport Lough and kept my companions from their suppers while we searched for it. There is a very sacred island there where St Maedoc of Ferns is said to have been born and many hundreds of stanzas of verse, many pages of prose in Latin and in Irish, have been written by medieval monks about him and about the dues and duties which the small tribes of west Cavan owed to his successors. When we found the lake it was not, I must admit, very different from all the other lakes. There is a Protestant church on the edge, but the rector lives in Swanlinbar and the rectory has been sold to some people who live half the year in Egypt. A big flat-bottomed boat is moored among the willow herbs and every now and then it is used to ferry mourners and coffins across to the island, for certain families are still buried there.

It is strange to reflect that it is an Englishman, Dr Plummer of Oxford, who forty years ago edited the lives of this Cavan and Wexford saint, both in Latin and in Irish, a task that demanded learning and industry and love. There is no reason to suppose that 'alien' settlers in Cavan would be any less respectful than he of the traditions and ancient language of those among whom they made their homes.

V. IN MONAGHAN

I have long wanted for a special reason to go to Donaghmoyne, and when a few weeks ago we found ourselves at Carrickmacross, we took the narrow road to Crossmaglen and after a couple of miles through a country of small lakes and small hills we were at Donaghmoyne Church. It is exactly the same as all the Protestant churches built 150 years ago: two pointed windows on the north and south side of a rectangular block and a belfry with pinnacles at each of the four corners. As often elsewhere it has been recently closed and the graveyard is waist-high with weeds. It was hard to decipher the names on the tombs so that it was not till later that I learnt that W. S. Trench, the author of *Realities of Irish Life*, lay there under a white marble Celtic cross. He was once a great local potentate, the land agent, successively, of Mr Shirley and the Marquess of Bath, who owned between them the barony of Farney and exercised an almost royal sway over its 44,000 inhabitants. His character has been variously interpreted. Canon O'Hanlon, writing of Donaghmoyne, refers to him as the notorious calumniator and exterminator of the people of Farney, and D. C. Rush, the historian of Monaghan, insinuates that he was a liar, who bribed *agents provocateurs*. On the other hand Lord Bath, a humane and progressive landlord, thought highly of him.

Trench's book, first published in 1868, suggests that his considerable literary gifts tempted him sometimes to colourful exaggeration but that on the whole he brought peace to the barony and served an unpopular régime with a loyalty that was tempered by humanity. His son illustrated the book with a superabundance of filial piety. In picture after picture Trench, a figure of scriptural beauty, faces alone and unarmed a mob of drink-sodden Paddies brandishing shillelaghs and hurling bottles and turnips. Though his shirt is torn from his back and his limbs are bleeding, he is undaunted. I like best the picture where he stands at bay on a dining-room chair in Mr Shirley's hall at Lough Fea. Above him a brace of elks' antlers, to his right an urn of aspidistras and all around him Ribbonmen and Molly Maguires. But he has quelled them with his manly eloquence and grace. How much of a liar was he? It is impossible to say. Rush's evidence is very inconclusive. But certainly Trench's sense of drama makes the book still very readable.

It was not, however, because of Trench, though I will come back to him, that I went to Donaghmoyne, but to see if I could find there any confirmation of a theory to which Donaghmoyne seemed to lend support. I am no Irish scholar but base my theory on everyday arguments and easily verifiable facts and so should be able to make myself intelligible to the ordinary reader.

When St Patrick brought the gospel to Donaghmoyne, we are told in the *Tripartite Life* that he found there a stiff-necked pagan called Victor, who hid from the light of the Truth in some blackthorn bushes (the word used for blackthorn is 'draighean'). But the apostle shed a supernatural radiance over the thicket and the pagan chief was exposed, converted and finally left in Donaghmoyne as its first bishop. Now it is my contention that the lives of the saints are a patchwork of tribal puns and that the writer was thinking of the Uí Draignean, a tribe principally located in Mayo, Sligo and Westmeath and linked by the philologists with 'draighean'. Were they also at Donaghmoyne? I listed all the places in Ireland called after blackthorns, for I believed that they too derived from the Uí Draignean. There were several dozens but not so many that the occurrence of three such places in the small parish of Donaghmoyne did not appear remarkable. There was Aghadreenan, Rosdreenagh, Drumdreenagh: the field, the wood, the ridge of the blackthorns. But to prove that they were not real blackthorns I had to find the Uí Draignean tribe there. Rush's *History of Monaghan* gave me what I wanted. He prints the Hearth Money roll of taxpayers for 1663 for the twenty-three parishes of Monaghan. In only one of them are the Uí Draignean, then O'Drynan or O'Dreenan, present and that is Donaghmoyne. Rush adds that the name was anglicized to Thornton in penal times.

The tombstones could not be deciphered and yielded nothing, so I asked an elderly woman who was walking past the church, 'Can you tell me is there a family called O'Dreenan or Thornton here?' She thought a moment and then said, 'No, but there were Thorntons at Rosdreenagh till last year.' This seemed to me conclusive. Clearly the Blackthorn family of Rosdreenagh had lived here for over a thousand years and it was of them that the hagiographer had been thinking when he wrote of St Victor's hiding-place. I found a little place in Donaghmoyne parish called Thornford and that surely also derives from the Uí Draignean. But will such investigations interest anybody now? It is only the local scholar who could disentangle these local facts from the ancient histories in which they are punningly embedded, but he is too intimidated by metropolitan learning to indulge in unconventional speculations. W. S. Trench belonged to a bolder breed. Though it has no relation to the rest of his book, he prints in it a map of all the tribes in Ireland and a four-page commentary, lively but extravagantly wrong, and his employer Mr Shirley not only gathered a famous library at Lough Fea but wrote a classic history of his native county. Is anything comparable being done in Co. Monaghan today?

Writing of the Thorntons, I recall that it was a Thornton from near Donaghmoyne, 'an idle, good-for-nothing fellow, weak, small and cunning', who plotted to kill W. S. Trench but later acted as informer so that two of his companions were hanged in Monaghan gaol. Trench devotes a chapter to a very racy account of the conspiracy furnished by this voluble informer. Indeed it is too racy to seem quite genuine, but it is not malicious and it is clear that Trench had a humorous understanding and indeed affection for his would-be assassins. In time he grew to love his warm-hearted, spontaneous, complicated neighbours, whose minds shifted so swiftly from murderous thoughts to kindly ones. There is evidence that he was loved in return, and certainly he tried to improve their lot and did.

When he first arrived in Farney as agent, the hills for miles around were ablaze with bonfires to celebrate the glad tidings of his predecessor's death, who by some miscarriage of plan had died in his bed. Trench had not inherited an easy situation. The week after his arrival ten thousand people marched to Carrickmacross and, surging round the agent's house, dropped all at once upon their knees and pleaded earnestly for a reduction of rent. It was shortly after this that Trench harangued them in the hall at Lough Fea, and though he lost his shirt, jacket and top hat he seems to have won their esteem.

Obviously it was preposterous that the welfare of a whole barony should depend on two families, one of them absentee (Farney had been given by Elizabeth to the Earl of Essex, and the Shirleys and Baths were his descendants), but an unjust system wisely administered sometimes has virtues which the just must admire. Trench was hard-working, scrupulous and a keen farmer, and even Rush and O'Hanlon would scarcely have denied that even at his worst he gave to the tenants the care that a good stock-breeder gives to his stock. They prospered and multiplied and the welcome which they gave to Lord Bath in 1865 was probably partially spontaneous. A prince returning to his principality could not have been more sumptuously entertained. Carrickmacross was gay with banners, inscribed with

'Céad Míle Fáilte', with festoons and evergreens. There were bands and cheering crowds as the Marquess drove behind four handsome greys to the Market Hall where upon 'superb carpets' a throne had been erected. There were addresses from the tenants, orations, banquets, coronets woven in ivy leaves and those two elks' heads of Mr Shirley's were brought to the Market House and decorated with 'Erin Go Bragh' and the coat of arms of the Baths. In the evening there were fireworks at the Court House, and 'a magnificent transparency' outside the sub-agent's house. There was a vast banquet attended by the tenants and the clergy of all denominations at which toasts were drunk in champagne while the band played 'Nora Creina'. Lord Bath was a boring speaker but Trench's reply is even today very interesting and informative for he analysed with unusual candour and a minimum of post-prandial unction the relationship of landlord and tenant on the Bath estate.

If Donaghmoyne churchyard were to yield him up for half a day, how would Trench report on the changed situation? One would not need to adapt very much his after-dinner speech. He would admit that the people were more sophisticated, better fed and clothed. But he would say: 'Where have you all gone? Why are half your farmhouses derelict? In my day, the Famine had already taken its toll, scarcely anyone emigrated from the estates of the Marquess of Bath. Often I would urge a tenant to leave an uneconomic holding, offering him his fare to America and ample compensation for his stock, but he seldom accepted. The Marquess spent £50,000 in sixteen years on his tenant farms; he engaged an agriculturalist to give free advice. And you were a real community then. Whether you wanted to murder me or applaud me, you were all, Catholic and Protestant, bound by common interests. There was no sectarian bitterness!'

Only the local worthies who sat at the banquet would now be able to tell us if what he was saying were true. Undoubtedly it was a very smug occasion, well garnished with blarney and red, white and blue ribbons. But a lucid mind should still be able to recognize what was good in the old system and disentangle it from the bullying and toadyism in which it was embedded.

VI. THE BRITISH ISRAELITES AT TARA

All my life I have heard how a band of British Israelites dug into the mounds of Tara in order to discover the Ark of the Covenant, and so muddled up everything for future excavators. The story has been used as a cautionary tale about the evils of unauthorized excavation and to justify the official regulations prohibiting it. These have always seemed to me to favour the farmer and the miner, who may demolish ancient earthworks in order to grow turnips or export minerals to Germany, and to insult and discourage the local antiquarian, who is assumed to be a barbarian. So I was delighted to learn in 1969 that the whole story was fictional from beginning to end.

My informant was my old cousin Synolda French, who like myself belonged to the lesser Irish gentry and was one of the Butlers of Dunboyne. I will relate our conversation just as it occurred, because she had a lively mind and an excellent memory and because the Meath of her childhood now seems as far away as Melchizedek, who, it is said, brought the Ark to Tara. It all took place in 1898, when Cousin Synolda was just grown-up.

'Tell me, Cousin Synolda,' I asked, 'about the band of British Israelites who excavated the mound at Tara.'

'Well, there wasn't any band but just one young student, and he was not a British Israelite and he didn't excavate the mound.'

'How did you come across him?'

'When Uncle Whitty died my father came to live at Staffordstown near Navan, but my mother died when I was seven (she was one of the Rothwells of Rockfield) and, as my father had difficulty about governesses, I went to live with Aunt Mary at 3 Leeson Park, Dublin, where I went to school, and only came home to Staffordstown for the holidays. I was born in 1881 and I was just seventeen when our neighbours, Cecil and Shirley Ball, told us about the young man from London. Cecil's father was a retired captain who hunted and farmed at Gerardstown Castle (that place is now gone); his wife was a Humphries from Ballyhaise in the north of Ireland. They were tickled to death about this young man, Mr Groome he was called, and we were all very interested.

'You see he was lodging in a hotel in Navan and he enquired there how to get to Tara and they told him he must get in touch with Gussie Briscoe at Bellinter, who was a great friend of Cecil and Shirley's.'

'Did Gussie Briscoe own Tara?'

'Yes, he came by it in an odd way. You see old Mr Preston of Bellinter had one daughter; she married a Mr Smith and had two or three children. He and his wife and children got scarlet fever, which was very hard to cure in those days, and they all died. Mr Preston was very lonely in the big house and when Mr Briscoe, the rector of Bective, died, Mr Preston asked his widow and her little boy, his godson, to come and live at Bellinter. And Mr Preston made Gussie his heir.

'We were great friends with Gussie's children. They are all dead now except the youngest, Baby or Bay she was called, but I think her real name was Muriel. Now Bay would be able to tell you a lot about that Ark of the Covenant. I was just engaged to be married at the time and, of course, I was thinking of other things.

'So this Mr Groome took a side-car out to Bellinter and told Gussie he wanted to dig for the Ark of the Covenant. Gussie was fascinated and said 'Of course!' and told two of his men to dig for him and paid their wages, for the young man hadn't a penny. And they dug three big holes near the wall of the Protestant church at Tara a long way from the mounds. We were all highly delighted and amused. There were all kinds of jokes. We were very hard up at the time and we were saying that we would turn Staffordstown into a hotel for all the Jews who would come to see the Ark and we would make a lot of money. Shirley and Cecil hid all kinds of things for the young man to find, teapot lids and so on, and Shirley hid Lady Dillon's napkin-ring. But the young man was very good-humoured and just laughed.'

'Did he explain to you what he was after?'

'Yes, he did. Everyone laughed at me for taking him seriously but I was interested. One day we had tennis at Staffordstown and Cecil and Shirley brought him along. He was very gauche and badly dressed and he tried to make excuses for not playing tennis. He hadn't shoes or a racquet. But we said we'd lend him them. He played very badly and I was sorry for him; he looked so odd. He had a grey shirt with red braces and all the others had white flannels and I said, 'Won't you come and see the garden?' So we walked off but I could see he wasn't at all interested in the garden either. So I said to him, 'Tell me about the Ark of the Covenant.' And after a bit he saw I was really interested and not just laughing at him as the others were.

'It was this way. He had been studying hieroglyphics and he found that there was a record that, wherever the Ark had rested, a stone with a certain hieroglyphic on it had been set up and these stones had been traced all the way from Palestine to the Atlantic coast. It had ended in mystery. Then one day he had been rummaging through some second-hand books on a stall and had found a small fat illustrated book about Freemasonry and there, on one of those ornaments that the masons wear, he had seen the very same hieroglyphic. He had gone then to the British Museum and found that there were stones in Ireland reaching from near Dundalk to Tara with the same hieroglyphics on them. So he'd come to Tara. He never said one word about the British Israelites. There was just himself and he'd no money. If they'd sent him, surely they'd have given him some?

'Well. Mr Groome was digging by the church wall just the right distance (he had all the measurements) from the stone which he thought must be the one locating the Ark, when an old man called Richard Wilkinson, whose father had been killed in the '98 rebellion, came up to him and told him that the stone had originally been the other side of the road on Lord Somebody's property (I forget his name) but it had been moved over near the church to commemorate the men who had been killed at the battle of Tara. Their names are on it. So Mr Groome saw he had been digging in the wrong place and he wrote to Lord Somebody asking him if he could dig on his land and Lord Somebody had just written back, 'Go to Hell!' So the poor young fellow went back to London having wasted his time and found nothing.

'But when we told Dr Praeger and the others that this was what had happened, they just wouldn't believe us. And some of them got quite angry about it. They'd made up their minds that Tara had been messed up by the British Israelites and nothing we said could make them change it.'

The old story cropped up in *The Irish Times* before she died and Cousin Synolda wrote contradicting it. But I don't think she made much impression, as one still hears it again and again.

[1948, 1949, 1956]

11

INFLUENZA IN ARAN

When I arrived in Aran by the *Naomh Éanna* at Kilronan I was sneezing and by the time I had raced to St Enda's church at Killeany and seen the stone on which he had floated in from Connemara I was feverish and coughing. I spent the rest of my time in bed reading the only two books on Aran and its saints which I could find, a big one by Mr Ó Síocháin and a small one by Father Scantlebury.* I also studied Irish with my landlady's daughter, a little girl of four called Teresa. These lessons started when she had her hands behind her back and said, 'You can't see my fingers!' I said, 'No more I can! But say it in Irish!' She replied immediately, 'Ní féidir leat mo mhéaranna a fheiceáil!' And so it went on. She was as instantaneous as an interpreter at the United Nations Assembly and she asked no salary. She taught and I learnt with pleasure and indeed joy. That is how Irish should have been. Yet in 1987 40,000 Irish are leaving Ireland every year, cursing their elders who forced them to learn Irish instead of something 'useful' like business management or word-processing or nuclear physics.

But to come back to those two books: Father Scantlebury is cautious and a little dry, Mr Ó Síocháin is exuberant and daring. He says that Aran might well be the tail-end of Hy Brasil, the wonderful island which, like Plato's Atlantis, is lost beneath the sea. He adds that Aran was once 'the greatest spiritual storehouse the world has ever known'. When the Celts first settled there, they had a mighty empire in Europe behind them and 'centuries of civilization of the highest order'. Of St Enda, the doyen of the spiritual storehouse, Mr Ó Síocháin says: 'He was

P. A. Ó Síocháin, *Aran Islands of Legend* (Dublin 1962); Rev. C. Scantlebury, S.J., *Saints and Shrines of Aran Mór* (Dublin 1926).

probably one of the greatest teachers the Church has ever known.' Father Scantlebury says the same thing more cautiously. There is much of interest in both these books. Mr Ó Síocháin writes perceptively of John Synge's brief but memorable sojourn in Aran, and of the many owners who collected rents from the islands but never visited them.

I too am tempted to use the language of hyperbole about Aran. It seems to me one of the most enchanting and interesting spots in Europe since it has held on to a precarious beauty and simplicity which the rest of the world is disastrously discarding. But it is St Enda and the spiritual storehouse that chiefly arouse my curiosity. When my friend Dr Simpson came out from Galway to visit me on the Whit Monday excursion I hoped to communicate some of my enthusiasm to him but I failed miserably. He dismissed Ó Síocháin scornfully and Scantlebury patronizingly, and talked to me in terms of the Latin *Life of Enda*, of conflations, collations, recensions. After a glance or two he slapped both my books down on the counterpane. 'I see they repeat that old error, which Zimmer exposed, of Conall Derg being the father of Enda. Conall was a purely fabulous person.'

'Of course,' I agreed, 'he was the wicked King of Clogher, who brought the poisoned ox to St Lassar on Devenish Island.' (I should explain that I enjoy the ancient Irish habit of explaining with an entertaining anecdote any proper name that puzzles them, as so many do. Devenish [Damh Inis] on Loch Erne, means Ox Island.)

'But surely,' I added, 'even if it were a different Enda who was son of Conall Derg and spent his youth burning churches and plotting to murder his grandfather, did the real Enda of Aran ever do or say anything that we would recognize as even faintly Christian? Weren't he and all the other saints of Aran merely very successful magicians?'

He dodged this and talked instead of folklore and comparative religion and then his voice tapered away into something about the charm of innocence. We both of us began to yawn and after a bit he got up to catch his boat.

He left me with the impression that Enda is sliding gently out of history on the heels of Conall Derg and that the whole spiritual storehouse is in danger of collapsing. Just as Enda had much in common with his church-burning namesake, so many of the other saints of Aran had either a sinful past or a sinful namesake. Moreover they are almost all Enda's relations and so are the saints of Wales, Cornwall, Scotland and Brittany. Three generations ago Father Shearman accommodated all the most important ones into three or four intertwined family trees. If one goes, and there are many hundreds of them, they all go. For they support each other like a house of cards in which no single card can stand alone or can safely be pulled away and if Enda, the greatest teacher in the greatest spiritual storehouse, were to go, a hundred spiritual storehouses would collapse with him, leaving a forest of interrogation marks behind.

For different reasons, romantic, religious, academic, tourist, no one wants this to happen. If Enda and his storehouse were to disintegrate, they would do so without any sort of explosion. No tremors would be recorded on Aran. *Naomh Éanna* would not sink or have to be renamed. Nor would Dr Simpson bother to force his new perceptions on Father Scantlebury or Mr Ó Síocháin.

This absence of explosion is a proof that learning, which in Ireland has always flourished best in the country, is dead. It has not transplanted well to the universities. Real learning is dynamic, dangerous, exhilarating. It is built on curiosity, not on knowledge. When it explodes, someone feels liberated, someone else is hurt. At present in place of curiosity there is textual criticism, and philology and scientific excavations, which are all highly skilled crafts like apiculture and hairdressing. No bombs are thrown at Atlantis or the spiritual storehouse, but there is much silent and salaried sneering.

Dr Simpson and the textual critics are at present working on Enda. When they have amputated what is fabulous or corrupt, there will be almost nothing left of the great teacher and saint. But because of their fine finicky methods, his will be an almost painless extinction. Every sentence is analysed separately and any attempt to judge truth by everyday criteria is deemed amateurish.

Mr Ó Síocháin argues like this too but more artlessly. He relates how Enda in his warlike, church-burning phase had tried to abduct a virgin from his sister St Fainche's convent and how the virgin, on a hint from Fainche, had said she would prefer to be the bride of Christ and had composed herself on a couch and died. Mr Ó Síocháin finds this too extreme and says that it was a clever little trick of Fainche's to make Enda repent. The girl was not really dead; her deathly pallor was due to shock and the dim conventual light. In fact he euphemizes her as Dr Simpson would say. Enda repented and built his sister a church in Co. Louth which, rather oddly, he called after himself, Killany. He built several such churches.

Were Enda and his colleagues just 'folklore', the unmotivated fabrication of country people? I do not think so. The travels of the saints, their friendships and quarrels, their kinships, their prophesies and cursings, have a close-woven consistency in which a pattern is dimly discernible. They cannot be the product of local and arbitrary fantasy. Behind the fiction lies truth of some kind. What is it?

I have a rough idea of what happened and Enda, like the others, offers clues. His story, though odd, is not chaotic. It is like the agitated and mysterious shadow thrown by a tree on a windy, moonlit night. In the daytime the mystery disperses; the tree is seen to be earth-bound and all its movements occur in a prescribed orbit. Our predecessors wrote history in a primitive picture-language. How is one to interpret it? My guess would be that the saints were the fabulous pre-Christian ancestors of pre-Celtic and proto-Celtic tribes and amalgamations of tribes, and that in their pilgrimages and pedigrees and in the multiplicity of their names, nicknames, cult-centres, we can read the true story of the wanderings of tribes. But since on this early pattern of history-writing later patterns have been superimposed, we have a palimpsest that is very hard to decipher.

Was Enda or Enna, as he is often called, an ancestor? And if so, can one guess what his tribe was? Before the Celts came to Gaul and it was populated by Iberians, Ligurians, Ilyrians, who knows what tribes invaded Ireland? After the Celts, it was the Eneti-Veneti who had easiest access to Ireland.

Thomas O'Rahilly, speculating in his Rhys Lecture on how the Q-Celts came to Ireland, since he knew of none in Gaul, suggested that in the mass migration of the Q-Celtic Helvetii from Switzerland, which Caesar had arrested with immense slaughter, a remnant might have escaped to Ireland, ferried across by the Veneti.

In this many-tiered conjecture what interested me was that so distinguished a scholar accepted the travels of the Veneti to Ireland quite casually. However, in his book *Early Irish History and Mythology* he took it all back, acknowledging that the

Helvetii were not Q- but P- Celts and that there *were* Q-Celts, the Quariates, in Gaul. His manner of saying 'I was wrong' is interesting.

'My suggestion', he wrote, 'had the fatal merit of picturesqueness, which impressed itself on people who were not in a position to appreciate my arguments.' If his lecture were reprinted, he said he would relegate it all to a footnote 'in the hope of preventing the less experienced reader from drawing lopsided conclusions'. But if the Helvetii were not, as he thought, Q-Celts, why mention them at all?

If the Veneti, who were also called Eneti, never came to Ireland and had nothing to do with Fintan and Enda, well, I was wrong and I apologize for my lopsided conclusion, but a few years later they did have a better reason for coming than transporting the Helvetii. They lived on the coast of Britanny leaving their name at Vannes. They were the most accomplished navigators in Gaul. They had a fleet of over 200 ships and, when Julius Caesar attacked them, they were able to summon allies from Britain and all the maritime tribes of northern Gaul. They felt themselves to be invincible and dared to imprison the two ambassadors that the Romans sent. This was an unforgivable outrage and, when Caesar had built a more formidable navy than theirs at Bordeaux and defeated them, none was spared. In his words (he always writes in the third person):

> Caesar thought that punishment should be inflicted the more severely, in order that for the future rights of ambassadors might be more carefully respected by barbarians. Having, therefore, put to death all their senate, he sold the rest for slaves.

So he says, but there were many thousands of Veneti and I do not doubt that many escaped to Britain and to Ireland. Gwynedd in Wales is supposed to owe its name to them, and some have suggested Fenit in Kerry and Fanad in Donegal.

Early tribes had eponymous ancestors: the Moabites had Moab, the Hittites had Heth, the Ionians had Ion, the Persians Perseus, and we do not doubt that the Gaulish tribes had them too, though the Romans, intending that Roman Gaul should be unified, aimed at the suppression of all the old tribal loyalties, in which the Romans showed no interest at all. Caesar did not view the Celts as Mr Ó Síocháin does. The Gauls to him were all just 'barbarians'.

Yet we know that the Esuvii had Esus as ancestor, the Lepontii had Lepontius, the Salassi had Salassus. Who was the ancestor of the Eneti-Veneti? Surely someone like Enetus or Venetus. But we know these proper names only in their Romanized form where the singular ended in -us, the plural in -i. The Gaulish form could easily have been, or become after several generations in Ireland, something like Enna or Enda and Fintan.

When St Enda arrived on his stone in Aran he found a very wicked King Corban in control. When St Enda approached, Corban's subjects all fled in wonder and horror to the coast of Clare, 'for the sun cannot abide with darkness nor heathendom with the light of the Gospel'. Only Corban himself stood his ground, 'a second Pharaoh, *obduratus in malicia*', but finally even he was convinced by a miracle and Enda took over the island. He divided it at first between nine other saints but then, to their anger, decided to keep half for himself. This and some other questions about procedure were settled by two doves flying from Rome. One dropped a missal into St Enda's lap, the other flung a cape over his shoulders to indicate his primacy. Only St Brecan at the Kilmurvey end of the island disputed this.

A different story is told of the division of the island between St Enda and St Brecan. They agreed to start Mass at the same time, one at Cill Éanna, the other at Teampall Bhreacáin. They were then to walk towards each other and where they met the island was to be divided between them. But St Brecan cheated and began Mass before St Enda and so was able to start sooner. However, St Enda quickly caught on to the deception and prayed to the Lord. As a result, when St Brecan and his disciples reached the sea at Kilmurvey their feet stuck fast in the sand and Enda came up to them and so got his fair share of Aran.

Who was this Brecan who held onto his corner of Aranmore when Enda routed Corban and his followers? The late Anne O'Sullivan, my dear friend Neans, edited a poem put into the mouth of a supposed Brecan of Aran. He was pictured as an old bishop dictating his life-story to a young man with special reference to the dues owed by the various families, especially the O'Muldowneys and O'Hallorans, to him and his successors. He relates how his original name was Bresal and his first mission was to Aran where he once destroyed the reigning idol, Brecan, and himself took his name (*Celtica*, Vol. XX, p. 28).

The story delights me for I have always maintained that the Irish saints were tribal ancestors Christianized, and here we see it actually happening.

The newly sanctified Brecan had said, 'The fierce Brecan was in Aran before me, I undertook to expel him and I sanctified his place.'

Anne O'Sullivan suggests that the 'fierce Brecan' was 'an idol', but in the pre-Christian saga there is little talk of idols and much of ancestors. St Brecan and St Enda, competing for territory with Corban and his flock, are behaving like tribes, not like individuals, and in historical retrospect the ancestor, a revered figure, symbolizes the tribe and when in time the tribe dissolves the ancestor, still a revered figure but without a vocation, easily turns into a saint. In Gaul the ancestor, losing his tribe under the Romans, became a god. Thus the god Esus was ancestor of the Esuvii of Normandy, while the goddess Nantosvelta was surely the amalgamated ancestress of the Nantuates and Svelteri of south-east Gaul.

Another inmate of the spiritual storehouse was St Grigóir of Aran. The great Celtic scholar, Rudolf Thurneysen, was baffled by an ancient prophecy that Pope Gregory the Great would be descended from the tribe of Curoi Mac Daire, the famous chieftain of the Dingle Peninsula in Kerry. '*Wie der Verfasser auf diesen Gedanken gekommen ist, ist unbekannt,*' he wrote. It is not, however, at all unknown. Father Shearman, a Victorian country scholar, knew all about it and wrote at length in 1876 in the *Kilkenny Archaeological Journal*.

He writes that there was an Irish St Grigóir or Gregory, a native of the Blasket Islands opposite the Dingle Peninsula, who went with another saint, Faelcu, to Rome; he dismisses as idle talk the story that while in Rome the pontiff died and a dove settled on Faelcu's head and he was offered the papacy, but he believes that on return they settled in Inishmaan in the Aran Islands, where as canons regular they founded Cill na Cannanach, or the Church of the Canons.

It was natural, he thinks, that because of this visit to Rome the Aran islanders should confound their St Gregory with Gregory the Great, and make him share a feast-day, 12 March, with the great pope. And it was not surprising that they should call after him Gregory's Sound, the strait between Inishmore and Inishmaan, through which he and Faelcu passed on their return from Rome. And he says that in 1876, when he wrote, the fishermen who voyaged down the sound on their way to Galway still lowered their sails in homage to the Irish pope.

Father Shearman thinks it quite natural that in Kerry, Grigóir's native land, the strait between the Blasket Islands and the Dingle Peninsula should also be called Gregory's Sound and that St Gregory the Great should be given the Kerry pedigree of his Irish namesake.*

Father Shearman had done better than Thurneysen but his argument should be carried a little farther into regions where he would be unwilling to follow me. Opposite Aran on the Clare coast were the Grecraige or Gregraige, with one ancestor called Grecus and another called Grec mac Aarod. There are Grecraige on Lough Gara in Co. Sligo and their territory is called the Gregories, so obviously Grecraige turns easily into Gregory and makes St Grigóir-Gregory look like a Christian incarnation of the pagan ancestor Grecus.

But to learn more about St Grigóir-Gregory I must go back to Kerry, his native land, and the southern Gregory's Sound. At the base of the Dingle Peninsula is Castle Gregory and inevitably I would claim it for St Gregory, but an Anglo-Norman family called Hoare once lived nearby and it is alleged that one of their number was called Gregory. Yet St Gregory's claim is stronger because he was patron of a church at Glenbeigh in the next barony of Iveragh and in Father Shearman's time his feast-day was observed there on 12 March. But even here, like mocking spirits from the pre-Celtic and pre-Christian past, the Grecraige are recorded in Inis Grecraige or Beare Island, a few miles off in Bantry Bay.

The Grecraige appear in many forms in many parts of Ireland with many ancestors and heroes and saints. To mention one of each, there were Gracraige in Munster with Grac as their ancestor; as hero, there was King Grig of Scotland, the ancestor of the Macgregors, who was also confused with Gregory the Great; there was St Colman Grec of Fermoy, whom Canon Power, the historian of the Decies in Co. Waterford, thought at first must be a Greek but then decided was one of the Grecraige.

* You will find the great pope's Kerry pedigree in Shearman's *Loca Patriciana*, p. 273.

I made it my duty to hunt them all down, but I must come back to Aran and the spiritual storehouse.

St Cybi (also called Cuby) was a Cornishman who founded several churches in Cornwall and Wales and then went to Ireland, where he spent four years in Aran. He took with him two disciples, Maelóg (31 Dec.), the son of Caw, and Cyngar (7 Nov.), an elderly relation of failing health who could take no food but milk, so St Cuby brought a cow and a calf with him.

They straightaway fell out with an irascible saint called Fintan. Maelóg quarrelled with him initially by digging the ground outside his house and they had to get Enda to make peace between them.

Then Cyngar's calf strayed into Fintan's cornfield and Fintan's people tied it to a great tree. Cuby sent one of his disciples to beg Fintan for the return of the calf but Fintan refused. Then St Cuby prayed that the calf should return to its mother, for without it the cow would not give milk and old Cyngar would die. The Lord heard his prayer and the calf returned to the cow dragging the great tree by the roots behind it. Fintan then prayed to the Lord that he would drive away Cuby from Aran and an angel of the Lord came to Cuby as he slept, advising him to go eastward. And Cuby answered, 'May God destroy Fintan from the island!' And the angel said, 'So shall it be.'

Then Cuby went eastward to Meath and on the way he built three churches; the third was the great church of Mochop. But Fintan pursued him farther east till he reached the sea and Fintan said, 'Cuby, go beyond the sea.' And Cuby turned on him and said, 'All thy churches are so much deserted that there are scarcely three to be found in the whole island of Ireland where there is singing at the altar.'

So Cuby and his disciples built a boat and Fintan said to prove he was a saint he must cross the sea without covering the planks with hide. The Lord aided Cuby and he crossed in a skinless currach to Anglesea. His adventures in Wales and back to Cornwall were many and varied. To commemorate his Welsh activities, there are Caergybi at Holyhead, Llangybi in Carnarvonshire and Llangybi in Monmouth.

Two aspects of this are interesting. Another version of the story describes Fintan not as a saint but as a rich landowner. Secondly, one of the churches which Cybi built while he was fleeing from St Fintan was called Kilmore Mo Cop, that is to say 'the big church of St Mo Cop' (for 'mo' [my] is said to be a prefix of affectionate respect: 'My Cop'). Now St Mo Cop has an Irish pedigree and is culted three days later than St Cybi, and it is very strange that a church which the great St Cybi founded should be called after an insignificant successor. The fact is that both St Cybi and St Mo Cop clearly belong to the great family of Goban saints, who are very difficult to distinguish from each other, and several of whom are called Mo Coppoc or Mo Goppoc Artifex.

St Gobban or Goban is usually thought the most fabulous of the Irish saints, although he only behaves as all the others do. The critics of his sanctity connect him with Goibniu, the Celtic god of smithcraft. This god had a Welsh counterpart, Goibnenn or Gwydion, who was responsible for Abergavenny, became St Govan in Pembroke and Sir Gawain of the Round Table. The critics believe that god and saint and knight developed out of the Irish word 'goba', a smith. There was a St Goban in Suffolk and a St Gobain in Picardy. In Aran St Cybi, St Goban and the virgin saint Gobnait of Inishere made a family party, for Cybi's first cousin, St David, had a sister Magna, who lived in the Galtees and was Goban's mother, and Gobnait was culted the same day as a St Goban. If they could be distinguished from each other there must have been about twenty of these Goban saints. They were mostly craftsmen and builders, and Petrie has fused them all into one real architect who built the round towers of Antrim, Ferns, Kilmacduagh and Killala. But even remote Gobans, like St Gobain of Laon, built their own churches, as did St Cybi. Order comes into this confusion only if we assume an ordinary tribal ancestor, whose name incidentally suggested smithcraft. What was the tribe?

I suggest they were the Cubi of the Upper Loire, a primitive tribe overrun by the Bituriges who gave their name to Bourges and were the only Celtic tribe in Aquitania.

Further, I suggest that in Ireland the Cubi were hard pressed by the Veneti, as in Gaul they were pressed by the Bituriges. I cannot otherwise explain why the Fintan saints treated the Goban saints so badly. St Fintan of Clonenagh once exposed his disciple, Presbyter Goban, as an appalling sinner at the very moment when he was celebrating Mass. He was ejected and died miserably and in sin.

Another Goban saint was chased away by a St Fintan in

Wexford and many other saints treated them harshly or displaced them. St Abban blinded Goban, his church-builder, for overcharging. Another Goban was such an ignorant man that he had to have his hands blessed by St Maedoc before he could build.

All the Aran saints had lives as adventurous as Enda's. I must write of St Ceannfionnán, or Concannon, because Concannon was Teresa's name. His name means Whitehead and his sister Ceanndearg or Redhead is also culted in Aran, but Mr Ó Síocháin thinks she must have been a male because no nun could be called Redhead. St Ceannfionnán was the son of a king and, like three other saints of Aran, went to Rome and was offered the papacy.

Ceannfionnán was beheaded in Connemara, the only Irish martyr; many Irish heroes with 'ceann' (head) in their names had an adventure with their head. I should mention too a lake near Kilmurvey once called Stagnum Genanni or Ceannfionnán. (The Gennani, an ancient tribe, once lived in the west.) It has not been connected, though, with St Ceannfionnán or the Concannons, but with a white-headed cow of St Enda's. It turned round three times in honour of the Trinity and disappeared into the lake.

Was Ceannfionnán a saint or a cow? I suspect he was neither but as no tribal ancestors come to mind perhaps someone else will take up the question.

Who was the wicked Corban who was turned out of Aran by Enda? He and his people were surely some scattered half-forgotten community. For example, in the midlands St Ciarán of Saighir also had trouble with a wicked king called Corban or Cobran, who had an evil eye. St Ciarán and his mother, St Liadán, who lived nearby, had two erring disciples called respectively Gobran and Cerpan, who died miserably. St Ciarán dealt with them all as Enda would have done. King Corban or Cobran was struck blind at Rathdowney in Co. Laois, where he gave himself and his property to St Ciarán; Gobran was redeemed from Hell and Cerpan was revived. It is natural to say that Corban, Cobran, Gobran and Cerpan never lived and their names are four regional variations of the same name. It is harder to say that they were invented for there is still at Rathdowney a place called Killcoran or the church of St Cobran. There is a large rath round the ruins of a church and a mound beside it was removed a hundred years ago and found to contain a mass of human bones. Did a saint or wicked king ever live there? Surely it is more probable that it was a settlement of an ancient, widespread tribe, submerged by later invaders, the Corban tribe in fact. Was there any known primitive tribe whom they represented? To speculate about that would take me far away from Aran.

Let us go back to Aran and St Caradoc Garb, who left his name at Cowragh and Port Caradoc between Kilronan and Kilmurvey. I know only one Caradoc saint and he was Welsh and twelfth century and possibly real. Many saints and heroes have been called 'Garb', which means rough. In a saint, Canon O'Hanlon suggested that it meant he was 'somewhat abrupt in his manner of rebuking sin', but the early hagiographers had far odder explanations. For example, St Enda's sister St Fainche Garb is said to have got her nickname because she swam under Loch Erne to avoid a suitor and St Diarmaid, seeing her emerging with shells and pondweed clinging to her skin, said, 'That is rough.' In fact no one knows, or has ever known, what 'garb' really meant and the reason is that it meant nothing; it was a tribal element applied to the ancestor or ancestress of the tribe by his or her descendants. There were two saints and a pagan hero called Senach Garb and the mountain in Kerry, which is called after the latter, had three other heroes called Senach Garb on it and a river Garb nearby. But the proof that it was tribal is offered by a Scottish hero, Fergna Garb, who was the eponymous ancestor of the Garbraige tribe. Now, however rough his manners or his skin may have been, a whole tribe would not be called 'the rough' on his account. So we must ask not 'What does "garb" mean?' but 'Who were the Garb-folk originally?' Since a certain hero Garb was also called Carpad, the best guess I can make at the moment is that they derive from the Carpetani, a very large Iberian tribe of the Upper Tagus.

I wrote, of course, most of all this when I got home. I worked out my general theory about Enda and his colleagues in Aran itself but developed it when I got back to my library in Kilkenny. The book which I have used most and enjoyed most is *Silva Gadelica* by Standish Hayes O'Grady, published in 1892. It is a collection of ancient Irish tales in two volumes, the first in Irish, the second in translation.

Till recently, I had not read his introduction and realized what a highly idiosyncratic and independent-minded man he was. His biography has never been written but I have heard that, a great Celtic scholar, he lived in London and worked in the British Museum. Here is a short passage from the introduction:

> This work is far from being exclusively or even primarily designed for the omniscient impeccable leviathans of science that headlong sound the linguistic ocean to its most horrid depths, and (in the intervals of ramming each other) ply their flukes on such audacious small fry as even on the mere surface will venture within their danger. Rather is it adapted to the use of those weaker brethren who, not blindly persisting in their hitherto blissful ignorance, may be disposed to learn, if but a little, of an out of the way and curious branch of literature.
>
> It would be no less instructive than easy to point out how and where lordly Cetaceans of philology, enviously invading shallows in which the humble Celtic whitebait sports at ease, lie stranded (as Milton has it) 'many a rood in length'.

He calls himself 'a humble quarryman' who brings up the raw material for the 'Keltologues' and 'philologists', the folklorists and others: 'Personally, I cannot boast of being anything that ends in either -logue or -ist.'

Did he have some grievance against them? I don't think so. The other Standish O'Grady, as I described in *Escape from the Anthill* ('Anglo-Irish Twilight', pp. 75ff), had a vision of a society which in our century and here in Ireland was governed by intellectual aristocrats. Standish Hayes O'Grady believed that Irish scholarship could be liberated from the combination of the -logues and -ists and that the impeccable omniscient leviathans of science should work fraternally with those who merely rescue the past without bothering themselves unduly about the language within which it is recorded; the whale would disport itself with the whitebait.

I believe O'Grady might, had he lived, have seen O'Rahilly as 'a lordly Cetacean lying stranded in the shallows'. As a humble whitebait he might have had sympathy for me.

I started this investigation in Aran so I shall end it in Aran. I decided that, when I passed through Galway on my way home, I would try and goad Dr Simpson into some interest in all this. He was very friendly but nothing came of it. I was embarrassed by not being sure how to pronounce Fainche and finding that he had scarcely heard of her or, for that matter, the Carpetani. They were gatecrashers, like myself, at a party to which only the Celts and Celticists were welcomed.

'I gather', he said, 'that you are saying that toponyms are frequently tribal in origin. That of course has been allowed for. But certainly the systematic study of onomastics has often been helped on by free-wheeling methods like yours. Splendid! But see that they don't degenerate into uncontrolled folk-philosophizing like poor Ó Síocháin's. Names have no more generality of behaviour than the pertinent dimensions of the specific culture of which they form a part.'

Simpson always expresses himself with great lucidity, but he has a curiously numbing effect on me. He paralyses the curiosity on which my confidence is based. My convictions do not seem wrong but in the wrong place. Corban may have felt like that when the fierce light of the gospel beat down on him, but he may have stammered out a few unpleasant things before he disappeared.

'But what about the spiritual storehouse?' I said.

'My dear fellow,' he answered a little irritably, 'all that you are arguing is really very old stuff. You'll find that Jorgensen of Wisconsin noted the chronological difficulties about Enda and others in *Gelehrte Anzeigen* fully forty years ago. As for Gobban, I wrote only last week for the Bollandists that it is no doubt a hypocoristic form of 'goba', smith, with geminated b.'

'Then Ó Síocháin is wrong?' I persisted. 'There weren't really any saints?'

'Ó Síocháin!' he snorted. 'What in the world does he know about anything? Ó Síocháin is utterly unimportant.'

'Well,' I answered, 'about a thousand copies of his book are sold to one of yours. Would yours have been published at all without a university subsidy?'

He looked very much hurt and so I did not finish what I was going to say, that country scholarship had deteriorated hugely since archaeology was professionalized.

Neither of us wanted to quarrel so he did the only thing he could do, which was to pour me out a geminated whiskey and say that I must look after my cold.

As I walked to the bus I reflected that Jorgensen and his colleagues had made a vast gulf between life and scholarship, between living and knowing, and that it would take a generation or two to fill it in. Educated Irishmen are now bored with the saints, who intrigued so intensely the sceptical antiquarians of our great-grandfathers' day. The question, 'Who were the saints?' had aroused curiosity then. There were theories and counter-theories and local societies had grown up as arenas in which fierce battles could be fought about them. Now all is still and dead, and the saints have been laid away in lavender in a bottom drawer. And curiosity has no status unless it is paid.

Yet for the Irish people to forget the saints is for them to forget their childhood. We are emotionally and intellectually committed to them. They beckon us along a private road that leads not only to the Irish past but to the past of Europe. It is through them that we can learn about the youth of the world and the infancy of religion. Whether they really lived or not, they belong to us more than to anybody else.

[1987]

12

GRANDMOTHER AND WOLFE TONE

Brian Inglis, former editor of *The Spectator*, is one of the most articulate of living Anglo-Irishmen. This is not saying much, for that once voluble people seems now to be stricken with aphasia. The title of his book, *West Briton*,* was a name which, in their late prime, attached itself to the more corrupted of the Anglo-Irish. As their fortunes declined, they tried to shed it but it had stuck and in the days of their collapse it was flung as a taunt at the whole community. Now Mr Inglis, a sophisticated, guilt-ridden exile, wears it as a sort of comic hat. His swan-song of the West Britons in Malahide is first-class. He is amusing, impartial, compassionate and his book is as cheering to the remnant that still hangs on in its native land as a nice cup of Ovaltine to the victim of disseminated sclerosis.

I read *West Briton* on the Barcelona express, but was not sure what was wrong with it till I picked up a discarded French literary magazine from the seat, and read an article, 'Où sont les polemicistes?' The writer complained that paralysis has overtaken us all because we have made an idol of 'objectivity'. No educated man now dares take up a cause till he has mastered 90 per cent of the facts and all the background. 'Would Zola ever have defended Dreyfus, if he had been objective? No, he would have waited till he could examine all the files at the French War Office.' It seems we cannot move without a professional lead, so we wait for an academic to lose his temper. But an academic is *ex officio* never angry. He is paid to be objective. While he is being scrupulously fair to the Romans and making allowances for the Jews and balancing the claims of law and order against those of charity, the thirty pieces tinkle unnoticed and unneeded

* Brian Inglis, *West Briton* (London 1962).

in his letter-box. Then, this sour Frenchman continues, Professor Iscariot, Ph.D., gives his trifling windfall to the Save the Children Fund and settles down with relish to a *fait accompli*. Once more he has facts and dates to handle instead of the chaos of unregulated passion through which the rest of us must pick our way by the flickering light of indignation or sympathy.

While reading this engagingly objective book, I listened for the familiar tinkle and heard it once or twice. Inglis does not betray a country or a cause but has he not sometimes consciously and frankly betrayed himself? Let's leave that till later and begin by repeating that the Malahide story could not have been better done. In that prosperous little Dublin suburb they talked of Fairyhouse and the Fitzwilliam Lawn Tennis Club and Gilbert and Sullivan, and reached for Ireland through George Birmingham and Percy French. They were proud of the width of Carlisle Bridge, the size of Phoenix Park and the world supremacy of Guinness. They disapproved strongly of the Black and Tans. But Grandmother told the children how a despicable gang of cowards and cutthroats had shot policemen in the back and driven away Uncle So-and-so, who had always been so good to his employees. Consequently they cheered madly for the English Army Riders at the Horse Show and jerked the hats off the seditious who did not stand up for 'God Save the King'. They prided themselves that the word 'Dunleary' never crossed their lips and made jokes about 'Erse' and 'Telefón' and 'Aerphort'. What dull provincial jokes they were! Surely the Anglo-Irish could have found a place for these sad cinders of a once blazing enthusiasm in the overflowing ash-pit into which whole centuries of their own misdirected idealism had been thrown? For whereas the Irish nationalists had been wrong about most things, the Irish unionists had been wrong about everything. Had they any option, a defeatist might argue, except to fade away – or become editor of *The Spectator*?

No whisper of self-criticism was ever heard in this tight little society and characteristically it was when he was studying the Irish Famine for an Oxford essay prize that Inglis first became aware that Kingstown had been called Dunleary till George IV set foot in it and millions had in fact died and emigrated through English incompetence so gross that recent English historians have had to explain it as the genocidal yearnings of the subconscious mind.

Family loyalty and class loyalty are not so obsessive as we grow older. For an Irish Protestant, national loyalty is a difficult and fragile growth. It may bolt into useless flowers like a summer lettuce or it may germinate hardly at all. Brian Inglis cherished his nationalism, once he had discovered it. His pages on *The Sham Squire* show what a good historian he can be and, though what he says of Galway and the Irish countryside could have been written by any English tourist after a summer holiday (the Little People, Grace O'Malley and so forth), his account of working on *The Irish Times* is unique.

His analysis of the slow social transformation of Malahide is also fascinating. He describes how the West British of the Pale got 'mixed' and how it came about that natives slid into the cavities of its decaying golf clubs. Impeccably well-born Britons, fleeing from the Labour government and unconscious of the gradations of Irish society, had swept into all the social sanctuaries, carrying with them in the backwash of their wealth so many people who were 'not our sort' that 'we' had become hopelessly contaminated. The rot had set in.

Having apparently vomited up Malahide, Inglis found that he had exchanged a firm loyalty for a wobbly one and that life is full of strain and misunderstanding and frustration for the hybrid, who works in Westmoreland Street and is expected to call it West Moreland Street. (In fact, of course, West Moreland Street is just as ignorant a solecism as Drogheeda or Yoggle!) If he is a defeatist, he at least earned the right to be one by fighting his battles on Irish soil. I think he is a defeatist, because he once wrote in *The Twentieth Century* that, even if the Anglo-Irish were to vanish from Ireland, it would not greatly matter so long as the important contribution which they made to London journalism were sustained. I do not think he wrote this because he is an important London journalist, but because if he were to justify his retreat to himself, it was comforting to look 'objectively' at the handful of old country crocks, retired British servicemen, civil servants and suburban car salesmen in whom the spirit of Anglo-Ireland has its contemporary incarnation, and to assume that it would die with them. With an odd mixture of modesty and arrogance, he is oppressed by the lofty superiority of the dedicated romantic heroes of Protestant nationalism, Fitzgerald, Emmet, Parnell, but tries to bring Wolfe Tone, whom he finds the most congenial, 'within his reach' by lowering his stature a little. He suggests that Tone's Irish patriotism derived from pique with Pitt for ignoring his scheme for colonizing some Pacific islands, that like Inglis himself he tried to get a job in England, that he drank more Burgundy than was good for him and made a messy, unsuccessful attempt to dodge hanging by cutting his throat. But he misses the whole grandeur of Tone. Tone never allowed himself to be paralysed by 'objectivity' but forged a philosophy for himself out of the confused and conflicting aspirations of his day, out of his own untidy impulses and selfish ambitions, and having forged it, adhered to it and died for it.

Tone would remain great even if it were proved that his ill-success had delayed Catholic Emancipation and precipitated the Union. The only extenuation for the feebleness of the Anglo-Irish today is that no strong challenge is ever presented to them. Mr Inglis's account of his experiences in 'the real army', as Grandmother called it, illustrate this. When he was training for the RAF in Rhodesia, he decided that, supposing the British invaded Ireland to recover the ports, he would present himself for internment as an untrustworthy alien. But was he really untrustworthy? Would he ever have used his aeroplane to bomb the British out of Spike Island? If he had been interned there would have been so much gentlemanly understanding about it that the distance between Theobald Wolfe Tone and Brian Inglis could be measured only in light years.

Clearly Inglis accepts in a general way Tone's social philosophy. Tone's political ideals are now largely realized and would inflame nobody; his unorthodox Protestantism is that of most British intellectuals today. Yet in that one direction where Tone's leadership is still needed, Inglis and most of his compatriots hang back as though they were paralysed. Obviously Tone, who had seen the American Revolution and its consequences, would have been in favour of the absolute separation of Church and State, which for the first time brought religious tolerance to America and made the United States possible. Can one doubt that every Protestant revolutionary nationalist who has ever lived, Emmet, Fitzgerald, Davis, Parnell, would have favoured it? In our century, Horace Plunkett and Yeats and the Protestant rebels of 1916 would have agreed that it was the only way to end partition and annihilate bigotry, both Catholic and Protestant.

I think that Inglis believes this too, for he says that 'the future relationship of Church and State is sooner or later going to become the most serious issue in Ireland', and he hints at the possibility of future bloodshed if the problem is not solved. And anticipating his own departure from Ireland he says: 'What else was there to retain our interest in politics if the subject of the future of Church and State was barred?'

Why should the subject be barred? There appear to be two reasons according to Inglis. Irish Protestants have lost their stamina and no Protestant or Anglo-Irishman, being an outsider, can help solve the Church-State relationship: 'Irish Catholicism must be left to come to terms with itself.' He does not see that the principal evidence that the Irish Protestants have lost their stamina is that they so constantly reiterate this paltry excuse for apathy.

Irish Protestants constitute 25 per cent of the population of Ireland, north and south, yet those of the Republic enjoy telling each other and being told either that they have no stamina or that they would 'only do harm by interfering'. In this way they can free their minds from the unglamorous complications of Ireland and the dreary forms of bloodshed which they foresee. They have an excuse for whatever form of disengagement may be comfortable and for devoting themselves agreeably to what they call 'wider issues' in a larger society. But for a small historic community can there be any issue wider than survival and the prevention of bloodshed?

'Outsiders only make things worse by intervening.' Chicago gangsters have grown fat on this repulsive old sophistry . . . moral cowardice dressing herself up in a diplomat's bemedalled frock-coat. The great Protestant nationalists did and said what they thought to be right and never argued that they could help their friends best by withholding their support from them. Nor did they consider themselves 'outsiders'.

The argument for non-intervention is ignorant as well as base. Jefferson and the Founding Fathers who introduced the separation of Church and State, did so in an atmosphere of tense religious rivalry. They could have been called 'outsiders' for Jefferson and John Adams, at least, were Unitarians, but if they had left it to the orthodox and the respectable to compose their differences nothing would have happened and America would be a more deeply divided country than Ireland is today.

Nor could a move to separate Church and State be called sectarian if the Anglo-Irish supported it, for hundreds of Protestant ecclesiastics, north and south, would oppose it passionately, as did their colleagues in America. Nor would it lead to 'irreligion'. Of all the great powers the USA has the highest percentage of churchgoers.

There are in fact only two forms of escape from the dilemma of the Anglo-Irish who wish to express themselves freely. One is that chosen by Mr Inglis: 'Go to England!' The unpopular alternative still remains: 'Go back to Wolfe Tone!'

Mr Inglis rightly places a great deal of blame for our dilemma on Grandmother, a totem-figure beside every Protestant hearth. She would have detested Wolfe Tone, who stabbed the real army in the back and chose a messy, unchristian death. But Inglis takes the wrong way of exorcising her since it ends in disengagement. He follows the will-o'-the-wisp of objectivity, saying: 'How could we Irish Protestants blame our fellow countrymen for bigotry? We had taught them how.' This argument which appears to lead to unity and brotherly love really leads to London.

Besides it is false. Grandmother with the real army behind her had, as a Catholic, oppressed the Irish for four centuries; as a Protestant she had oppressed them for only three. When Inglis says that, because of the penal laws, Irish Protestants can never give disinterested advice he is only searching for an excuse for not sticking his neck out. If Tone and Emmet and all the others did not by dying close that chapter, what profit is there in Mr Inglis's cosy penitence? And where does 'objectivity' begin? Where does it stop? The Catholic Church prides itself on its universality so it must be judged by its universal and not by its local activities. Why not say the penal laws started not in Ireland in 1688 but rather in France three years earlier, when after the Revocation of the Edict of Nantes several hundred thousand Lost Sheep were bayoneted back into the Fold? Why not recall that at the battle of the Boyne William III had eleven hundred Huguenot officers with him, fugitives from a Catholic persecution which, unlike the relatively tolerant affair which he instituted, was genuinely annihilating? Why not admit that scarcely twenty years ago countless Lost Sheep of Central Europe were driven back into the Fold with a Belsen-model crook and that their sufferings, though briefer, far surpassed those of the Huguenots or the Irish Catholics? Mr Inglis has seen the reports of their leaders; he knows them to be true, but considers it 'injudicious' to publish them.

All these facts prove is that collectively even kind and intelligent men are always ready to put pressure on their neighbours to make them conform, that Catholics and their 'separated brethren' still have excellent reasons for fearing each other not as individuals but as organized groups, and that real danger only arises when the state also ranges itself on the side of conformity.

There is only one way out, the way of Jefferson and Tone. In the North the Protestant Parliament for the Protestant people must go and in the South the separation of Church and State must be introduced and adhered to absolutely. Through not recognizing this, Inglis wandered down many strange bypaths before he admitted himself lost. He was a rebel without a cause, since, rejecting all those offered him by the Malahide Golf Club, he could find none in his warm, honest heart. So he window-gazed in Ireland in a discriminating way, but in the late forties each exhibit seemed more shop-soiled than the last. Yet Ireland still offers opportunities to the countrymen of Tone. On the way to them there is a rich crop of slights and misunderstandings to be harvested, but it is better to be arrogant like Yeats and to stay than to be deprecating like Inglis and to go. As Yeats knew, Irish independence, like American, was primarily the notion of a small Protestant minority. It is in stark opposition to the imperialist universalism of the English and to the Catholic universalism of the Irish and derives from a handful of unpopular Trinity students and a few Belfast radicals. Similarly, American independence was principally the work of some unorthodox Anglicans from Virginia, some unorthodox non-conformists from Massachussetts and Thomas Paine, a renegade English Quaker. The two groups made contact in revolutionary France and their affinity has often been underlined. When, for example, the American War of Independence broke out, Belfast Protestants lit bonfires and sent congratulations to George Washington while Dublin Catholics sent loyal messages to George III. Ireland might not be the dull, divided little island which it is today if those groups, north and south, to whom the idea of national independence is chiefly due, had played a greater part in its realization.

But the longer Inglis stayed in Ireland the further he strayed from his hero, Wolfe Tone. One of the causes which he adopted on behalf of the Civil Liberty Association, that of Baillie Stewart, is intelligible only as a hysterical come-back at dead, defeated Grandmother. When Irish liberals campaign on behalf of the illiberal and secure an Irish passport for Artukovitch (as Foreign Minister he introduced gas chambers into Yugoslavia) and country refuges for Skorzeny and sympathy for Lord Haw-Haw and Amery and Baillie Stewart (Inglis thinks that all these three were badly treated), they have started to sell their freedom and it will not be long now before Grandmother is called back from the shades and, heavily shrouded by NATO or the Common Market, once more takes things in hand.

Fortunately for Inglis, deliverance from all this came in the shape of the managing director of Associated Newspapers, who enabled him to transfer from a good Irish newspaper, *The Irish Times*, to a bad English one, *The Sketch*. *The Sketch* was a low rung on a lofty ladder, which led to a distinguished editorial chair and to the view that the Anglo-Irish, except for export purposes, are as good as dead.

The last words but six in this sad and honest book are 'an assured monthly cheque'. They are deliberately ironical.

[1962]

The Editor,
The Kilkenny Magazine

Sir,
There are two points in Hubert Butler's remarkable review of my *West Briton* on which I would like, if I may, to correct him.

He hints that because I thought Baillie Stewart was unfairly treated, I might have felt similarly well-disposed to Artukovitch. My point about Baillie Stewart was simply that however repellent his opinions, he was entitled to a fair trial, which he did not get.

Mr Butler quotes me as saying that it was 'injudicious' of him to publish reports of what went on in Central Europe twenty years ago. If Mr Butler had published them in *The Irish Times* – or *The Kilkenny Magazine* – I should have applauded him for doing a public service by bringing into the open a particularly unsavoury episode; his reports, if exaggerated or inaccurate in any respect, could there be rebutted. The occasion and the company in which Mr Butler chose to air his views seemed to me at that time to be injudiciously chosen: that was all.

I recalled the incident in *West Briton* not to reopen old wounds, but to illustrate the difficulty that confronted any Protestant and liberal at that time – less, I am sure, now – who wanted to retain freedom of speech but who realized that to speak freely in certain circumstances might only revive old prejudices and acrimonies. It still seems to me a clear example of How Not To Do It. In my book, however, I made it clear that my decision to leave Ireland, though prompted by difficulties of this kind, was basically economic – like that of most emigrants. If I had been enjoying a private income, very probably I would have refrained from denouncing those of my fellow West Britons who have elected to go into exile, as deserters.

Yours etc.,
Brian Inglis.
20 Albion Street,
London W.2.

Mr Butler writes:

I am sorry that Dr Inglis should think that I called him a deserter. I really did not. Like several millons of our countrymen he has left Ireland for economic reasons. No one has a right to blame them, but it is legitimate to quote Lord Charlemont on the subject of absentees: 'Let it not be said that Ireland can be served in England. It never was. It is the nature of man to assimilate himself to those with whom he lives.'

Contrary to the usual belief, the absentee landlord was popular in Ireland. On his brief visits he was always very affable and lived in a whirl of tenants' banquets and bobbing curtsies. He left behind him a 'rascally' land agent to collect the rents, to evict the tenants, to be shot at. The intellectual absentee nowadays bears the same odd relationship to those he leaves behind to collect the dues.

I had known, of course, that Dr Inglis had no sympathy for Artukovitch and only defended Baillie Stewart, who *was* a sympathizer, on legalistic grounds. But Eichmann, kidnapped from the Argentine, also had an 'unfair' trial. So what? Surely Dr Inglis should have left these small illegalities to the jurist and concentrated on what mattered. For example the Association of Civil Liberty would have served liberty better if it had tried to discover the name of the kindly Irish official who enabled

Artukovitch to escape the hangman with an Irish identity card, under an assumed name. Why should we bother to track down the murderer of, say, Miss Hazel Mullen of Shankill if our officials facilitate the escape of a man who was guilty of a hundred thousand deaths?

Dr Inglis apologized for opening old wounds in *West Briton* but I am not clear whose wounds he meant. He seems to think that the views I once expressed at the International Affairs Association were mine alone: 'Mr Butler's King Charles' Head' . . . 'Mr Butler chose to air his views'. All I said on the subject under discussion, *The Pattern of Persecution in Yugoslavia*, was as authoritative as it could possibly be since I was quoting from *The Martyrdom of the Serbs*, which had been published in Chicago by the Hierarchy of the Serbian Orthodox Church. Its findings have since been endorsed by Dr Georgevitch, the Bishop of Dalmatia, and in 1961 by Archbishop Leonti, Metropolitan of the Russian Orthodox Church in the USA. Georgevitch, who escaped to America, was the only Croatian bishop to survive massacre.

In 1941 the Serbian Orthodox Church was, with the Church in Greece, the only strong outpost of Orthodoxy in free Europe, so the attempt to exterminate or convert its three million adherents in Croatia (tea-tabled by Dr Inglis into 'an unsavoury episode'), could not fail to rouse the apprehensions of all Orthodoxy. Those I have named believed it was a major factor in bringing Communism into Central Europe, has possibly sowed the seeds of a third world war, and made the task of reconciling men of good will in the East and West infinitely harder.

I am completely baffled by Dr Inglis's suggestion that the place for discussing such remote problems could ever have been *The Kilkenny Magazine* (it did not then exist and even in these few lines I feel I have already strained the patience of the editor and his readers). I quoted the Orthodox evidence in the most appropriate place, The International Affairs Association, which was modelled on Chatham House as an interdenominational fact-finding society. Arnold Toynbee had come over to give his blessing to the first meeting. How can such a society function if three-quarters of the facts have to be suppressed and how can Dr Inglis, a historian and an editor, value tact so much more than truth as to find such suppression desirable?

Toynbee himself expressed the same views as mine but more

strongly in *The Survey of International Affairs* (1955); very few people read this and perhaps Dr Inglis, who has not scolded Toynbee, would argue that disturbing passages of history should be recorded only where no one who is likely to be disturbed will notice them. This seems to me the negation of history.

Dr Inglis is right in saying that in Ireland the situation has changed. He once honoured us by speaking at our annual Kilkenny Debate. I think he will have sensed that he could then have spoken his mind here with complete freedom. I hope he will come again.

PART TWO

POLITICS AND CULTURE IN EUROPE AND AMERICA

THE CITY

You said: 'I'll seek some other land, far off, with
sails unfurled.
I'll find a worthier town than this and some
serener clime.
For here ambition foiled is like a crime,
the quickening impulse of the heart is dead,
and sluggish thoughts entomb the past like
lead.
Whichever way eyes glance or footsteps go,
the embers of a burnt-out ardour glow,
the scorched and broken years into the ash-pit
hurled.'

You'll find no other lands, my friend, speeding
with sails unfurled.
Your city will go with you. Through its streets
and squares
you'll still be strolling, as you strolled, despite
your prayers.
You'll age beside the hearth you once held dear,
thinking familiar thoughts. No ship will steer
your heart, new-fallowed, to a virgin strand.
You wrecked your life in this poor, stubborn
land.
It's wrecked beyond repair for all the world.

(Translated from the Greek of C. P. CAVAFY in memory of James Joyce and Trieste)

13

JAMES BOURCHIER: AN IRISHMAN IN BULGARIA

I wonder what is thought of my compatriot James Bourchier in Bulgaria today? Is there still a street called Bourchier Street: or have you become critical of the man who was once held in such high esteem in Bulgaria that when he was buried near Rilo Monastery in December 1920, a day of national mourning was declared in Sofia? An issue of postage stamps was made to commemorate him. Perhaps that is now of interest only to the stamp-collectors, or is Bourchier himself still remembered with affection?

Now, in every country, reputations change rapidly and we judge the great men of the past according to different standards. James Bourchier was a man of his time and the Bulgaria of a generation ago, with all its special problems, has passed away. I ask you, though, to think of him now not simply as a political partisan, a man whose strong championship of Bulgarian claims certainly changed history. Think of him instead as a warm-hearted and intelligent foreigner, an Irishman who rose above the prejudices of his nation, his class and his profession, and who tried always to speak the truth about Bulgaria even when it made him enemies.

It is not generally known that James Bourchier was an Irishman. The greater part of his life was spent in English service so his Irish origin escaped notice. Yet he was very much an Irishman belonging to the Protestant minority. Unfortunately for us who remain at home, the Protestant Irishman is often bound to England by close ties of self-interest and imperial service as well as of religion. His working days he gives to others. Ireland is a place for childhood and holidays and old age. That was what it was to James Bourchier.

The Bourchiers were a Huguenot family from Bruff, Co. Limerick, who had taken refuge in Ireland almost three centuries ago when Protestants were being persecuted in France. James's mother, Sarah Aher, came from my neighbourhood and her home, La Rive, became his home whenever he came back from Bulgaria. So when I was a boy I remember seeing him in the village of Castlecomer where his home was. It is a small mining village, the only mining village in Ireland, with one long street shaded with lime trees, and his house was comparatively new for the original house had been burnt down in the rebellion of 1798 when the Irish had tried to throw off English rule. Bourchier, as an Irishman born in 1850, must have heard from his boyhood of rebellion and civil war. He must have been familiar with the rival claims of nationalism and imperialism. The Irish problem is not unique, and those who have grown up with it will not be easily baffled by the problems of other small peoples who have powerful neighbours. Bourchier put all his gifts of imagination and understanding at the service of Bulgaria; he played no part in Irish politics. I say this with regret because I think in his own country he could have exercised a great and good influence where it was badly needed.

When I saw him he was already an elderly man, bowed and so deaf that it was almost impossible to communicate with him. It was in 1919 and at that time, as a century before, our neighbourhood was in the grip of civil war. Houses were once more being burnt down and Ireland was only in sight of that political independence which Bulgaria had reached a generation before.

It was a queer chance that brought Bourchier from Ireland to Bulgaria in 1888. When he had left Trinity College, Dublin, and King's College, Cambridge, to which he had won a scholarship, he became first a teacher at Eton. He was a bad teacher: for even then he was very deaf and he could not keep discipline. One evening, when he was taking class, the boys turned all the lights off and had a firework display. After ten years there his deafness grew worse and the school had reluctantly to dismiss him. He was greatly liked but he was obviously unfitted for his profession.

What was he to do? He chose journalism and soon he found himself as correspondent of *The Times* in the Balkans. He travelled in Greece, Romania, Crete and Serbia – but it was Bulgaria to which he finally gave his heart and in which he established his headquarters.

The work of a correspondent of a great paper is not easy. How can you tell the truth consistently and keep your job? Inevitably, the policy of the paper may be in conflict with the private views of the correspondent, and Bourchier was often charged with being unwisely pro-Bulgarian. But he never compromised. He wrote back angrily when he was chided, and a couple of times he was saved from dismissal only by the fact that he was known to be the most accomplished journalist in the Balkans. In any case he was no blind partisan. If he thought the foreign policy of the Bulgarian government at fault he said so, though this made him unpopular. King Ferdinand, for example, never forgave him for being too candid in his criticism of the King's ministers and their policy.

Bourchier's deafness was such an appalling handicap that only a man of supreme talent could have overcome it. Often urgent telephoning was necessary and he had to get his servant or a hotel porter to do it for him. All his private negotiations had to be conducted at the top of his voice. When he was on an important mission in Greece he chose the slopes of Mount Pelion for his private talks with Venizelos. Riding there every day, they were able to bawl at each other from horseback. It was in this way that Bourchier acted as intermediary between Greece and Bulgaria in forming the alliance that preceded the first Balkan War.

Bulgaria was, when Bourchier arrived, only just emerging into partial freedom and independence. Eastern Roumelia was still held for the Turks by a Christian governor. Macedonia was wholly Turkish. Every year Bourchier used to spend a few weeks exploring Macedonia, arranging secret interviews with the men who were conspiring to overthrow the Turk. Bourchier was passionately pro-Bulgarian but he was an even more passionate advocate of the truth. Let me explain how he fell out with King Ferdinand.

The Moslems were constantly attacking the Bulgars in Macedonia and inevitably the Bulgars would retaliate with reprisals on the Moslems in the territory they controlled. On one occasion the village of Dospat was burnt to the ground, and many Moslems, as Bourchier wrote in *The Times*, were massacred. The Bulgarian government published an indignant denial but Bourchier stuck to his guns. *The Times* insisted that the report must be verified or withdrawn. Bourchier received threats of assassination.

Finally, the Bulgarian government permitted Bourchier to go to the spot and investigate himself. He went and found the village a charred and looted ruin, as he anticipated, but he also found the number of massacred greatly exaggerated. As usually happens, neither side was satisfied with his revised account of the massacre. But though Bourchier made enemies, yet even they ultimately began to respect his integrity and his desire for the truth at all costs. He cared nothing for popularity with the powerful and often he would intervene when he found, for example, that some village was being encroached upon by the authorities. It was seen that he was not out for profit and that he did not change his loyalties easily.

To the staff of *The Times* Bulgaria was a remote and unimportant country. The problems of Macedonia were insignificant compared to those of India. 'Is it wise', the editor once wrote to Bourchier, 'to risk annoying the Moslems, subjects of the British empire, by supporting the Bulgarians against the Moslem rulers in Bosnia?' Bourchier argued out this point with heat. He hated all this high diplomacy; *The Times* was not, he maintained, a branch of the British Foreign Office and should not reflect its policy. As for the need to placate the Indian Moslems, had they been in the least gratified by the British protests against the annexation of Bosnia by Austria-Hungary? Had they been annoyed when the British had supported the Greeks in their expulsion of the Moslems from Crete? '*Magna est veritas et praevalebit.*'

Bourchier was, as you will have deduced, rather a lonely figure – or perhaps I should say not 'lonely' but spiritually isolated. He never lacked warm and loyal friends, either in England or Ireland or Bulgaria. But he was always at war with the cynical imperialism of the great powers to which small peoples like the Bulgars were continually sacrificed. He was repelled by the commercial competitiveness of great newspapers like *The Times*, which valued early news more than true news. His life was soured for years by 'an infamous telegram', as he called it, which *The Times* sent him; in it he was blamed because another paper had forestalled *The Times* in announcing the proclamation of the total independence of Bulgaria by the King in 1908. As a matter of fact, by an odd chance, the news had first been released in Paris and Bourchier was not even technically to blame. But Bourchier was deeply wounded that the telegram dismissing him was sent for all to read and that another English journalist was sent to replace him. However, Bourchier was, it proved, the only man for the job and soon he was at it again. But a year later he noted in his diary: 'Today is the anniversary of the infamous telegram.' Bourchier was too sensitive and scrupulous to make an entirely dependable journalist and there were frequent breezes of this kind. But he was irreplaceable and he knew it. He stayed on.

As mentioned, Bourchier played a very influential part, acknowledged by all the Greek and Bulgarian leaders of the time, in cementing the Graeco-Bulgarian alliance of 1911-12. It was a fine achievement, for Bulgars and Greeks had been enemies for close on eight centuries and there were still bitter memories of the attempt by the Phanariot Greeks to suppress Bulgarian culture. Bourchier's tact and persuasiveness turned the scale in favour of the alliance.

It was not only the prominent Bulgarians who were grateful to Bourchier. A group of Macedonians sent him as a prized gift a horse called 'Yaver' and a letter which ran as follows: 'The Bulgarians will never forget your defence of their national ideals and your fight for their realization in past and present, when the whole world has turned against the suffering Bulgar nation.' Bourchier cherished this horse all his life and used to ride it every day from the Boris Gardens along the Constantinople Road.

Bourchier was distressed when the Greeks refused to withdraw from Adrianople which had been awarded by treaty to Bulgaria, but he was equally taken by surprise at the Bulgarian attack on their former allies which led to the disastrous Treaty of Bucharest, when Bulgaria lost almost all that she had gained. Had he known, he would have tried to avert this quarrel by those methods of conciliation at which he was such an adept. He believed strongly in the friendship, perhaps the federation, of the Balkan peoples, but at that time the enemies of Bulgaria regarded Bourchier as the leader of a conspiracy to keep them apart.

A Greek newspaper, *Atlantis,* in February 1914 wrote how Bourchier had been given a vast estate from a confiscated monastery and how he used to spend hours in the Bulgarian Foreign Office concocting and circulating faked atrocity stories about the conduct of the Greek troops in Macedonia. Of course there was not a word of truth in all this.

One amusing episode occurred illustrating the great influence of Bourchier, and the efforts made by the Greeks to counteract it. A well-known London actor called Arthur Bourchier was approached by some prominent Greeks and invited to go to the Balkans at their expense. From there he was to send articles to a rival English newspaper. He was to sign them 'Bourchier', but he need not, they kindly explained, write them. That would be done for him. It was hoped that the British public would be so confused by seeing the famous name affixed to Greek propaganda that they would think that the great man had either gone out of his mind or else changed it. The tempting offer of a free holiday was declined.

When the war of 1914 broke out Bourchier tried to make the Allies promise to Bulgaria the provinces that were hers by right of population. He was bitterly disappointed with his failure. When Bulgaria sided with Germany, as a British subject Bourchier had to leave. But he left with the goodwill of the Bulgarian people. In gratitude for Bourchier's service the government released Ivan, his old servant and friend, from conscription in the army, so that he could look after Bourchier's affairs for him, and in particular his horse Yaver, given him by the Macedonians.

From Bucharest Bourchier wrote: 'Though you have chosen the wrong side in the war, I do not forget your cause is just and, when peace comes, I shall defend the legitimate rights of the Bulgarian nation.'

But by the time peace arrived Bourchier had become an old man and tired. In the violent passions aroused by the war there was little scope for his calm, well-instructed intervention. He returned for the last time to Bulgaria and there he died, at Sofia on 30 December 1920. He was buried, as he wished, in a valley near the monastery of Rilo.

How did it come about that an Irishman could exercise so great an influence in the affairs of a foreign people? An Irishman would not be puzzled by that question, for Ireland too owes much to foreigners, who have sympathized with her cause and presented it truthfully and generously in the press and parliament of more powerful nations. And Bourchier not only served the Bulgarian cause but he loved the Bulgarian land and its people, and described them in prose. He gave an unforgettable account of Trnovo with 'its houses clustered like sea-birds on the ocean crag', and studied the birds, the flowers and the antiquities of Bulgaria. His paper on the Pomaks of Rhodope still has value. He wrote well and persuasively.

The days when a single man could exert so big an influence in a country not his own are perhaps long passed. We cannot wish them to return. Bourchier would now appear a very outlandish figure to most of us. Many of his views would strike us as old-fashioned and wrong. But it is not his views for which I ask your attention and respect but his loyalty, his warm-heartedness and his devoted search for justice and truth.

[1948]

Endnote This talk was written rapidly in London to be delivered in Sofia or, as a secondary choice, on the BBC or Radio Éireann. It was 'intended to suggest bridges for friendly intercourse' and drew principally from Lady Grogan's *Life of J. D. Bourchier* published in 1924. In a note to the text the author has added:

> I've tried to give an objective account of Bourchier as a man who was by temperament tied to no particular régime. Obviously his traditions and upbringing were such that he would not have been friendly to Communism, but that is a point I have naturally not stressed. Indeed it is irrelevant. His sense of justice often overcame his traditional conservative outlook. He would, I think, have remained today a firm and valuable, though probably critical, friend of Bulgaria.

It was never broadcast. *(Ed.)*

14

MEIN KAMPF, MR ELIOT AND MR FORSTER

The triumph of a certain set of ideas over Europe has had several contradictory effects. . . . It is to the more passionate and illogical passages of *Mein Kampf* that I return with the greatest satisfaction. Certain kinds of silliness are reassuring and even endearing. The personality which is revealed is tempestuous, tormented, fascinating. The sentiment of the early pages is vulgar, derivative and false, the images are hackneyed, and yet it is clear that some great unhappiness is trying to express itself. Emotionally impoverished, too impatient to value truth of feeling, it has the violence of disorder not of strength. Such anguish as that we have heard in the past expressed in personal terms. It is not the cry of the oppressed or the hungry, it is of the excluded. How else can we explain the tremendous influence of this book which in its analysis seldom goes below superficial appearance, and which is without intellect, charm or vision? It must clearly express the universal, it is no private vengeance for which it clamours, it finds an echo in a thousand hearts.

Truth of feeling is something different from truth of expression . . . it is more important for it compels attention, support, enthusiasm. The deepest feeling is often the most careless and reckless in its expression. The cry that comes from the heart is often a misleading one, for it does not make its appeal to the reason, which is slow in action, but directly to the heart. We can acknowledge and respect the inevitability and sincerity of this amazing work; I believe that till we can feel, we shall not be able to reject these conclusions. We shall think on a superficial reading that the obvious overstatement, absurdity, prejudice and venom are their own disproof. Nonetheless the book as a whole we shall not be able to reject, and hunting to locate some truths in it we shall be teased by qualifying afterthoughts. We shall remember some statistics, we shall be impressed by the docility with which facts and history have bent themselves to these imperious, exorbitant programmes, and now and again from some unexpected quarter we will hear some prim and scholarly confirmation of the frenzy: 'Reasons of race and religion combine to make any large number of free-thinking Jews undesirable,' says Mr T. S. Eliot [in *After Strange Gods*, 1934]. Detached from its context, and the context of this emotional statement is in this case not [?] . . . but Mr T. S. Eliot himself, this soberly stated opinion impresses us deeply, dims the clarity of our belief that 'There is neither bond nor free, Jew nor Gentile.' Such thoughts seem platitudinous, unreal, unsophisticated. But then another great English writer, Mr Forster, has respectfully undermined Mr Eliot's objectivity, his 'attempted impersonality':

> *The Waste Land* is a poem of horror . . . and the horror is so intense that the poet has an inhibition and is unable to state it openly. . . . If I have its hang, it has nothing to do with the English tradition of literature or law or order, nor, except incidentally, has the rest of his work anything to do with them either. It is just a personal comment on the universe, as individual and as isolated as Shelley's *Prometheus*. . . . He is not a mystic . . . what he seeks is not revelation but stability. Hence his approval of institutions deeply rooted in the State, such as the Anglican Church, hence the high premium he places on statesmanship. . . . Hence the attempted impersonality and (if one can use the word here) the inhospitality of his writing. . . . Mr E. does not want us in. He feels we shall increase the barrenness. To say he is wrong would be rash and to pity him would be the height of impertinence but it does seem to emphasize the real as opposed to the apparent difficulty of his work. He is difficult because he has seen something terrible, and (underestimating, I think, the general decency of his audience) has declined to say so plainly.
>
> *Abinger Harvest* (1936)

Though it is a commonplace of our generation that all judgment and creation have a psychological basis, only a writer of equal stature would venture to analyse Mr Eliot in this way. But once the analysis has been made it is possible to note that Mr Eliot has acknowledged it in other ways. He refers once to the fact that certain truths he can express only in cryptograms. Hence his attempt to express very intimate personal thoughts, such intimate thoughts as have seldom been uttered before . . . and his aloofness we see to be the recoil of a sensitive spirit from a world which he has taken too deeply into his confidence. In his heart he does not believe that it is safe to expose one's soul to the savagely competitive race of men; they will surely take advantage of it . . . he expresses himself in parables to the select few.

[from Hubert Butler's Notebooks, 1936/7]

15

YUGOSLAVIA: THE CULTURAL BACKGROUND

Some years ago a Yugoslav professor came to lecture on his country in Ireland. The Central European intellectual has a passion for information and, even before he reached our shores, he was an expert on the Language Question, the Annuities and the Northern Education Act. He returned home with so many anecdotes and opinions that he decided to give a lecture on Ireland in the Dalmatian port where he was employed. It was well-attended and rather feverishly applauded. As he left the hall, he was accosted by two members of the secret police and marched away to the police-station, where he was sharply cross-examined. That was an old dodge, they told him. Clearly he was a Croat Separatist and his audience understood that 'Ulster' meant 'Croatia'. Was he advocating partition for Yugoslavia or wasn't he? He was not released till he had produced a copy of the *Irish Independent* with a report of his Dublin lecture. It was found, on translation, to contain no heresies. He proved that he did not like partition either in Ireland or in Yugoslavia.

The Yugoslav intellectual has, in fact, a keener sense of the common interest of small nations than has his Irish counterpart. He is used to foreign analogies and the story of the Anglo-Irish struggle has often been studied as a textbook of rebellion, much as Arthur Griffith studied the manoeuvres of Hungarians against the Habsburgs. Even in peacetime a drastic censorship accustoms him to the oblique approach. The most celebrated comic paper in Yugoslavia was called *Brijani Yezh*, 'The Shaven Hedgehog'; in this ingenious journal words never bore their obvious meaning and innocent expressions like 'Eire' might be charged with subversive innuendo.

Unfortunately there is no trade union of the oppressed. The

brave little Hungary which inspired Sinn Féin by its nimble resistance to the Austrian oppressor used its new freedom to oppress the Croats even more than before. This was not surprising. In the centre of Zagreb, the Croatian capital, stands the statue of the Croatian general who fought against the Hungarian patriots for his Austrian overlord. To the Croats the resurrection of Hungary and the Magyar aristocracy had a different message to that which it held for the leaders of Sinn Féin.

Griffith was right, all the same, in seeing that all small nations are menaced by similar forces. The great powers have been able to obscure this fact by the manipulation of local rivalries. Centuries of Austrian diplomacy lie behind the failure of the 'Succession States' to achieve solidarity in themselves or friendliness with each other. Yet except through collaboration there is no future for the small national state.

During the war a mayoress of Dublin asserted that Czechoslovakia was an English invention. There is more than ignorance behind this remarkable statement. A genteel snobbism has often kept oppressed nations apart and attracted them to the oppressors of others. Many Czechs and Serbs still think of the Irish as an obscure cross-breed of the liberal and cultured Englishman. The Irish have, in the same way, always rated the Austrian above his uncouth Slavonic subjects and for centuries the Irish Wild Geese assisted the Habsburgs in oppressing them. The mayoress was true to type.

Still, we cannot deny that in each of the new states the same pattern recurs. In Yugoslavia a simple and indigenous society appears to have defeated a sophisticated one that was privileged and anti-national. Yet both societies are equally moribund and more akin to each other than to the mechanized and impersonal civilization which is likely to succeed them. The cultural conflict has more significance than any other, but to follow its development in Yugoslavia a little knowledge of the political background is necessary.

In 1918 the small kingdom of Serbia became a great state by the accession of six historic Slav regions – Croatia, Slovenia, Montenegro, Bosnia, Herzegovina and Dalmatia, as well as territory in Macedonia and in the northern plains. Of these provinces Austria, Hungary and Italy had formerly been dominant in the north, Turkey in the south, including Serbia itself. Montenegro alone has resisted every oppressor and most external influences.

The common bond between all these peoples is the Serbo-Croatian language with its Slovene and Macedonian dialects. It is a very frail bond but without it Yugoslavia would certainly fall apart. That much must be conceded to the language enthusiast.

The kingdom of Serbia is chiefly responsible for the liberation of all these peoples. For generations all their energies have been directed to this end and, after two Balkan wars and the first German war, it was finally achieved in our century. Unlike the Slovenes and Croats, the Serbs had little time or opportunity for culture and education, nor are they noted for diplomacy. Courage and cunning were more valuable weapons against the Turk.

The history of Yugoslavia since 1918 has been a struggle between the Serbian 'racial' conception of nationalism and the mellower, more cosmopolitan nationalism of the north-west. One might say that the latter is based on regional sentiment and, as such, is uncongenial to the more unsophisticated Slav, who still has nomadism in his blood. In moments of tension the Quisling with his myth of cultural superiority appears in the north, the chauvinist among the Serbs; and a familiar pattern repeats itself.

In 1929 King Alexander attempted to create a new Yugoslav patriotism by an attack on regional sentiment, replacing with modern departments the old historic territories. He drew upon himself the hatred of the Croats. In 1934 he was murdered at the instigation of Pavelitch, a Zagreb lawyer. The complicity of the Italian and Hungarian governments was suspected.

On the collapse of Yugoslavia in 1940 Pavelitch was appointed 'Poglavnik' (Duce) of the puppet state of Croatia which was given an Italian king, the Duke of Aosta. Many prominent Croats were collaborationists, for example Stepinac, the Primate of Croatia, and Sharitch, the Archbishop of Bosnia (who published a poem to the murderer Pavelitch, hailing him as 'the sun of Croatia'), and many industrialists and former landowners. The evidence for this comes from anti-Communist sources. We must think of Zagreb and Belgrade as much farther apart in sentiment than Dublin and Belfast. Only a very little manoeuvring of religious and cultural antipathies by a great power is necessary to set hatred ablaze.

I heard the news of the surrender of Yugoslavia from the German-controlled station of Belgrade on a Yugoslav boat moored on the Liffey. The crew sat round listening. They were friendly with each other and seemed united in their grief. At the end they divided up into two groups, Croats and Serbs. One walked off to the German legation and the other to the UK office to learn their destinies. So easy is it to divide a people whom only a common language unites.

Will it be possible to consolidate the diverse elements of Yugoslavia into one people without spectacular abdications at both ends of the scale of civilization? As we go north from Montenegro to Slovenia, we pass from primitive and traditional communities to a sensitive and highly civilized society where racial loyalties are qualified by more sophisticated pieties. All the northern districts of Yugoslavia are still irradiated by the sun of Vienna, which has not yet set. Zagreb is a charming and civilized city with theatre, opera, ballet and art gallery. In addition it has one of the best folk museums in southern Europe. It was to cosmopolitan Trieste, in Slovene territory, that James Joyce withdrew to write his epic of Dublin. From Trieste to Macedonia and Montenegro an immense gulf of cultural experience is spanned by the frail bridge of a common language. The formula for spiritual unity has not yet been discovered, for the cultural elements, which must be reconciled, are seldom analysed.

Starting from the south, Montenegro is the Gaeltacht of Yugoslavia, where the last traces of a southern Slav culture survive. We find communities so self-contained that Western civilization encroaching on every side has not yet decomposed them. Yet the mountains which protected them so long from the Turk are no longer a barrier to subtler agents of destruction. The patriarchal society of Montenegro is doomed as surely as is the Gaeltacht, and yet something perhaps can be salvaged. Before the war two codes of justice, Montenegrin, which was personal, and Yugoslav, which was abstract, ran concurrently. The last 'izmirenje' or reconciliation ceremony took place at the monastery of Grbalj in 1935. (I described it in my book *Escape from the Anthill* – see 'The Last Izmirenje', pp. 261ff – and perhaps it revealed some of the spiritual torment of Yugoslavia.) Those who can recall a society which took forgiveness rather than punishment as the true atonement for crime will not adjust themselves easily to ordinary codes of law. Why should they?

The murderer, Stevo Orlovitch, had served his term in prison for the murder of Stjepo Bauk, when he returned to Grbalj.

Montenegrin law took no account of his sentence or imprisonment, his enemies had refused to bear witness against him. It was the duty of a member of the Bauk clan to kill him in vengeance for their kinsman's death. Only by soliciting a 'reconciliation' could Orlovitch escape. It happened on Easter Day. Outside the chapel one hundred Orlovitches lined up opposite one hundred Bauks, all in their gorgeous Montenegrin dress. They sang the Easter hymn. The priest read out the solemn words of reconciliation by which Orlovitch was forgiven and his first child adopted into the family of the Bauks. When it was ended, Mirko Bauk, the brother of the murdered man, stepped to one end of the two confronting lines. At the other end the murderer slipped quickly from behind the priest. He was a thin trembling figure in a cheap blue suit from Tivar, the wholesale clothier, and Bata shoes. A fountain pen was clipped to his breast pocket; he had learnt civilization and a useful trade in prison. He fingered the pen nervously to give himself confidence. Suddenly he ducked down his head and ran blindly between the ranks. 'Forgive me!' he cried, when he reached Mirko Bauk. Mirko raised him from his knees and embraced him and the hundred Bauks stepped forward and embraced the hundred Orlovitches. To those who had experienced this tremendous moment, any ceremony in the lawcourts would seem frigid and meaningless. I may appear to attribute great significance to what is only an interesting piece of folklore, but I believe that the democracy and even the Communism of the southern Slavs is still coloured by a sense of personal responsibility for each other which we have long forgotten. They adopt unwillingly and inexpertly the impersonal code of ethics which the administration of a large national state demands.

At the invitation of one of the Bauks, I sat down at the long table outside the chapel door on which the Orlovitches had prepared a meal for them. A Bauk, magnificent in crimson and gold, seated himself beside me. Tuning himself into the English tongue with a poem beginning 'My 'ome is the ocean, my 'earth is the ship,' he then said to me, 'Excuse the primitiveness of this! It is custom!' He told me that he had been, like many others in Grbalj, at the copper mines in Butte, Montana. Higher up the Dalmatian coast I had come on valleys associated for several generations with San Jose in California and with Lima in Peru. The returned exiles recover their old solidarity with their people quickly enough, but the presence of an Anglo-Saxon or an Iberian is disturbing to them, they become self-conscious and boastful. My companion had heard about the 'Liberty Irish State' and a mayor who had starved for forty days.

Conditions were very bad in Montenegro, he said. The Serbs had cheated them. 'Montenegrin men', he said, 'should do like Irishmen, raise hell, holler!' He was blaming on Belgrade the sterile rocky soil of Montenegro which had shaped the character of his race and guaranteed their independence. Butte, Montana, had made him dissatisfied with his home but given him no idea of a society better than that which he had begun to despise.

'What will the murderer do now?' I asked a judge from Kotor, one of the two who had sentenced Orlovitch in the lawcourts; 'He won't stay here anyway,' the judge replied. 'He learnt to type in prison and he is looking for a clerk's job in Belgrade. His relations are trying to get him to Montana but it's hard because of the quota.'

'Why did he bother about the izmirenje then?'

'Just because of the rest of the family. The Bauks would persecute them. You know,' he added, putting on an up-to-date expression, 'it's a unique ceremony. The Press Bureau in Belgrade should have sent a chap to film it.' Looking at the murderer crouched with the priest behind the buttress of the chapel, I thought that even without being filmed he had had as much publicity as he could bear. Yet could one tell what the effect would have been on this quivering little pariah of a few jolly words and a fat cheque from an experienced cameraman? What repulsive bastard will commerce beget upon ancient custom?

I drove back to Kotor with the judge in a lemon-coloured sports car. Half a mile from the town a stretch of blackened waste lay between the road and the lovely bay with its fringe of violet mountains and lacy acacias. 'That', said the judge 'is where they lit a bonfire to welcome Edward VIII and Mrs Simpson. It set alight to a plantation by mistake.'

Dalmatia, which stretches along the Adriatic from Montenegro to Slovenia, is another of Yugoslavia's problems, and the judge's remark is a good introduction to it. Except as a tourist resort, there seems to be no future for these lovely barren shores, but tourism raises difficulties. Here is the shop window that Yugoslavia presents to the enquiring West and it is unfortunate that, though all the salesmen except 2 per cent are Croats, the goods displayed are, despite the labels, unmistakably Italian. The great palaces that fringe the shores of Kotor and Gruz were built when Venice controlled the carrying trade of the East. Her wealth filled the churches with gold vessels and fabulous vestments. The lion of St Mark prances over town gates and on castle doorways. But Yugoslavia is fortunate to possess in Mestrovitch a great European sculptor. The fine plaque of King Peter of Serbia over the town gate of Dubrovnik, the Racic Mausoleum at Cavtat, the striking statue of Bishop Gregory, too aggressively placed in the ruins of Diocletian's Palace, are evidence that Italy has no monopoly of culture along the Adriatic coast.

The Yugoslav patriot is morbidly sensitive and in Dalmatia his feelings are constantly bruised. He has no status with the tourist of the luxury cruise. To the average American all the territory from the Carpathians to Corfu is inhabited by 'Hunkies' and little has been done to glamorize them. No one has edited them for the shilling seats, as Mr Bert Feldmann edited the Irish with 'Tipperary' and 'When Irish Eyes Are Smiling'. The Yugoslav must blow his own trumpet and he does it without skill. When some years ago an American company proposed to film Dalmatia, the Belgrade government eagerly collaborated, even putting the navy at their disposal. A final polish by a publicity expert had to be given to the film in America. He knew his job. The uncouth Croatian names and terms were exchanged for melodious Italian ones, familiar to the film-goer's ear: Antonio instead of Zvonko, Spalato for Split. It was inevitable but sad.

At the head of the Adriatic lies Trieste, which will be a focus of discord for some years. Roughly speaking it is about as Yugoslav as Belfast is Irish, and no Italian, Austrian or Slovene can discuss its future calmly. Once a powerful race interferes with a weaker one, it is hard for it to withdraw when a milder mood prevails. Too many hostages must remain behind. Trieste was built on the site of a Slovene fishing village by a Rhineland Baron Bruck as a port for the Austro-Hungarian empire. It became the harbour for the greater part of Central Europe as well as for the Slovenian hinterland. Austria-Hungary, a polyglot imperial state, made no attempt to impose a German culture upon it. Italy was weak and divided before the Risorgimento, and the Habsburgs, to keep an equilibrium in their empire, used to favour minority cultures. In Trieste, as in Dalmatia, there were very few Italians, but, indulged by Austria, it rapidly became a city of Italians and Italianized Slovenes in the middle of a Slovene countryside. On the building of the port of Trieste, Austria-Hungary sunk over a hundred million pounds. The railway which she made opened up the whole of Slovenia and increased its prosperity enormously. Blasted through the Julian Alps, it can be rivalled as an engineering feat only by the vital mountain railway that the Austrians built from the Sava valley to the coast. An immense amount of Austrian wealth, enterprise and talent has been sunk into Yugoslavia. After the defeat of Austria in 1918 Italy was awarded Istria with Trieste, and half a million Croats and Slovenes passed under her control. Italy, unlike Austro-Hungary, was a fiercely nationalist state. She determined that Istria and Trieste should be unmistakably Italian. All Slovene schools were closed, newspapers and books banned, and the public use of the language prohibited. Slovene-speaking clergy and doctors were expelled. An Italian doctor, who was told that his patients could not explain their symptoms to him, replied, 'Nor can the cow explain her symptoms to the vet.' When the Abyssinian War broke out the Fascist government conscripted the Slovenes among the first. A clear Italian majority was ultimately secured. In the dispute now raging the voice of Austria will not be raised but the Italian and Yugoslav arguments are of a type so familiar to us in Ireland that they need not be repeated.

There is no solution of this problem so long as cultural nationalism is identified with political and economic nationalism. Marshal Tito is probably an internationalist who, in claiming Trieste for Yugoslavia, finds it opportune to use a nationalist argument, but an internationalism which tries to reconcile divergent peoples by ignoring the sources of their culture can bring no permanent pacification. Nor are the histories of Fiume and Danzig so encouraging that another Free City at Trieste could be risked. Trieste will probably be granted to Yugoslavia, and in this, at the worst, there will be a certain retributive justice.

Trieste is a danger point because it lies upon a frontier, but in fact there is hardly a town in northern Yugoslavia about whose nature a similar dispute might not be raised. Yugoslavs, like Irish, are not by temperament originators of towns, railways, factories. It was as employees and colleagues of Austrians and Venetians that they gathered into the cities. Where they have lived relatively undisturbed by the foreigner, as in Montenegro, the pattern of their lives is based upon the rural community. The Turk, who unlike the Austrian was purely predatory, without the power to assimilate, has sometimes left this primitive pattern intact. The 'Zadruga' of the Serbian countryside is a family co-operative society, which is dying only because all village communities are everywhere dying beneath the impact of urban civilization. The forward-looking Serbian peasant, no longer able to emigrate, looks to the city for advancement. Torn from his own social traditions, he jibs at new ones. He is so little hampered by the sense of civic responsibility that his economic progress is often as rapid as his moral decline. It is not unusual to find a peasant, who can neither read nor write, the proprietor of a block of up-to-date flats in Belgrade. How does he manage it? Possibly there are not yet enough hereditary go-getters to block the path of the enthusiastic amateur. Immense power has fallen into the hands of wealthy and ignorant peasants and to this, in part, is due the naïve egoism and corruption of the Belgrade politician, which has often alienated Croats and Slovenes to the pitch of sedition.

'Innocent' is sometimes a better word than 'ignorant' to apply to the ruling classes of Balkan lands. Ignorance implies vulgarity, but the flats built by illiterate peasants are often full of the same taste and refinement that their own homes display. For centuries they have made their own clothes and their own furniture, the larger farmers have made their own pottery. Their natural taste for colour and form does not desert them as quickly as their morals. At present only the established middle classes have access to the mass-produced commonplaces of Germany and America. No doubt this restraint about domestic architecture is a transient phenomenon and would speedily be corrected by the opening of Yugoslavia to the West, but it is so striking that it deserves comment.

In such a society the word 'Communism', so freely used and abused, needs careful interpretation. It is not in the first place greatly assisted by Pan-Slav sentiment which so long favoured Church and State. Both King Alexander and Prince Paul, the one by education the other by marriage, were closely associated with Czarist Russia. On the collapse of White resistance, a hoard of generals and ex-landowners and former administrators with large treasury chests descended on Belgrade. It was natural that they should be asked to assist in the government of the young and inexperienced state, natural also that they should raise a hue and cry about Communism. Unfortunately they thought they were dealing with Mouzhiks speaking a Slav patois, who could be made to understand Russian if spoken to in peremptory tones. Every Serb, on the other hand, knows that he belongs to a race of heroes which fought for centuries against the Turk and ultimately won, and in our century fought against German, Austrian, Hungarian and Bulgar, and also won. Russian superciliousness was resented. Except among Montenegrins ('We and the Russians are 170 millions!'), Serbian royalty and a handful of Croatian illuminati, Pan-Slav sentiment has had little influence. Romantic nationalism, patriarchal traditions and peasant proprietorship may retard the spread of Communism. Yet obviously there is a very strong possibility that the Balkan states, Slav and non-Slav, will pass under Russian influence and that Communist Quislings will replace Fascist ones.

Clearly the Churches can do much to bring to the Balkans a unity based on brotherly love rather than on economics but so far their contribution has been meagre and disrupting. The Catholic Church is accused of having played the Fascist and Italian game in Slovenia and Croatia and, by its clamour for privileges and concordats, of jeopardizing that brotherhood of southern Slavs which is the keystone of Yugoslav unity. The Orthodox Church still retains its prestige because it rallied the Serb against the Turk, but it is an easy-going community, more notable for its feast-days than for its doctrine or its discipline. At the time of the concordat the faithful rallied round it with fervour, but without the halo of persecution it cannot long retain its hold over the flock. Except for an understandable assault on the Moslem at the time of the liberation from the Turk, the southern Slav believes in religious toleration: 'Brat je mio, koje vere bio'– 'He is my brother whatever his faith.'

There remains the old aristocracy. Though they are negligible in numbers and power, I believe that much depends on them if Yugoslavia is ever to become a cultured European state. Their loyalty has, like that of their Anglo-Irish counterpart, often been qualified, yet where it has been given it has been of inestimable value. They derive mostly from the old Austro-Hungarian provinces of Yugoslavia and are of hybrid Croatian and Austrian blood, for the Turk prevented the development of an aristocracy in the south. Such princely families as survived in Serbia owed their authority like the royal dynasties of Karageorge and Obrenovitch to military prowess. They united the virtues of the patriarch and the courage of the bandit. The Croatian nobility stands at the opposite pole; they are sometimes called over-civilized and useless, but some blame must rest with the inexperienced state which failed to use them. Many of them are highly educated and cosmopolitan, thinking in three languages, often witty, intelligent, liberal. Of Slav descent and Viennese culture, they should be the natural interpreters between Yugoslavia and Western Europe. Though they have long ago lost property and estates, from fastidiousness and snobbery, they have, many of them, held aloof from the Nazis and the Quislings. It is among the professional middle classes of Croatia, solicitors, doctors, auctioneers, that the doctrine of race superiority and disdain for the Serb has flourished most, small men who have to feed their self-esteem on contempt for others. There are scores of their brothers in the smarter Dublin suburbs. Foreign cultural bodies such as the British Council and its opposite number, the Deutsches Haus, made converts among this class, but at the expense of Yugoslavia. Only an educated minority, whose patriotism is reinforced by sensibility or pride, has the power to assimilate foreign culture without being overwhelmed or corrupted by it.

Like every hybrid aristocracy the Croatian nobility has had its rebel minority which has inspired the subject peoples with the dream of liberty and rallied them to its attainment. In the Austrian provinces the Yugoslav ideal was first fostered by the great Bishop Strossmayer, an aristocrat of Austrian descent. He was an amazing personality, as fervent as Thomas Davis, as practical as Horace Plunkett, as lavish and eccentric as the Earl Bishop of Derry. He revived the national spirit of the Croats and shaped their demands for independence.

I shall describe one of these hybrid families, typical except in one particular. They are doubly alien in descent. Like the Nugents and Kavanaghs of Slovenia, they are of Irish ancestry and name. This, however, is only of historical significance. German is their mother-tongue and they have the dark mobile features of the Croat. Their ancestor, an Irish Catholic, forfeited his estates under Cromwell and took service with the Habsburgs in the regiment of Irish Dragoons, quartered at Prague. He rose to be a general and was granted estates in Croatia by the emperor, for it was the habit of the Habsburgs to award their foreign subjects with land in the Slav marches where they could be trusted to keep order without partiality. He must have married into Schloss Pischatz, the vast castle where his descendants lived, because it is far older than the seventeenth century. It is surrounded by acres of dark pine forest which the von Buttlar Moscons still own, though, by the ingenuity of the tax collector they derive nothing from it but firewood. Outside the castle gates is a village or rather one long broad street of farmhouses. Rudi, the elder Count, showed me the spot where, a century ago, the gallows stood on which his great-grandfather strung up insubordinate villagers. 'They bore us no ill-will,' he said. 'In 1918 after the liberation, when they burnt Perovitch's house, they did not molest us at all.' The von Moscons dislike Perovitch. He is very up-to-date. He worked in America before he inherited his family home, and acquired there a lot of go-ahead ideas, none of them, strange to say, either democratic or original. A specimen remark would be, 'What these chaps want is a Hitler to wake them up.' He is certainly a Nazi. With a small adjustment of vocabulary and opportunity, he is to be found among the Philistine ruling classes of every country.

The old Count von Moscon was a Minister of Franz Josef and they lived all the year in Vienna, except for a month of summer holiday at Schloss Krnica. Therefore they never bothered about the plumbing. Servants carried water all over the castle. On the collapse of the central powers they found themselves all at once Yugoslav citizens with Krnica their only property, and no water and no servants. Dick, the elder son, who was in the Austrian navy, transferred to the Yugoslav navy; Rudi, who was gay and expensive, recoiled from so dowdy a destiny. After a search through the family archives, he wrote to the representatives of the Moscons in Ireland and asked them to get him a commission in the Free State Army. In Ireland only one branch of the family had emerged from the forfeitures of Cromwell and it had long ago made its peace with authority. The Irish army seemed to them as comical as the Yugoslav army. They sent Rudi £2 c/o Thomas Cook, Stefansplatz, and put his letter into the curio table. In despair Rudi took a job in the First Croatian Savings Bank in Zagreb.

It was their sister, the Countess Wanda, who had the brains of the family. After dealing with the family finances so that Krnica could pay its way, she took a job in an American shipping office. Simultaneously the Queen made her a lady-in-waiting, for decorative and honorary jobs were still at the disposal of the old nobility. She was worried about her brothers, though. Dick was unhappy in the navy. He had rather elaborate manners and his new shipmates thought he was putting on airs. She got him a job dubbing gangster films in Belgrade and he left the navy. He liked the work but did not do it very well. Though he spoke Serbo-Croatian fluently, he could not write it well. He had been brought up to consider it a language in which one gave orders to servants. His sister had to assist him. Meanwhile Rudi found the bank insupportable and he left Vienna. There was a theory that he intended to marry a rich Viennese commoner. Anyway he became an Austrian citizen and asked for his share of the family property. Wanda had for years been working unsuccessfully to have Krnica taken over as a national monument. Now the furniture, which was the only thing realizable, would have to be sold and the proceeds divided. This was a difficult as well as a sad task. In the days of Maria Theresa a celebrated Italian cabinet-maker had travelled round Croatia and Slovenia, staying a few years in each castle, building magnificent furniture from the local timber. In the salon at Krnica there were priceless wardrobes and chests, so vast that without dismemberment they could not be brought down the narrow winding stairs unless a breach were made in the salon walls. The breach was made. Rudi, abandoning Yugoslavia for good, refused to pay his share for the repair. 'Let them use the castle for road material, if they choose, the ignorant boors! I, thank God, am an Austrian.' He became a Nazi and put his knowledge of Yugoslavia at the service of its enemies. He was a very ordinary person. The challenge presented to him by the young state was crude and unimaginative, and so was his response. Their failure to be reconciled was disastrous to them both.

Dick was not ordinary. He did not sell his furniture but had it brought by lorry to Belgrade. It was to him a symbol that he was a Croatian gentleman and not a mere Austrian colonist. The problem of adjusting his furniture to a tiny labour-saving flat had a spiritual counterpart. The framework of the new Yugoslav society is crude, without the dignity of the peasant or the culture of the nobleman. Dick was good and loyal; he had that rare perceptiveness and candour which sometimes develops behind a shelter of security and privilege. He was constantly misquoted and distrusted. He did not fit in. A small group of pushing Croat businessmen cultivated him and imperceptibly he too drifted into the ranks of Yugoslavia's enemies. They were Croat separatists and the brand of Slavophile Fascism which they preached was not at all crude. Ljutic, their philosopher, was a mystic and Dostoievsky was his prophet. The contacts with Italy and with the White Russians seemed to be on a spiritual plane, the political pledges were ingeniously disguised. If it had not been for Wanda's good sense Dick would have committed himself irrevocably. His fine gifts have been wasted by his country but not used against it.

This unimportant family history is a parable applicable to any new national state with an unassimilated minority. Minorities, which from some scruple of pride or cultural superiority refuse to assimilate, often accept with resignation the choice of two destinies, exile or extinction; a handful attempts to survive by becoming Quislings. The upper classes of Yugoslavia and the other Succession States are not merging, they are disappearing. This would not matter if they left behind them the rich and fertile civilization which they acquired through generations of privilege as mediators between Slav and Teuton. Rightly this hybrid culture belongs to Yugoslavia and should be claimed by it. Otherwise it will be appropriated by Vienna. With every fresh access of educated *émigrés* from the new states, the cultural magnetism of Vienna, so long irresistible in Eastern Europe, will be reinforced. This magnetism has possibly even been increased by political decay. Attracting unappreciated talent from all the border countries, Vienna has, like London, been able to disturb the consolidation of new civilizations politically beyond her control. Only by the free crystallization of all cultural elements, old and new, can these new civilizations become strong enough to hold their own.

I have shown how the old south Slav way of life, as exemplified by the 'izmirenje', is inevitably doomed. The survivors of it are not sufficiently sophisticated to resist the encroachments of middle-class Western civilization, nor, except in the educated classes, is there any real cultural toughness and integrity to form the basis of a distinctive Yugoslav civilization. Even though the new intelligentsia may appear to take their politics from

Moscow, it is probable that, as in the past, they will take their culture from Vienna. Typical examples of this inevitable Austro-Yugoslav culture are the Zagreb Communist playwright Krleza, and Mestrovitch, the Dalmatian peasant boy who made contact with Rodin and the sculptors of the West in the Viennese art schools. The remnant of the ruling classes, if they can be won over, are far better qualified by hereditary fastidiousness to select and transmit these external influences than is the more easily deluded middle-class majority.

For there is no such thing as a pure national culture. In the monasteries of Pec and Decani and Gracanica there is evidence of a lofty Serbian art, inspired by Byzantium, yet the promise of a greater future was destroyed by the Turk as catastrophically as were even greater Irish hopes by the Norman. A few frescoes and ballads and some rapidly dying social traditions are all that the Serb chauvinist has to build on, and he is building badly after the cheapest standards of the West, scorning the assistance of those who understand the West. A common language survives, it is true, and a language unites men, so long as you can close the frontiers, mental and physical, but it cannot give the spiritual unity from which great cultures develop. If you looked before the war in the popular bookshops or in the cinemas in Zagreb or Belgrade, you would see that men follow the same fashions, dubbed and adapted, as in Dublin or Cardiff. Despite all the talk of national culture, Edgar Wallace and Garbo and their Viennese counterparts have a more potent educational influence on the average Serb and Irishman than Decani or Cormac's Chapel.

I have scarcely mentioned Mihailovitch and Tito, and the unbelievable cruelties and heroisms which in Yugoslavia have for four years usurped the place of normal development. At the moment of writing the political foreground is blurred, but I have tried to give some account of the constant forces, social and cultural, with which any Yugoslav government, of whatever complexion, will have ultimately to reckon.

[1947]

16

YUGOSLAV PAPERS: THE CHURCH AND ITS OPPONENTS

It was surprising to find in Communist Yugoslavia how elementary and almost perfunctory was the criticism of the Christian Churches. It seemed to be based almost exclusively on Charles Darwin and certain clerical misdemeanours of recent date. I suggested to a friend who was a translator that it might be a good plan if the works of some freethinkers, like Bertrand Russell or Arthur Weigall, who are Christians and humanists as well as distinguished scholars, were translated. He told me, however, that there would be no demand for such work. The policy of both the Church and its opponents in Yugoslavia was 'all or nothing', and no attempt to salvage Christian conduct from the mythology in which, in the view of many, it had become entangled, would be countenanced. The baby, in fact, must be drowned in its bath-water or thrown out with it.

It is a very tragic situation which might, I think, be relieved by extreme candour and truthfulness on behalf of the Churches. They would have to avow more explicitly than hitherto that Christian virtues existed and could exist outside their ranks, and that, in fact, the representatives of the Churches had, in Yugoslavia, done a disservice to the Christian way of life by claiming to be its unique exponents. Their weakness and subservience had compromised fatally those in their flock, or outside it, who were neither weak nor subservient.

In Ireland interest has focused itself disproportionately on Archbishop Stepinac, whose trial was only a small episode in a struggle for Christian values which lasted for four or five years and in which the Churches were as deeply divided as any other branch of society. At the very start the Protestant Church, which was very small, accepted the Nazis with enthusiasm, as did the

Evangelical Church in Austria. The ecstatic welcome given to Hitler by the Viennese Evangelical clergy is recorded in the Dean of Chichester's *Struggle for Religious Freedom in Germany* (1938). But some effort has been made to prove that the Catholic Church in Yugoslavia was the backbone of the resistance to totalitarianism. Such an extraordinary notion could scarcely have gone unchallenged if it had not been feared that any admission of guilt would help the Communists. To do this would seem to be a greater crime than falsehood.

A large volume was published in Zagreb in 1946, called *Dokumenti O Protonarodnom Radu (Documents about the anti-national activities and crimes of a part of the Catholic Clergy)*. Some of the innumerable documents contained in it were used in the controversy. By most Churchmen they were held to be spurious. The Communist Yugoslav government was accused of faking the evidence. When I was in Zagreb I looked up ten or twelve of the most significant passages in the back number of papers published during the Occupation. They are stored in the University Library and many other libraries easily accessible. I found them all, without exception, accurately recorded. Moreover, I found that the Yugoslav government had not used a tenth of the material at its disposal. The Catholic Church in Yugoslavia for the most part received the invaders not with resignation but with transports of joy, and many of its prominent priests and friars had been preparing the way for them for many years.

Archbishop Stepinac, by his many brave sermons in defence of Jew and Orthodox, did something to redeem the welcome which he gave to Pavelitch on his arrival and the appeal which he broadcast to his clergy for submission (I saw his appeal, which has been called a fake, both in the diocesan paper of Zagreb and in two other papers.)But unquestionably his conciliatory attitude influenced others who were not capable of his restraint. So it happened that the man who organized the murder of King Alexander and was later responsible for the attempted extermination of the Serbs as well as the Jews in Croatia, was received with rapture in convents and monasteries and ecclesiastical seminaries, as well as being idolized in the Catholic press. Here is an account in a Church paper (*Nedjelja*, 17 May 1942) of a visit of 140 Zagreb theological students to the Poglavnik (or 'Leader'):

And then He entered. Himself, He opened the door of His room and stood before us. A kingly face, He raised His arm and greeted us with His wonderful deep voice, commanding and fatherly.

'Za Dom!' (For Fatherland!) 'Spremni!' (Alert!) [This corresponds to the Nazi greeting 'Heil Hitler!'; 'Poglavnik' corresponds to the Italian 'Duce' and the Nazi 'Führer'.]

A roar from 140 youthful throats, and then there stepped before Him the president of the Council of Young Clerics, Stephen Krisovitch, and addressed Him.

While He spoke our eyes rested on the heir of the great Croat heroes of the past, on Ante Pavelitch! We try to watch the meaning in every feature of His face, every flicker of His eyes. And He – our sovereign – stands before us, wonderful in His simplicity. His was the holy calm of the grotto.

The president finished his speech and handed to the Poglavnik our gift, five Roman missals in the Croatian tongue, and the Poglavnik enfolding us in His glance exclaimed: 'Brothers!' We held our breath from excitement and a strange exhalation seemed to flow towards us from the Poglavnik. His words sketched out a new page, the loveliest and most precious of all in the history of the Seminary Youth of Croatia.

Then they sang to him the Ustashi hymn and there was a further exchange of heartfelt cordiality and they went away.

As you see, capital letters are used throughout in the pronouns referring to Pavelitch. There is a photograph of Pavelitch in the midst of the 140 students. They look mild and submissive young men and I do not think they would have ventured on this demonstration if it had been displeasing to their ecclesiastical superiors or likely to prejudice their careers in the Church.

The following month there was a solemn gathering in honour of Pavelitch at the archiepiscopal church of Sarajevo, at which a choir sang Ustashi hymns and Archbishop Sharitch's 'Ode to the Poglavnik' was recited; also, a young cleric recited a declamation on the Poglavnik's heroic deeds in the 'Barbarous East'. At that time the mass slaughter of the Serbs in Bosnia was in progress with the Poglavnik's approval, so the young man's reference to the Barbarous East was highly topical.

The pages of those papers published during the Occupation are full of such astonishing stories. Many of them are illustrated because the Poglavnik, who claimed to be religious, obtained great advertisement for himself by his association with ecclesiastics and there was usually a photographer nearby. And so he is seen as a sturdy, strutting figure surrounded by gentle nuns or eager theological students inhaling his loving kindness with eager smiles.

I have quoted hitherto the more serious papers of Yugoslavia. There are also innumerable smaller papers, like *The Messenger of the Heart of Jesus, The Guardian Angel, St Joseph's Herald,* etc. etc., which reached a less literate public. One and all they have photographs of the Poglavnik in strange proximity to angels, doves, lambs, little girls, and poems and prayers of sickly piety extolling his virtues.

It would be wrong to deride the simplicity of these people, whose fault lay in believing what they were told, if it had not had terrible consequences. We read in *St Antony's Messenger,* June 1941, the calm announcement that 'There are too many Jews in Zagreb with their aims of world domination and their perfidy and destructiveness. The Poglavnik has decided that the Jewish question must be radically solved.' A few weeks later an announcement of an anti-Jewish exhibition and an article that might have been inspired by Streicher appeared. Almost the whole of the Jewish populations of Zagreb were, in fact, in those days plundered and taken to the camps of Jasenovac and executed. I believe that in spite of the Christian papers, the population regarded their fate with horror and revulsion. In the diocesan magazine of Bosnia and Slavonia for June 1941 parish clerks are notified of an important new decision: 'Today it is the solemn duty of every citizen to show proof of his Aryan parentage.'

It has been said that these papers were forced to print these articles under threat of suppression. But a healthy Christianity could only have been invigorated by the suppression of *St Antony's Messenger* or, when it became a travesty of Christian principles, would have prevented its circulation. Nor do I think that 'political' pressure is a sufficient excuse. Those who read *Katolicki List* will find that the editorship of the paper did not change at the time of the invasion. Its new policy was merely an inflamed and exaggerated development of tendencies which had been evident before.

It is true that Archbishop Stepinac many times spoke against racial discrimination. Yet he must have been aware that such laws would follow quickly on the establishment of that government to which he had given his sanction and support. He seems to have had a curious detachment from the laws of cause and effect and to have believed that any crime committed against

Russia could be overlooked. He seems to have been scarcely aware of the crimes committed on a wide scale in the name of the Church and the connivance and condonation of which many of its leaders were guilty. It is not possible that the Church leaders were ignorant of the wild and murderous excesses of hundreds and perhaps thousands of fanatical priests and monks in Yugoslavia. Yet in their statement of 8 March 1945 there is one solitary reference to these misdeeds: 'When in exceptional cases a mad priest has assailed his neighbours' rights, we have not hesitated to lay a church punishment on him, and even to take away his priestly orders'!

In September the bishops also declared: 'There were isolated cases of priests blinded by national and party passion who committed offences against the law and had to be put on trial before a secular court.' In the same circular they tell how all the friars of Shiroki Brieg were executed without trial by the Partisans but they weakened their case against this brutal act by saying what is not true, that almost all the friars were known for their 'opposition to fascist ideology'. In the diocesan papers of Bosnia there are reports of ecstatic celebrations at Shiroki Brieg on the Poglavnik's birthday and other Ustashi festivals similar to that I have described. Many of the most prominent of the Ustashi leaders had been educated at Shiroki Brieg.

If the Church leaders had shown some penitence and cared about the wrongs they had done to unoffending people they might expect a more candid examination of the wrongs done to them and others in the name of Communism.

[1942]

17

FATHER CHOK AND COMPULSORY CONVERSION

Father Ilja Chok is a frank intelligent man of middle age, with a small black beard. He is the principal priest of the Orthodox community of Zagreb, and moved up here some years ago from the wild district of the Lika, where his parish lay. In the Lika the parishes are sometimes Orthodox, sometimes Catholic, and Father Chok found himself between two large Catholic communities whose priests were Father Morber and Father Mimica. Fortunately for him Father Mimica, the nearer of his two neighbours, was friendly and kind, while Father Morber, who was not, was busy with the affairs of another Orthodox parish, Shtikada. One day, after the government had announced its programme for the conversion of the Orthodox in Croatia, Father Morber arrived by car in Shtikada and ordered the villagers to assemble at the marsh where the ceremony of conversion would take place. He explained that in this way they would escape being killed. The Orthodox came trustfully, as they were told, but a few who did not come were brought by force. However, the rumour went round that they were going to be killed in any case and some of them escaped. The others had not long to wait for very soon a band of Ustashi arrived from another village of Gudur and started to shoot them. Some weeks later the Italians took over that portion of the Lika from the Ustashi and dug up 350 bodies. They said that the ammunition had evidently run short for some had been buried alive, others hacked and pounded to death with scythes and hammers.

The Italians withdrew once more and the Ustashi returned. Father Chok's parishioners became greatly agitated and they asked Father Mimica's advice. 'I could convert you,' he said, 'but it would not help you either in this world or the next.' Instructions to convert had come for him, but the situation was more than he could bear. He asked to be transferred to Zagreb and he helped Father Chok to escape too. Most of the Orthodox parishioners fled to the woods.

'Anyway the Italians were revolted?' I asked Father Chok. He shook his head vigorously. 'They pretended to be but that did not stop the Ustashi!' And he told how the commander of the 73rd Division had said to the local Ustashi, 'Go on with what you are doing but not so that I can see.'

Father Chok, smoking a great many cigarettes, went on with his reminiscences of the Lika in a quiet philosophical way. There had been good Catholic priests who had helped the Orthodox to get passports and escape; there had been bad priests. I could see that, like everyone who has lived in a small community, he was more interested in personalities than in generalizations.

The next year the situation had become slightly better, for Pavelitch, finding that the extermination and conversion policy was not successful, agreed to recognize an Orthodox Church of Croatia with a Croatian Patriarch. All the Orthodox bishops in Croatia had been murdered and so he felt himself free to choose an *émigré* Russian from the Ukraine called Germogen, who had been living in disgrace in the monastery of Hopovo since 1922. An Orthodox bishop could not leave his See without disgracing himself. Father Chok had the passion for minutiae and the faultless memory of country people, and he told me the history of Father Germogen with many fascinating details, only some of which I recall. In 1919 the Albanians, who had become independent, wanted to have their own Patriarch, but the Patriarch of Belgrade said that this could not be decided without a conference of all the Patriarchs. But the Albanians were impatient and they asked the refugee Father Germogen to come and consecrate an Albanian bishop as Patriarch. They sent an aeroplane for him and a present of 20,000 dinars. This was irresistible; Father Germogen came and then obediently went to do penance in the monastery of Hopovo. There he stayed until Pavelitch called him to be Patriarch of Croatia, a post which he held till he was hanged. 'Germogen was a real tough,' said Father Chok, 'The only time I saw him he had a row of military medals on his chest.' The story of the village of Shtikada was parallelled hundreds of times in Croatia. The heads of the Orthodox Church in

Yugoslavia are of the opinion that the campaign of forcible conversion had the assent of many of the heads of the Catholic Church. Whether or not that is so, the majority of the Croatian priesthood seems to have accepted with resignation the expansion and enrichment of their Church. Judicial statements were made that conversions had to be willing to be effective, but at no time did they face squarely the fact that their Church, its ritual and its dogma, were used as instruments of crime. There were small sophistries by which they were able to quiet their consciences. Many priests persuaded themselves that they were saving the lives of the Orthodox by converting them, some may have believed they were saving their souls. Unlike other Churches, they had in the Vatican an extraterritorial head which could have made known to the world how their faith was being degraded by Pavelitch. The weapon of excommunication was tried against Marshal Tito's government. Was it tried against Pavelitch's? Pavelitch posed as a champion of Christianity under whom Croatia returned to its ancient role of 'Antemurale Christianitatis', a bastion against the pagan East. If the Church had made known to the world how that role was being interpreted, Pavelitch would have lost all his influence over the devout. But instead of exposing it, the clergy of Croatia tried to belittle and ignore what was happening and to attribute the blame for everything to the Communists. Very little, either then or since, has been heard of this extraordinary chapter in the history of Christianity.

Meanwhile, overnight, Catholic parishes were doubled and trebled in size, churches were reconsecrated for Catholic use, abandoned monasteries were filled and adapted to a new ritual. To deal with the extraordinary situation a special government department was established to cope with the problems arising out of the conversions. The department's correspondence has been preserved and mimeographed so that it is possible for us to enter into its many perplexities and misgivings. Chief among them, perhaps, was the shortage of Catholic clergy to minister to the new converts, of whom over a million were anticipated, 'if things continue at the present rate'. Owing to the strongly nationalist character of the new Croatia, it was thought unwise to introduce Slovenes, and it was therefore proposed that some agreement be made between the parish priests and the Franciscans by which the latter would, on suitable terms, take charge of the new parishes till permanent incumbents could be found for them. The department also had the power to pay the expenses of the friars who were sent round the country for missionary work. Converts were expected to give them their keep and also to pay a preliminary fee of twenty dinars a head, but a central board paid their salaries and travelling expenses, also postage and the printing of leaflets. Prayer-books and rosaries, of which many thousands were issued, naturally fell to the charge of the converts.

A new trouble arose; Pavelitch had decreed that only the Orthodox Church in Croatia was to be dissolved and conversions could be made to the other three Churches, Evangelical, Moslem and Greek Catholic or Uniate. The Evangelicals were few and weak and the Moslems, for whom Pavelitch had a special tenderness, were too tactful to assert themselves but Mgr Shimrak, the head of the Uniates, did not hang back; whenever a large adjacent Orthodox parish was dissolved a Uniate priest was sent post-haste to celebrate Mass in the deserted church before a rival confession could intervene. But these were only passing differences; on the whole a spirit of co-operation between Uniate and Roman Catholics prevailed. Small difficulties were quickly surmounted. Where in some cases the ikonostasis was a fixture and could not be moved, a temporary altar was put up instead; but it was found that in many cases the Orthodox churches had been burnt or looted and the equipment and vestments were absent or could not be adapted. In that case the schoolhouse had to be used and all the necessaries, such as holy vessels and holy water, had to be brought from the nearest Catholic parish.

The newspapers give full details of these conversions, usually under some such headline as 'Return to the faith of their fathers after 250 years' and we learn of the comprehensive way in which several villages were converted at one time. For example, in *Nova Hrvatska* of 9 April 1942, we read how the then Mgr Stepinac received a telegram of 'devoted greetings to the head of the Church' from 2300 new converts from six different villages, assembled in the village of Drenovac. At a village near Karlovac three clergy performed the ceremony assisted by a company of 400 Ustashi, and Father Niksich, the preacher, told the new parishioners that Catholics would receive them with open arms and would accompany them every step. 'Alert for Fatherland!'

roared the 400. Mass was then celebrated. The band played the Ustashi hymn and the converts raised their hands in the Ustashi salute. Father Niksich afterwards had 'a long heart-warming talk' with the converts, who went back home bearing the Ustashi flag.

This ritual appears to have been followed at all the conversions. Something of the substance of the 'heart-warming talk' can be guessed from a leaflet headed 'Friendly Advice' published by the diocesan press in Djakovo. It shows that these conversions were not just barbarous raids between rival villages. The invitation to conversion came decorously from the towns in pious words. Abridged, the leaflet reads:

Our Lord Jesus Christ declared that there should be one flock and one shepherd. That is to say there must be one Church and one Head of the Church who is the representative of Christ on earth and the Chief Priest in the Church of Christ. Members of the Orthodox Church, we must introduce that unity into Croatia! The Bishop of Djakovo (Dr Aksamovitch) has already received thousands of citizens into the Catholic Church. As Catholics you will be able to stay in your homes and carry on your husbandry uninterrupted. In the Catholic Church you will be able to save your immortal souls according to the sacred words of Our Lord Jesus Christ.

Many will say that these missives had at worst the embarrassed connivance of the bishops, but though the concentration camps were full with men who opposed Pavelitch's New Order, there is no record of a bishop going there for violent opposition to the Poglavnik's intervention in ecclesiastical affairs.

As for the Uniates, Mgr Shimrak, the chief administrator, declared that, with the conversions, historic days had come for their confession. 'Every great work has its critics but that must not make us downhearted, for it is a question of a holy union, of the salvation of souls and the eternal glory of the Lord Jesus.' Mgr Shimrak died in prison and hundreds of priests, many of them perhaps innocent, have suffered because of the fury let loose in Yugoslavia by the compulsory conversions. Only the enemies of private judgment and Christian conduct have profited by the hypocrisy and intolerance shown by the Christian Churches under the Pavelitch régime. Only in one way could Christianity have made headway against Communism and that is by a frank admission of hideous faults. Yet such an admission seems unlikely. The Churches have made the world ring with the crimes committed by the Communists, but the great offences committed in the name of Christianity they have passed over in silence.

I have never understood the meaning of 'Return to the Faith of their Fathers after 250 years'. What happened to the Serbian Orthodox in 1692?

[1947]

18

SOME ENCOUNTERS: ZAGREB 1946

When the war was over and the Germans had withdrawn from Yugoslavia, I went back to Zagreb and visited old friends. Among others were the Drashkovitches, Countess Manya and her brother Yuritsa. They were members of an old Croat landowning family, reduced, since the collapse of Austria-Hungary, to living quarters in an outer suburb near Mirogoj, the cemetery. I remember the tram to the cemetery had hooks on its rear end on which the bereaved could hang their wreaths.

When I got to the Drashkovitch apartment, I was sad to find only Manya. Yuritsa had died: he was always delicate and had succumbed to the inevitable deprivations of the war years. I knew they were short of sugar and as I had been keeping bees all through the war I several times sent cans of honey to him and other friends. They had all written gratefully back.

It was dark when I started back to the city centre and I found only one person waiting at the terminus. She was carrying a striped Serbian bag full of what I at first thought were flowers, but then I saw they were vegetable-marrow thinnings, tiny fruit with their flowers still on. She must have been to see a friend in the country. We could hear the screeching of the tram in the distance but it never came nearer.

I commented on this impatiently to her and very soon she found I was no Croat and broke into fluent English. 'I love the English,' she said, 'it's almost a religion, and I went on loving them even after a Pen Club Conference I went to in Edinburgh with my husband, when we found they were just like everybody else only more fortunate. During the war it was a joy to us to hear the voices of fortunate, confident people on the wireless. I listen to them still. . . . But look!' she suddenly interrupted herself, 'I've remembered that after ten the trams finish three stops away from the terminus; we'll have to walk.' So we walked.

As it was dark and I was unknown and our language not likely to be understood by passers-by, she began to explain how sad and disillusioning life had become for elderly idealists, as she described herself. 'I have to keep reminding myself of all the wicked things that were done under Alexander and Stojadinovich and Pavelitch but it does not console me much. We expected nothing from them and had such great hopes from the Partisans. But everything is lies. We were given a wonderful Constitution but it's not observed.' She told me things which I have often read in English papers but did not know how to interpret: how, in spite of *habeas corpus* regulations, people were arrested and detained for months without trial; how in the elections there is only one party. 'If you choose to vote against it, there is a black box into which you can put your voting-ball, but there is always somebody there at your heels explaining which box is which and the little ball makes a small noise as it drops.'

I told her that friends of mine had assured me that whenever they had voted the room had been crowded and no single attendant could have managed to watch all those hundreds of darting hands and listen to the tiny noises.

'Most people are sure they are being watched all the same. Perhaps it is the Communists themselves who spread these rumours just to save themselves the trouble of spying. If people even think they are being spied on they are more likely to vote for the government. The worst spies though', she added, 'are not the Communists, they are the ex-Ustashi. They have bad consciences for collaborating with the Germans and they hope to get back into favour by denouncing others.'

'But would they be listened to?'

'It's hard to forget something you are told even if you don't believe it.'

'Why', I asked, 'are you not frightened of saying all this to a stranger?'

'Because I don't care what happens to me, and I think it might be a relief to those I am fond of if I am no longer here. My son is in Italy now and while I'm alive he worries what they may do to me because of him. You see, when the Ustashi came to Zagreb he joined Mihailovitch. My son Ivo never collaborated with Germans or Italians, whatever the other Chetniks [followers of the royalist, Mihailovitch] may have done, but he's best where he is . . . he works in a canteen for the Allied troops in Venice.

'My only other relation is my brother; he's a teacher and he's very generous to me. He gets a big ration, of course, as a Scientific Worker,* without his help I don't know how I'd manage. But I feel I'm a handicap to him because of Ivo, as well as a responsibility.'

'Is your brother contented?'

'Well, he likes to appear contented and that's another reason why I'm only an embarrassment to him, because I'm one of the few people who knows he couldn't really be contented. My brother has always been good at deceiving himself. I asked him the other day why he wasn't finishing his book on Mazzini which he went on writing even under Pavelitch, and he said "Paper rations". But there's loads of paper, and though they say publication is free the government only gives out the rations for the books they like. They ask to see the manuscript first "in order to estimate the quantity of paper required". He doesn't even want to show his manuscript in case it isn't liked.'

'But what could they do with him if it wasn't?'

'Well, I think he has a holy dread of the new Secretary of the school council, a young man who stalks about in front of them in high boots and lays down the law. The French master objected to being ordered about by an ignoramus in high boots and resigned, but my brother said: "You see he fought like a lion in the Fifth Montenegrin Brigade at Nevesinje. Unquestionably he is sincere and has a gift of leadership, a revolution is going on and we need somebody outside our petty academic quarrels to get something done," and so on and so on – '

'But aren't there always interfering fat-heads on school committees all over Europe?'

'Yes, but they're different,' she said. 'The French master can't get any work and is starving.

'You know, you mustn't think I'm a reactionary; when my husband and I went to the Pen Club Conference in Edinburgh ten or fifteen years ago, he went round lecturing about the way the Fascists were treating the Slovenes in Italy and he tried to get Galsworthy interested . . . and he fought against Fascism at

* This is copied from Soviet Russia, where every teacher is called *'Naoochni Rabotnik'*, 'Scientific Worker'.

home, too; he got up petitions for the release of imprisoned Communists under Alexander and Stojadinovich; he was always writing in the papers and then seeing his articles blacked out and feeling that he was under suspicion. He kept all those black strips and now they are all I have to prove what a fine revolutionary thinker he was. I burnt all the rest under Pavelitch.'

'Did the Ustashi trouble you?'

'Not at first, though I think they must have been watching us in case we were in touch with my son who was with Mihailovitch and the Chetniks. But in spite of Ivo, our hearts were with the Partisans as soon as we heard reliably that some of the Chetniks had come to terms with the Italians. We started sending the Partisans bandages and blankets and iodine through the milkman's brother, and we said that we would join them ourselves if we could be of any use. We were never Communists. My husband used to say that Communism would be all right if practised by saints but we are none of us saints. All the same, we thought that the Partisan movement was so incoherent it was necessary to accept the temporary leadership of a party with a positive policy and doctrine, and the Communists had that. So, when one day three Partisans drove up in a car and said, "We've come to fetch you, get your things," we were delighted. We got the three men to help us bury what we valued in the garden and we brought out the last of our stores and blankets and our wireless set and piled them in the car. And do you know where they drove us to? The Sava Cesta prison. They were Ustashi dressed as Partisans and we had been denounced to them by a gardener we had dismissed. He had been using my carnations to make wreaths for the Ustashi and keeping the money.

'My husband and I were separated and I was put in with some Communist women. They were so sweet and good to me, as for the first three days you cannot get food from outside and you must eat prison food, which is awful, so they shared their food with me and were pleased to find an educated person with them. I was there for three months and it was not till I was let out that I learnt that my husband had died. When I got back home I found that there was a German general in my house, so I just went to the garden and found what I feared I would find, that the three men who had helped us dig in our treasures had come back immediately and taken them away. I had relations near Senj on the coast and I managed to get down to them . . .

and I stayed there till the end of the war. It was peaceful enough and the Italians did not interfere with us. I came back to Zagreb soon after the liberation.

'I found that because a German had been living in my house the Partisans had confiscated half my furniture as German property, and allowed a Bosnian family to get into the ground floor and use what was left. The Bosnians expected me to be grateful for holding onto it and for paying a tiny rent. With difficulty I got enough of my furniture back to do up a couple of rooms but I never got compensation for what was seized.

'One of the first persons to pay a visit to the Bosnians was my gardener; he came when he thought I could not see him, but I did. Then I knew that it was he who had urged this family to take my ground floor. . . . I'm sure he was annoyed to see me upstairs; he wanted that for himself. He's probably thinking of some way to get me shut up again so that he can work the garden for himself for market.

'The Bosnians are no more Communist than he is; a good many of the Bosnian Ustashi came up here to Zagreb when they saw the time had come to change sides. They'd be too well known at home. The woman had no ideas in her head but lying on the sofa and eating cake and listening to the wireless. She's learnt a few catchwords by heart. She knows I'm a reactionary because I speak English and had a good education. Perhaps she knows about Ivo. . . . She cut down the legs of my beautiful bureau so that the child would be able to do his lessons at it. They are making it very hard for me to get my garden back into order because they leave the gate open deliberately and let their chickens in. All my seeds get scratched up. When I complained she just looked at me and I thought she had not heard. It is that she is so primitive she can't think of anything nasty to say straight away. She went away and then came back and showed me a hotel label on an old suitcase of mine . . . a very magnificent turreted place in Stockholm where we had once stayed for a conference, and she said, "Go back there then. We're not grand enough for you in Zagreb now." '

'But you are not sorry that you and your husband were idealists, are you? What went wrong, do you think?'

'I'm tired of thinking but perhaps we hoped too much from our international conferences and delegations and reports. We were always having to conciliate some group so that they should not walk out. I remember how it was considered politic for us to sit quiet while an Italian woman delegate gave a talk on how slavery was being abolished in Abyssinia, because she had sensible views on something else. Conferences are always like that. When anyone was spontaneous and vehement, as H. G. Wells was at the Pen Club Conference at Dubrovnik, he was regarded as irresponsible. Our nice societies are dead now in any case, so what would it have mattered if they had smashed themselves up for the truth a few years earlier? If we had not compromised I would look back on them now with pride, not just disappointment. I don't think the opportunities we once had will ever come back. All the international societies in Yugoslavia for peace and freedom have been abolished or absorbed into official ones.

'A friend of mine argues that we are being punished now for our selfishness. We lived contentedly for so many years enjoying privileges and opportunities which others lacked. If the others are hostile and distrustful now, it's our own fault, she says. And we talked of how when a Moslem came to the Anglo-Yugoslav Club before the war, not a soul would talk to him. It was rather swanky then to be Anglophile; people felt they were being very democratic if they went to the club and read *The Illustrated London News* and they wanted to forget that some of us Croats are Moslems like the Indians.

'All the same I find the idea that we are just getting what we deserve a dangerous one, it's a typical masochistic Slav idea. Among my friends the most resigned to the disappearance of the leisured, educated classes were the lackadaisical ones who were quite satisfied to be on top before. My husband and I were never satisfied and we tried to justify our leisure by the use we made of it. I am not resigned to effacing myself now or thinking of myself as a piece of past history. When I was in prison with the Communist women and we were all on a level, they respected me and listened to me because I was better educated and had more ideas about how to make prison endurable. I could make even Communism work better than they could; I know more about it.

'Even now', she said emphatically, 'I could play a part in our street committee, if I wasn't so worried by money problems and these people in my house. I know many of the people on our street committee are good and only treat the Marxist manuals as gospels because they have no ideas of their own and no experience of the interchange of ideas. I've no politics left now and no religion but I still have a few very simple notions, which these people find strange or frightening. I believe, for example, that we should be good to each other and put kind interpretations on each other's faults and failings, and not harsh ones. But these people have small vocabularies and not very flexible minds. They could not say anything like that without using Church words, and that, of course, would be out of the question.'

'Why could you not say it though?' I asked.

'Because they've not even left me the privacy to think, and when one is dependent on others for charity, as I am now, it is not in very good taste to preach it. Why, I had to beg even these vegetables off someone else, in spite of my lovely garden.'

She shook her basket of marrows at me mournfully and we drifted apart as we entered the well-lit street, in which the tram was moving towards us.

* * *

In Zagreb I found to my surprise that I was not shunned as a foreigner, whose company might be compromising. Many were glad to meet someone from beyond the sea, who would not be bored with the story of their extraordinary experiences and might listen to the new notions that these experiences sometimes generated. Their small world had just been turned upside-down and shaken and everything would have to be rearranged. One would have to be very cowed or stupid not to have ideas how this should be done. One would be eager to try them out on a stranger with an open mind.

I was buying some picture postcards in a bookshop, when I felt a small fat hand on my shoulder. I saw a man of about fifty, with sad eyes and an unshaven chin. 'I saw you at the Marionette Show yesterday,' he said, 'did you like it?' 'Well, I was rather far back,' I said, 'and . . .' 'Well, I will explain then,' he interrupted me. 'There were three brothers and the youngest one was terribly stupid, but he had made great friends with a horse. . . .' He told me the whole story of Ivanushka while I was choosing a card and then he said, 'May I speak to you for ten minutes? I want your advice.' 'Well, I'm going to the post office,' I said, 'and you can come along if you like.' He told me that he had had a shoe shop in Banja Luka but had run into debt, and his wife, who was a seamstress, had found the German Occupation so much on her nerves that she had become very neurotic. During the war he had thought it might be a good idea to go with the Germans to work in Essen. But it hadn't been a good idea. What did I think he ought to do now. Was England or America a good place to be? But he did not wait for an answer. All this had been a way of making an opening for his ideas. They weren't very clear, but I think he wanted a broad band of neutral countries down the middle of Europe and thought we should discuss things much more. He hadn't, as I supposed, wanted to abuse the government or borrow money. We came to the post office and I shook hands with him warmly with a gentle outward pressure, but when I had got my *poste restante* letters and turned round, I found he was still beside me. He handed me a name, Stanko Peritch, and an address on a slip of paper. 'This is who I am. I will write you my ideas. Give me your address please!' I don't remember how I got out of doing this but I did. He looked hurt and used to being hurt and, as he turned away, I realized he wasn't an *agent provocateur* or a government spy but what he said he was, a bankrupt shopkeeper with a neurotic wife. He was one of those people – it's not easy to detect them – who likes giving more than taking, and all he had to give was his life story.

There was still a row of shoeblacks on the pavement in Jelachich Trg but it was lunch-hour and I had to wait a bit for my turn. There was a dark-haired man without a hat with his shoe on the foot-rest. It was a good shoe and he was waving its fellow at the gaping old boots of the old man, who was bent forward doing the polishing. A woman was standing beside him and, as he talked, he swept us all three into his audience with gestures and glances. I had to ask him to start again and go slower if he expected me to catch up. 'I was talking about his boots,' he said. 'His boots are bad, mine are good. That is wrong. We must share things. There is not enough "grouping" in Zagreb, we all act on our own. It is not fair that you should have a shabby coat like this,' he tweaked at my overcoat sympathetically, 'and I should have a smart one. That is wrong and we can only change it by meetings and discussions. We must do it through our "syndikats".' He took his foot down off the stand and walked away briskly and buoyantly. Two or three of the words he used, like *'zajedno'*, together, were almost wearisomely familiar, so frequently did one read them on the posters and in the speeches in the wall-gazettes, and it struck me that his altruism, though no doubt genuine, had a rather official character. 'Was he wanting you to support the Five Year Plan?' I asked the woman, 'Yes,' she said without enthusiasm. She was a sad, preoccupied person. She told me her husband, a Serb, had been shot by the Ustashi and she had been taken to Berlin, where she had typed in an office. She said she had not enough to eat.

[1946]

19

TWO FACES OF POST-WAR YUGOSLAVIA: BELGRADE AND SPLIT

I. BELGRADE

A long, glass-fronted restaurant is attached to a smart hotel in Belgrade. To enter it from the hotel you must go through the small telephone room, squeezing past half a dozen arm-chairs which stand on their heads, and a couple of hundred empty bottles. In Belgrade you can count on a traditional and copious dinner and supper, but breakfast has always been a vague and formless meal. Because of the shortage of milk and butter I decided to forget about old prejudices and improvise. I had beer and salami and a hunk of dark bread.

The hotel guests who wriggled in through the telephone room looked mostly like delegates to conferences; non-residents came through another door that led onto the street. The two streams mingled incongruously and almost fused half-way down the room. There were lean, patriarchal peasants with big black moustaches, black sheepskin hats shaped like tea-cosies and embroidered brown felt coats. One of them at the table beside me had a basket in which something moved. He was talking to a hotel guest with a shrewd face and heavy jowls: the guest's wife, who was fat but elegant, was sorting a bunch of tea-roses. She went away for a moment and the old peasant thoughtfully picked up a rose and widened his buttonhole with a salami knife to receive it. At four or five other tables there were other mixed groups like this, and all over Belgrade you meet them. The patriarchs are usually perfectly at their ease and in no way abashed at the business deals, the ladies and the tea-roses, the chromium and glass.

The impact of these curious collisions is muffled and uncertain. Is it East meeting West, or science meeting superstition, or capitalism meeting Communism? The names are in fact unimportant and easily interchangeable. Town meeting country is perhaps the simplest way of describing it. It was from the poorest and most tradition-bound parts of Serbia and Montenegro that the principal emigration to Belgrade came and still comes. And they influenced its politics with their inflexible loyalties. Village life had its rigid taboos and its stern punishment for their infraction. The payment of debts, the moral obligation to your neighbours and kinsfolk ('brother' and 'sister' are terms that can be stretched to cover remote cousinship) were more binding and sacred duties than in the West. Coming to the city, the villager had to expand his narrow but exacting tribal code to meet the needs of a complex, heterogeneous community. He brought with him his sense of loyalty to persons rather than to principles and was often able to extend this to include the whole Serbian people; more than that he could not do. Yugoslavia remained an abstraction. His taut Serbian patriotism was invincible in the battlefield but in the later tasks of negotiation, compromise, co-operation, it snapped under the strain. It was an exasperated Serb from Montenegro who shot Raditch, the Croat leader, in the Parliament House and brought about in 1926 the collapse of the first democratic Yugoslavia. Today, in federated Communist Yugoslavia, the Serbo-Croatian tension is relieved but other tensions remain, and Belgrade is a city of extraordinary contrast and incoherence.

There is less than ever left now of the old Turkish Belgrade. After two appalling bombardments, streets and squares have vanished and in some places you already find lawns and flowerbeds where they existed. Repairs are going on at an intense speed and much of the work is being done by volunteer labour. In the main street some young men and women, who looked like students, were working away with picks and shovels. Part of the King's Palace had gone and the remainder has been turned into a museum. By the time I reached the Irish friend with whom I was lunching (Betty Duncan from Dublin) the workmen were taking their mid-day rest. Some collapsed loosely into wheelbarrows, others lay face downward high up on the scaffolding. A tall old man was queuing outside a cafeteria with a big brown sheep under his arm.

Betty works in Radio Belgrade and had managed to bring up two sons, lively and strong and intelligent, through the terrible years of the Occupation. Like everybody else in Belgrade, she has suffered extraordinary things. When the Germans reached Belgrade, as a warning to the inhabitants they strung up the corpses of a dozen who resisted on lampposts in Terazia, the central square. Betty's Serbian husband Sava Popovitch said that it was their duty to go and see these corpses so that they could bear witness later to the crimes the Germans had committed. They were disappointed with themselves for feeling no particular emotion, the corpses just looked like dolls; her husband said, 'There's German culture for you!' and they turned away. He moved on alone and at the same time a small woman, who had been beside them, scuttled across the street. When Betty went to join her husband it was a moment before she could see him. Then she saw him a hundred yards off. He was being marched away between the two Gestapo men to whom the little woman had borne her tale. Betty followed after him and discovered the prison to which he had been taken. Three days later Sava was let out and crawled home. He never recovered from the beating which he had been given: his kidneys had been injured and after a short time he died.

Children endure acknowledged horrors which they can describe in words quite as well as adults, and Betty's children did not seem at all warped in temperament by what they had seen. They had seen a lot. One day they were bathing in the Sava at the time when the Croats, incited by the Ustashi, were murdering the Orthodox: a wedding party came floating down the river towards them, the bride in her white dress, the bearded priest in his black robes, the bridegroom and a couple of friends. The huge bundle was corded round and skewered through with an iron prong. Another time it was a barrel of babies' heads.

In their school they were obliged to be precociously critical of their teachers, for some were more subservient to the Germans than others. I have never heard characters so patiently yet ruthlessly dissected; and it struck me that their comments on their elders were far more tolerant and imaginative than those of schoolboys usually are. They may find it hard to adapt themselves to a more normal life with its discreet taboos and veiled horrors.

I spent the afternoon in Kalemegdan, the lovely park which

runs down to the confluence of the Sava and the Danube. On my way there I had to call in at the Press Bureau. As I climbed the stairs I heard shrill screams of agony approaching me. I went on rather apprehensively and round the next corner met a woman coming downstairs carrying a good-sized pig under her arm. I was not able to find out what she had been doing with it in the Press Bureau.

There is an old red-brick Turkish fort at the point of Kalemegdan and the remains of a Roman bath, for there was a Roman town here on the site of the old Celtic settlement of Singidunum. The museum beside it used to be principally devoted to trophies of the murdered King Alexander and had the atmosphere of a mortuary. There were photos and letters, favourite books and favourite thoughts, his bullet-pierced jacket and blood-stained shirt, Bibles, penwipers, trousers, swords. There was the car in which he and M. Barthou were murdered at Marseilles. I do not know if the Germans replaced them with their trophies. Now the rooms are full with mementos of dead Partisans or National Heroes, the name by which the bravest were honoured. In addition there are excellent maps and plans explaining the development of the campaigns. There are small blurred news-sheets printed in the woods in 1942 and 1943 which have now become the great daily organs of Belgrade.

It was impossible not to admire the adept arrangement of the exhibition, but I could not see the emergence of new ideas or any reflection of the intellectual ferment in which the revolution had its rise. It seemed to be merely a skilful transference of sentiment and mythology from one kind of hero to the other. It was like any other national war museum and there was no trace in it of the Communist belief that all men, even Italians and Germans, are brothers divided only by ignorance, exploitation and mistrust. Nor was there an attempt to suggest the complex character of the struggle and the economic and military assistance of Britain and America. Such an enterprise would not have been possible in so small a space, but even a modest gesture in the direction of international thinking would have been encouraging. War is evidently not a good introduction to social revolution. Ideals that were vigorous and soaring begin to droop over the graves of dead heroes and too much attention is paid to the reflections of the physically brave.

The Americans have a display room in Prince Michael Street.

The idea is to make it a window on the Western world for Yugoslavs with claustrophobia. Clearly they find some difficulty in knowing what to put in it that is both edifying and advantageous to themselves. It was closed when I passed, but I could see the windows. One was full of pictures of spring fashions from New York dressmakers, and in another was a big hand putting a vote into a ballot-box very secretively. The meaning of both these is clear but I was not sure of the intention of a large display and description of the Cathedral of Science (which is, I think, at Pittsburgh) in the third window. This building has a nave and transepts and a soaring Gothic spire, with many floors each devoted to a different science. Thus you could do mineralogy, say, in the belfry, gynaecology in the Chapter House. I think the idea behind the cathedral and its reproduction in Belgrade is that science is the religion of the modern world and can with a little ingenuity be fitted reverently into the framework of the old religions. A gentle reproach is conveyed at the crude iconoclasm of the Communists. The Americans do not realize that the Yugoslavs are a deeply serious people.

II. SPLIT

If one were to make a study of Yugoslav problems, Split would be a pleasant and propitious place to choose as a headquarters. It is an ancient town proud of its tradition but not, like Dubrovnik, withdrawn self-consciously from the confusion of the present. ('We were a republic for centuries,' say the citizens of Dubrovnik. 'There is nothing now to get so excited about.') Ideas, influences, enthusiasms new and old, foreign and native, percolate freely at Split; fresh syntheses seem possible and daring experiments are made that do not usually lead to bloodshed.

Diocletian's Palace, into whose walls much of the modern town of Split has been skilfully fitted, is a good symbol of this adaptability. In the centre of the palace is the Roman peristyle round some of whose fluted columns a church was built by the Venetians. In front of the church used to stand Mestrovitch's huge bronze statue of Bishop Gregory of Nin, who preached there in the tenth century. He is a symbolic figure. It was Bishop Gregory who stood up for the rights of Croatian against Latin culture and won from the Pope the privilege for all Croats from the coast inwards to read the Mass in Slavonic rather than Latin. For a long time, by concessions such as these, a tolerable cultural relationship was established between the Croat and Latin peoples and it was possible for a Croat, without disloyalty to his race, to admit the great part that Rome and Venice had played in building up the cultural communities of the Dalmatian coast.

All this changed when the Fascists came to power. In 1919 d'Annunzio seized with his Arditi the Croatian island of Krk, which had been awarded by the Treaty of Rapallo to Yugoslavia. On Christmas Day 1920 a group of them stormed the church where Father Bonefachitch, now Bishop of Split, was preaching and commanded that henceforth Latin must be substituted for the Slavonic tongue. The man who attacked Father Bonefachitch was battered to death by the congregation and in the reprisals several people were killed, but Slavonic was never abandoned. The same campaign was carried through with greater success in Istria, which fell to the Italians. It had disastrous results all through the Dalmatian coast. Incensed by Mussolini's parrot cry 'Dalmazia Nostra', Croat hooligans started to smash whatever reminded them of Venice. In the lovely little town of Trogir, for example, the Venetian lions that surmount the archways had their heads hammered off. Then the Fascists tried to win the sympathies of the Croat opposition to Belgrade by maintaining Pavelitch, the future Quisling of Croatia, in Italy and supporting him financially. But the art of Mestrovitch is the best reply that Yugoslavia ever offered to Italian bragging, for his genius proved that Croats could renew the sculptural beauties of the Dalmatian towns. When the Italians came to Split the statue of Gregory of Nin, the symbol of the successful struggle of the Slavs for cultural freedom, was removed from the peristyle. It was feared that it would be broken up for war material, but the Italian commander was not as barbarian as that; it was taken and stored in the basement of Mestrovitch's house outside Split.

Mestrovitch was at that time in America but his house was being looked after by an old friend of mine from Zagreb, Dr Milan Curcin; he was the editor of *Nova Evropa*, the best of the Central European journals. With the problems of Serbia and Croatia in mind, he had visited Ulster.

Mestrovitch's house lies on the northernmost side of the harbour. To reach it you must walk down the whole sea front with its venerable row of palm trees, and out for about a mile along a road lined with dusty ilex and poplars. The house stands high above the sea, approached by a long flight of steps that climb up three terraces to a long portico with eight Ionic columns. In front of the steps is a bronze woman playing a guitar in a big open space (where there were to have been lawns and flower-beds). She gazes out at the masts of a small fishing-vessel which was bombed close to the shore in the early days of the invasion. (Beside her are some huge wooden packing-cases containing sculpture which Mestrovitch has requested for exhibition in America.) Inside, the house suggests a sculpture gallery rather than the country villa for which Mestrovitch intended it. Maybe it is true that he intends to bequeath it to the town of Split. Three or four large rooms are filled with huge pieces of sculpture, many of them familiar from exhibition or reproduction. Mestrovitch was working on two colossal wooden statues of Adam and Eve when the war broke out, and they soar in their unfinished state in the studio. The dining-room has a sort of recess at the end whose roof is supported by caryatids dressed in the costume of Mestrovitch's native village. Similar caryatids are on the War Memorial which he built at Avala near Belgrade. An outside studio is still being used by a pupil of Mestrovitch and in it I saw some recent sculpture of remarkable promise; a tomb-stone for a young man killed by Italian soldiers, a Roman wolf tearing at his breast; a wounded Partisan being carried away by the women of his village.

When the war broke out Mestrovitch returned to Zagreb to look after some work he had left there. Pavelitch tried to gain his support but failed and the sculptor was imprisoned for several weeks. Soon after that he escaped on the plea of a visit to the Biennial Exhibition at Venice, where Croatian work was to be exhibited under Italian auspices. He obtained through the Vatican a visa to Switzerland and never returned.

At the other end of the town lies the museum. It is one of the most charming I know. A great number of the Greek, Roman, Croatian and Venetian exhibits are displayed in a long cloister which extends round a garden full of mimosas and oleanders. Earliest are the graceful Greek tombstones from the islands, later the large and numerous urns and sarcophagi from Salona, a very large and prosperous Roman provincial town just north of Split which was destroyed by the Avars 1300 years ago. The pompous busts of the dignitaries of Salona and their wives and children, the elaborate scenes from Greek and Roman mythology and legend which are deeply carved on their tombs, recall the secure and self-satisfied life that must once have been lived on this barren shore. Their only enemies had been the Liburni and Illyrians. There is a fragment of a huge triumphal arch which celebrated the victory over these tribes, and their weapons are carved on it. There is the tomb of a Roman legionary and a door closed by massive handles to show that 'He is gone' and above it the tokens of a soldier, medals and military badges, straps and ornaments. Later on come doves and lambs and other ambiguous symbols carved on the sarcophagi, which hinted to the initiate that the dead man was a Christian. Diocletian, the great persecutor of the Church, became a near neighbour, and there were many martyrs. It was not till the last days of Salona that the cross and specifically Christian symbols were openly displayed. All the sarcophagi have huge holes in their sides where they were plundered by the Avars at the fall of Salona. After the Avars came the Croats, and of the Croatian work before the arrival of the Venetians there are some elegant examples in altar-rails and arches; they are simple and graceful with interwoven tracery, not unlike Celtic work but without naturalistic or animal ornament. Finally comes the Venetian sculpture, rather brutal and grotesque.

The Yugoslav government has already done much for archaeology. A row of houses that masked the western wall and entrance to Diocletian's Palace has been pulled down and a large ethnographical museum is to be built at Split, similar to the magnificent museums at Zagreb and Belgrade. The new museum is going to be used for educational purposes; the study of their country and its past is to be included in the curriculum of schoolchildren. A memorandum on the new museum suggests that it will be used to illustrate the diverse currents of race and culture which have contributed to form the Dalmatian communities. There is evidence in the Yugoslav museums of great skill in the use of maps, diagrams, models, photographs; Russian influence will, perhaps, be strong but Russian museums are passing through that early crude phase when every exhibit must have a Marxist explanation, and if the new museum at Split develops on the generous lines indicated, it should do much to bring order and sanity into the cultural and emotional tangle of Dalmatia.

Yet one thing made me fear that the curators of the museum might have much silly chauvinism to fight. Outside the Belvedere Hotel I found that the large eighteenth-century fountain had disappeared and was nothing but a pile of rubble from which stone fragments of dragons' jaws, snakes' heads and human limbs protruded. Enquiring, I was told that it was ugly and had been built by Italians. Yet it was not as ugly as much else that had been allowed to survive, and it was old enough to illustrate the history of Split as well as any museum. I learnt that before it had finally disappeared it had constantly been masked with planks for processions and demonstrations, so that slowly the public had been indoctrinated with the idea that it was an eyesore, unnecessary, an obstacle to the march of progress. The same thing has been happening to the statue of Ban Jelacic in the central square of Zagreb, who, with his horse, disappears from time to time under more and more comprehensive extinguishers. Yet Jelacic was a great and patriotic Croat nobleman who did much to revive the independent spirit of his countrymen, and scored a resounding triumph against the Hungarian oppressors. It is true he was betrayed by the Habsburgs whom he served, but he is a splendid symbol of the Croatian will to resistance. By removing him the authorities will show that they are more frightened of history than the Hungarians, who allowed him to stay there; and that like small-minded Philistines they do not like or trust any greatness of character or intellect that has not been produced in their own workshops.

A museum is a good index of the cultural problems of a country and the chances for their solution. The tragedy of Fiume is illustrated poignantly in its museum. It is 'closed for repairs' but a knock at the door brings out a baffled, exasperated scholar with a three days' beard. All around him in dumps on the floor lies the wreckage of history, once thought glorious, now dishonourable. What is to be done with all these photographs, busts, pictures, manuscripts, Austrian, Hungarian, Italian? In the lumber-room there are the double-headed Austrian eagles taken from the town buildings, cameos of archduchesses, medals and illuminated addresses and all the paraphernalia of the Habsburgs, covered in cobwebs. Sometimes, as in Torre Civica, the Italians sawed one of the heads off a carved eagle and made him a lopsided Italian fowl, but mostly they sent them here. Now a huge white marble bust of Victor Emmanuel has joined them. 'The provinces of Italy to their newly recovered little sister Fiume and the Quarenero' is the inscription. There are multitudes of pictures and photographs of d'Annunzio with his sallow hairless face and jaunty green hat. Only the pictures of the Hungarian governors of Fiume have been left on the walls, both by the Italians and the Yugoslavs, whiskered self-confident noblemen covered with medals. What are the Yugoslavs to do? Only in country crafts were they permitted by their overlords to create anything worthy of a place in a museum.

I anticipate that the small nations of Europe will take a lead in the creation of folk-museums. In this the Yugoslavs are like ourselves in Ireland and have to look back for a purely native inspiration to distant periods of history and prehistory before their ancestors were enslaved: the modern Yugoslav, like the modern Irishman, must, now that he is free, acknowledge the rich cultural deposit left by the invader. Only by such generosity of spirit can the long years of human tragedy and loss be made good in the future.

[1948]

20

THE FINAL SOLUTION

THE FIRST PHASE

When you talk to people about the Eichmann trial, 90 per cent of them (and in Ireland 95 per cent) will say, with some parade of originality: 'Personally, I think it a great pity to rake it all up now. What an opportunity it would have been for the Jews to make a generous gesture!'

There are even eminent Jews like Martin Buber and Gollancz, who, for more complex reasons, disapproved of the trial. Yet if one were to investigate, one would find that a large proportion of these vicariously magnanimous people had at the beginning been sceptical about the extermination camps. What we are asking the Israelis to forgive and forget is not so much Auschwitz and the rest as our own former indifference and incredulity.

I remember, when the film of the liberation of Belsen was shown in Kilkenny after the war, it was considered in very bad taste. Someone wrote to the local paper complaining that the pleasant wholesome film which preceded it (about cowboys or married love) had been spoilt for him by this morbid intrusion of horror propaganda. He suggested that the film director had gathered together a crowd of starving Indians to impersonate the Belsen inmates. No one contradicted him, and the same paper printed a letter complaining, 'As regards the cigarette situation, Kilkenny is a regular Belsen,' together with an announcement that a man had won a prize at a local fancy dress ball as the Beast of Belsen.

In fact, whether you believed it or not, the whole affair was utterly beyond our imaginations. We had to treat it as either a lie or a joke. And this was happening all over Europe. Yet Belsen was one of a score of similar camps and genocide and deportations were practised by no means only on the Jews or by the Germans. They had become quite respectable and might at last have reached ourselves. Himmler was intending to transfer eight and a half million Dutch to East Poland but, because of stomach cramp, was advised by Kersten, his doctor, to postpone this exhausting enterprise. What had Himmler in mind for *us*?

The most effective criticism of the Eichmann trial which I have read is by Hannah Arendt and was published this spring in five long instalments in the *New Yorker*. She blames Ben Gurion for staging the trial as a pageant of horror to floodlight an epoch and the long torment of an ancient people. It was really the trial of a man, and that was how the three very scrupulous judges insisted on treating it, but they were constantly forced to admit evidence that had no conceivable bearing on Eichmann. He had had nothing, for example, to do with the killing of the Eastern Jews, for this had been a military responsibility and did not require the services of an expert negotiator like Eichmann. Yet when some eloquent survivor of the heroic battles in Poland or Estonia pleaded to be heard, it was very difficult to cut him short.

The trial was undoubtedly a muddle and hard to justify legally, yet Dr Arendt concedes that it had some very notable results. Unprecedented things happened in West Germany as soon as it was known that the trial was impending and that a fresh crop of war criminals were likely to be named in Jerusalem. Baer, the commandant of Auschwitz, was arrested, as were a dozen or more of Eichmann's and Himmler's closest associates who had been quietly working as foresters, printers, lawyers, without even troubling to assume false names. It is true they are being given only small sentences for enormous offences, but at least the reproach of sheltering them was removed from West Germany.

Also the trial disclosed an extraordinary amount of fascinating facts not only about Jews and Germans but about all Europeans and about twentieth-century man.

What was most terrifying about Eichmann was that he was not terrifying at all. Had there been no social cataclysm he might have lived out his days in some quiet German town as the local agent for an oil company. He was immensely ordinary and it was, in Dr Arendt's view, an unfortunate outcome of the Jerusalem trial that he has been presented so stagily as one of the Monsters of All Time. He had had his early schooling in the YMCA. He was and remained an excellent and devoted husband and father, and a loyal and conscientious employee. He had a great sense of propriety. When a young policeman in Jerusalem lent him *Lolita* to entertain him in prison, he returned it coldly after a glance or two: 'A most distasteful book!' He was in no sense a sadist rejoicing in the mass exterminations which he organized. Physical violence made him sick as it did Himmler, who used to shake the nerves of firing squads with his compassionate sighs. The prosecution tried to make out that he had once beaten a Jewish boy to death but there was no real evidence and the charge was dropped.

He spoke of himself continually as 'an idealist' and in the sense that he was not vindictive or particularly greedy, and that he was more concerned with principles than most people are, the word could be applied to him. He said that he had always liked Jews and wished them no harm, and that his mother had Jewish relations. Like all genteel Nazis he strongly disapproved of the coarse Jew-baiting in which vulgarians like Julius Streicher, editor of *Der Stürmer*, indulged.

He went to his death with dignity, refusing the black hood and saying at the foot of the gallows: 'After a short while, gentlemen, we shall all meet again. Such is the fate of all men. Long live Germany! Long live Argentina! Long live Austria! I shall not forget them.' As exit-lines rather clichéd perhaps but respectable. As an agent of evil he was unutterably banal.

Was he a demoniacal anticipation of the Organization Man, that phenomenon of our mechanical civilization that is troubling American sociologists? He had certain traits that suggested this. He was extremely well-adjusted, he was wonderful on committees, knowing the right people to approach and the right 'public image' to present. With the minimum of friction and hysteria he manoeuvred his Jews on to the conveyor belt that bore them to destruction. Their co-operation was, he said, the 'corner-stone' of his work. He wanted to make things as 'palatable' for them as possible, and to be 'fair to both sides'.

It is this aspect of the Jewish tragedy that is hardest to grasp, despite the abundant evidence from every land. The Jews have always had their Gideons and Solomons. If so brilliant a people, practised in survival both by fighting and by diplomacy, could be manoeuvred into collaboration, no people in the world is safe.

It happened by stages. Acting on principle, but adapting it gradually to altered circumstances, millions of respectable men and women, by no means all of them Germans, became accomplices in mass-murder and received right up to the end a measure of 'understanding' from their victims. The Jews, like their persecutors, had the Organization Man's fatal respect for orderliness. They had in 1935 mostly welcomed the Nuremberg Laws, because they seemed to regularize a chaotic situation and guarantee them certain limited rights. They co-operated therefore. Then these rights no longer protected them and they were advised to emigrate. Again they co-operated. The war started, frontiers closed, voluntary emigration became impossible. But new lands were available in Poland and forced evacuation – it was called 'Resettlement' – became necessary. They co-operated. Finally the fourth stage, the *Endlösung* or Final Solution, was reached. By that time they had lost the art of resisting. Jewish policemen rounded them up, Jewish technicians built gas chambers, extracted gold teeth, dug graves. Jews dug them up again to destroy the traces of crime and then were exterminated themselves.

But even this degree of co-operation had its apologists. For example, Chief Rabbi Baeck of Berlin, the leader of the Jewish community and a cultivated sensitive man, believed that Jewish policemen would be 'more gentle and helpful' and 'make the ordeal easier'. And he thought that the deported should not be told the truth since 'living in the expectation of gassing could only be the harder'.

This was not true.

THE ORGANIZATION MAN

Eichmann himself moved only by degrees towards the Final Solution. He never exceeded his orders or treated them cynically. To him 'resettlement', till the Final Solution had been decreed by Hitler in August 1941, had always meant simply resettlement. He had studied the possibilities of Madagascar and of Nisko in Poland and he was, until the end, a great admirer of the Zionists, considering them 'idealists' like himself. They were allowed great freedom of movement and were excused wearing yellow stars. He had read 'the basic books', Herzl's *Der Jüdenstaat* and Böhm's *History of Zionism*; he had learnt a little Hebrew and had accepted an invitation from some Zionists to visit Palestine.

It was in Vienna, 1938 to 1939, that Eichmann, in the interests of the emigration of the Jews, perfected his system of co-operation, which he was later to use again and again for their extermination. It attracted the attention of his superiors; he was made an officer and later rose to the rank of Lieutenant-Colonel. Luck had favoured him at the start. In Vienna he found, as he was to find elsewhere, that the local Nazis had in an excess of zeal imprisoned all the leading Jews. Eichmann promptly let them out and formed them into a Jewish Council and asked them to advise him. After their experiences they were naturally very eager to leave Austria and here was Eichmann ready to help them. He got the head of the Jewish community, Dr Löwenheiz, to write down his 'basic ideas' on emigration and he put Rabbi Murmelstein in charge of the Viennese scheme. Even humble Jews who knew him in those days say he was very friendly, called them 'Mister' and asked them to take a seat. He worked out a plan by which the rich Jews were able to furnish money for the poor Jews to emigrate. To help 'resettlement' he set aside little plots round the city, where the future settlers could practise agriculture. I think the twenty or so members of the Kagran Gruppe who came to Ireland before the war (see *The Children of Drancy*, pp. 197ff) may have been lent the small swampy patch of land near Vienna which they tried to cultivate, on Eichmann's orders.

He was a wonderful organizer and negotiator and the Jews, at first, had reason to be pleased with him. If they wished to emigrate, they had had to fill in endless forms and stand in queues at different offices. There were officials to be bribed and insults and humiliations to be endured. Complicated inventories of property and effects had to be made out. Eichmann changed all this by assembling all the necessary offices in the one building and delegating to the Jewish Council the job of collecting in an orderly way all the data about funds and goods and furniture.

The Jews now swept rapidly through the offices, going in at one door full of problems and coming out at the other, stateless and propertyless, but with only one problem: how to get out of Austria. But here again Eichmann was at hand to help them. He had sent Jewish functionaries abroad to collect the Vorzeigegeld, which they needed for their visas, from some Jewish Relief Society. It all ended for him triumphantly. In eight months more than twice as many Jews left Austria as left Germany in the corresponding period, and in eighteen months half the Jewish population had gone. Once in a fit of impatience at some temporary delays he had slapped Dr Löwenheiz in the face. He apologized to him in front of his staff (he was very conscious that with his commission he had become a gentleman), but he reproached himself with his rudeness to the end of his days.

If we accept that he was genuinely attached to his Jewish 'helpers' we get closer to the horrible complexities of human life. Is one to laugh or to cry at the story of Commercial Councillor Berthold Storfer? Abandoning his post on the Viennese Jewish Council, which guaranteed him immunity from deportation, Storfer had gone into hiding. The Gestapo had ferreted him out and sent him to Auschwitz and he had persuaded the commandant to send a telegram to Eichmann appealing for his help. I have regretfully to abridge Eichmann's fascinating account of what happened then.

I said to myself, 'OK. This man has always behaved well. I'll go there myself.' So off I went to Auschwitz and found Storfer in one of the labour gangs. He told me all his grief and sorrow and I said to him, 'Ja, mein lieber guter Storfer, we certainly got it! What rotten luck! But what a silly thing to do to bolt, when you didn't need to! No one can be got out, once he's put in. That's Reichsführer's orders and I can't help you.' Then I asked him how he was and he said couldn't he be let off the work – it was heavy work.

Eichmann went to the commandant but was told that everyone had to work.

So I said, 'OK. I'll make out a chit saying that Storfer has to keep the gravel paths in order with a broom (there were little gravel paths there), and that he has the right to sit down with his broom on one of the benches. Will that be all right, Dr Storfer?' He shook hands and was very pleased and then he was given the broom and sat down on the bench.

It was a great inner joy to me that I could at last see the man with whom I had worked for so many long years and that we could speak with each other.

Thus it happened that, through Eichmann's intervention, Dr Storfer was able to muse on a bench with his broom for six weeks before he was incinerated. This story of Eichmann and his feelings surely has the ring of truth in it.

At his trial everyone must have hoped that Eichmann would stammer and lie and contradict himself, but he never really felt guilty or fully understood what had happened. He had been completely integrated into a criminal society so that the demands it made on him in the name of duty could not be recognized as crime. One could no more shame him than one could convince a faithful old family butler that he was 'a lackey of the bourgeois' and 'a traitor to his class'. Just like the old butler, Eichmann always called his Nazi employers by their formal titles even after they had been hanged. For him Himmler was always 'Der Reichsführer'.

The lessons Eichmann learnt in Austria he applied in every other country where a Jewish Council could be established. He told them how many Jews were needed to fill the trains and the Councils made out the lists of deportees, tabulating their property so that it could be easily collected and arranging for them to board the trains. Then when all the smaller people had been gathered and taken away, the Council itself was deported and their property confiscated. They were sent to Theresienstadt, a Czech town from which the Czechs had been evicted. Privileged Jews stayed there 'till overcrowding made thinning out necessary'. It was an entirely self-supporting community. There was a resident Jewish hangman.

In three or four countries it was impossible to form a Jewish Council. In Belgium, for instance, all the prominent Jews who would have been appointed to it had fled before the Occupation, and there was no routine way of registering the 5000 Belgian Jews who remained. The result was that not one of them was deported.

In Holland, by contrast, appalling disaster fell upon the Jews. There was a very strong Dutch Nazi party, and the proud Dutch Jews long established there were confident that it was only the immigrants that the Nazis would dare to attack. A Jewish Council or Joodsche Raad was formed to list and assemble the deportees and Jewish police were enlisted to help the Dutch police in rounding them up. The Dutch themselves were brave and kind and as many as 25,000 Jews survived in hiding. But three-quarters of all the Jews living in Holland were killed.

THE DREAMS COLLAPSE

The Nazis discovered that all the states of Europe, except Italy and two small ones (Bulgaria and Denmark), would under pressure accommodate themselves to their racial programme. Save in Romania and the East, one cannot attribute this to anti-Semitism. It is surely an aspect of modern war. As our mechanical weapons multiply, our powers of moral resistance, as though superannuated, become feebler and feebler. When the Maginot Line collapsed it looked for a time as though Eichmann could do what he liked with the French. The French prefer to forget this or there would today be some great monument at the Gare d'Austerlitz to one of the most sickening crimes in which they have ever been implicated. I wrote of this in *The Children of Drancy*.

François Mauriac has told how one grey August morning in 1942 his wife had seen crowds of children packed into cattle wagons at the station. There were 4051 of them between the ages of two and fifteen. They had been seized with their parents in July and kept for four days without food at the Vélodrôme d'Hiver. Then their parents were moved to Auschwitz and the children were to follow but there were transport difficulties and they were detained for ten days in the camp at Drancy, north of Paris. Compassionate policemen handled them and sad little stories are told by neighbours who heard the children crying every night across the camp. There was a little girl with a bleeding ear who had not been quick enough in removing her earrings when the children and their bags and parcels were being inspected for valuables.

Such stories seem obscene, for has one a right to witness such things and survive? Bus-drivers, engine-drivers and porters were all deeply moved but a dozen trainloads of children rolled on across France and Germany and Poland. No one stopped them. At the end of August the children were incinerated.

Mauriac wrote that an era had ended for him that day at the Gare d'Austerlitz. The dream of a happy future to be attained through science and enlightenment, which the thinkers of the eighteenth century had conceived, had dissolved for ever. Some era certainly should have ended there but which and how? The

Nazis who ordered the deportation of the children, the Vichy government which sanctioned it (the authorization came from Laval), were hostile to the dreams of the Enlightenment. On the other hand the Danes, who alone resisted the Nazi racial policy on principle, are often scolded for their prosy devotion to the Age of Reason. The issue is by no means clear.

It was in Hungary that Eichmann achieved his most spectacular successes, and it was here too that he demonstrated most clearly that he was not a monster but merely the well-adjusted child of a monstrous age.

The Hungarians had first of all in 1941 been too impetuous, hurling some thousands of foreign Jews into occupied Russia before the Germans had camps and extermination facilities prepared for them. They had had to take them back into Hungary and kill them themselves.

The next year they had been equally unco-operative, for though the Hungarian government had agreed to the deportation of a further 300,000 refugee Jews, they would not surrender their own 500,000 native Jews, even though Eichmann explained that it would be too costly to set up the elaborate machinery of evacuation for one category of Jew alone. On grounds of economy the purge was postponed for two years. But in March 1944 the Germans occupied Hungary because, with the Red Army approaching through the Carpathians, they feared that Hungary might sue for a separate peace. It is surprising that at such a moment they should have bothered with 'the liquidation of the Jewish problems', but they did. The problem had by now become colossal. Including converted Jews, there were now about 950,000 to be evacuated. The Russians were approaching and everybody knew by now that evacuation meant murder. The Zionists, more realistic than the others, had publicized the truth to the world, and the world was aghast.

But Eichmann knew that his moment had come. He arrived in Budapest with a large staff of typists and ten officials and he summoned his experts from all the occupied countries. He had expected difficulties but in fact, as he was later to recall, everything went 'like a dream'; the Hungarian police were co-operative and the government friendly and helpful, and most astonishing of all, he had gathered his Jewish Council together in a fortnight and had persuaded a prominent Jewish Privy Councillor, Dr Stern, to act as president. Never before had there been so great an exchange of small courtesies between the murderers and their victims. Typewriters and pictures were wanted to furnish the new office and the transport offices. Herr Novak, who was musical, wanted a piano. Original Watteaus came and eight pianos. Novak laughingly returned seven. 'Gentlemen! Gentlemen! I'm not opening a piano store. I merely want to play the piano.' Eichmann himself visited the Jewish library and the Jewish museum and had constant meetings with Zionists. Even at this stage he appeared to have persuaded himself and others that he wished 'to be fair to both sides'. It was all temporary, he explained.

The vast enterprise, so often repeated, seemed now to be working of its own momentum. There had been conferences in Vienna with the officials of the German State Railways and a new branch line was constructed so that the freight cars could come within a few yards of the crematoria. The personnel at the gas chambers had been quadrupled, so that it was possible to kill about 10,000 every day. Messrs Krupp had their representatives there to salvage able-bodied Jews for their Auschwitz fuse factory. The Reichsbank, the army, the Foreign Office, the mint, industry, everything was geared to the smooth fulfilment of the Führer's tremendous dream.

In two months 147 trains carried 434,351 Jews to Auschwitz, yet by good organization the gas chambers were just able to cope with this vast and sudden influx. In the East the Russians were still advancing but even the German generals could not clear the lines for their retreating armies. They were choked with freight cars carrying Jews.

Yet Eichmann had difficulties. They came not from the Jews, but from one of the SS officials in his own entourage. He had offended against all that Eichmann held most dear, for was not the motto of the SS, 'MY HONOUR IS MY LOYALTY'? Dr Becher, now a prosperous merchant in Bremen, was secretly sabotaging the Führer's dream and Himmler was behind him. Now that the war was going badly it had seemed to Himmler more politic and more profitable to sell Jews to relief committees than to kill them. The compassion of the Allies could be turned into trucks and food and arms for their destruction. But of course the idealists, the Führer and Eichmann, must not know. To mollify Eichmann, just in case he should hear of it, Dr Becher gave him a chauffeur-driven amphibious car. Meanwhile, he was able to sell 1684 Jews for 1000 dollars each and had prospects of 20 million Swiss francs from the American Joint Distribution Committee. On behalf of Himmler he had taken over some vast Hungarian-Jewish factories for aeroplanes and bicycles and in return had given the panic-stricken owners free passage to Portugal and some foreign currency.

To Eichmann, when he heard of it, this was all 'Schweinerei' and gross betrayal of the Hungarians who were paying the cost per capita for the deportation and extermination of the Jews and were entitled by agreement to inherit all their property. He was beside himself.

Every day the Russians drew nearer and Hungarians and Germans became progressively more 'moderate' in their views. At last Admiral Horthy, the head of the government, stopped all further deportations and arrangements were made for dismantling the gas chambers. Only Eichmann remained loyal to his Führer and in June 1944 by a clever ruse he got the better of Horthy and, illegally, sent one last transport of 1500 to Auschwitz.

After that Auschwitz was closed and even Eichmann had to realize that 'ideals' must be abandoned. The tottering Reich was in need of labour. Eichmann promised 50,000 able-bodied Jews and Jewesses, but there were no trains to take them, so in November 1944 he made them walk. The nature of these 'dead marches' need not be described.

When in 13 February 1945 Hungary capitulated to the British army, less than 160,000 out of nearly a million Hungarian Jews remained alive.

GROUNDS FOR HOPE

Is decency that is unarmed quite helpless in a modern war? I would like to hurry on to the proof that it is not. But the evidence for the other side is still far from complete.

When northern Greece was occupied by the Germans, Eichmann sent two trusted officials to Salonika in February 1943. There were 55,000 Jews there, many of whom had lived in Greece for centuries. Eichmann's two colleagues met with wonderful co-operation from the German military governor, Dr Marten, and soon were able to persuade Chief Rabbi Koretz to gather a Jewish Council. All the Jews were quickly concentrated near the railway station, and within two months the entire community, except the staff of the Council and a few others, had been evacuated to Auschwitz. Dr Marten and the Nazis met with great 'understanding' from the Greeks, and soon after the war he returned there to run a travel agency. He was arrested in 1959 and sentenced to twenty-five years' imprisonment, but as it was feared that his detention might injure the Graeco-German tobacco trade he was immediately released. He now lives in West Germany; he is loyal to his old colleagues and always ready to bear false witness on their behalf. He tried to help Eichmann by testifying that he had saved 20,000 Salonika Jews. This surprised Eichmann considerably as he had never been there.

The Romanians showed even more 'understanding' than the Greeks. Antonescu, the dictator, had, on joining the Axis, initiated such enthusiastic and ill-organized massacres of Jews that Eichmann himself urged the Foreign Office to intervene. The Romanians were proposing to dump 110,000 Jews across the river Bug in German-occupied Russia, where there were as yet no proper facilities for orderly extermination. They had invaded Russia too and begun vast pogroms there, killing 60,000 Jews in Odessa alone. Of their own native Jews they had killed 270,000 without German help, but in such a scandalous and disorderly way, sometimes exposing them on meat-hooks in butchers' shops, that Eichmann decided he must direct the final operations himself. To do this he had to rearrange his entire schedule, for Jewish problems were being settled from west to east and Romanian Jews would normally not have engaged his attention till much later. He persuaded the German railroads to organize transport for a further 200,000 Jews to the extermination camp at Lublin; all was prepared when he learnt that Antonescu had let him down and his labour was for nothing.

No Jews were to be sent to Lublin. Antonescu had hit upon an idea, later to be copied by Himmler in Budapest. He had found that by emigrating Jews to Palestine he could collect thirteen dollars a head from foreign relief committees. Overnight he became a Zionist.

All over Europe people sheltered Jews. Many met anonymous deaths on their behalf and the Jews themselves, in scattered groups, particularly in Poland, fought back courageously.

But most men need the stimulus of publicity for their heroism, and courage can be sapped by censoring every evidence of it. The Jewish fighters in the East got neither aid nor recognition from the Allies and the fact that they existed is now an embarrassment to be forgotten, even by the Jews themselves. Terrible reprisals were taken on the whole Jewish community for any act of resistance, so the Jewish Councils, believing that death could be avoided by diplomacy, surrendered their more militant members first for deportation.

As for the Germans, the names of only three German heroes recurred at the Jerusalem trial. There was the Lutheran, Propst Grüber, the Catholic, Dompropst Lichtenberg, and Sergeant Anton Schmidt, the last two of whom were executed. There was no mention of the 'Inner Emigration', those who claimed that they were best able to modify the Nazi movement by taking part in it. Dr Globke, for instance, Under-Secretary of State in the West German Chancery, was once, in his Nazi days, able to defend insulted Czech womanhood. They had been obliged to show nude photographs of themselves before marriage to a German soldier could be licensed. Dr Globke signed a new decree permitting them to wear bathing dresses. He has never had the gratitude that he thinks he deserves.

Miss Arendt believes that by exaggerating the blackness of Eichmann the Jerusalem court managed to bleach the dirty grey background against which he worked. Every social institution was implicated in crime. One instance of this should suffice. Like Krupps and I. G. Farben and many other large firms, Siemens Schückert, the engineers of the Shannon Scheme, set up factories at Auschwitz and Lublin for the employment of slave labour, paying the SS four to six marks a head for them at Ravensbruck. The intention of the camp authorities was to kill by toil. We do not know the figures for Siemens, but Raul Hilzbert in *The Destruction of European Jews* says that about 25,000 Jews out of 35,000 who worked for one of the I. G. Farben plants, died.

Yet one can end this record hopefully. One does not, in fact, have to be as tactful as Dr Globke or as business-like as Messrs Siemen and the Greeks in order to survive and win respect. Proof of this comes from three countries. The Italians and Bulgarians passed anti-Jewish laws but ceaselessly sabotaged them, whereas the Danes resolutely refused to take any part whatever in the campaign against the Jews. The story of Danish resistance cannot be told too often since it proves that a helpless defeated people can, by non-violent action, defend its integrity better than many a powerful military state. The government threatened to resign rather than legalize any measures against the Jews, immigrant or native. If the wearing of the yellow star were enforced, the King would be the first to wear it. The Germans accepted this decision until August 1943, when orders came from Hitler himself that all the Jews in Denmark were to be deported.

What happened then was astonishing. The German officials, who had lived for some years in Denmark, were themselves infected by the spirit of resistance and even the Jews took heart and courage. The German military commander refused to put troops at the disposal of Dr Best, the German governor, and Best himself showed an amazing lack of zeal. Seeking for a compromise he went to Berlin and secured a promise that all the Jews in Denmark would be sent to the camp for 'privileged Jews' in Theresienstadt.

It was privately arranged that they were to be arrested on 1 October and put on board the ships, which were waiting for them. But a German shipping agent warned the Danish government, and the government warned the leading Jews, who spread the news through the synagogues. All withdrew to hiding-places prepared for them in Danish homes. When the German police called, they found only 477 Jews out of 7800 at home. Shortly afterwards the Danes used their fishing fleet to transfer them to Sweden and paid the cost of transport (about 100 dollars a head) themselves.

In Bulgaria, as in Denmark, the German officials took their colour from their surroundings. The ambassador and his police attaché advised the Foreign Office that the situation was hopeless. The Bulgarians were showing no 'understanding' at all. The Jews next caught the contagion of 'non-co-operation' and when in 1943 Eichmann's agent, Dannecker, arrived in Sofia, he totally failed to form a Jewish Council. He could not even make contact with the Chief Rabbi, who was being sheltered by the Metropolitan, Stephan. Not a single native Jew was deported from Bulgaria.

The example of Denmark and Bulgaria shows that unanimous disapproval, openly expressed, still has power and that in a small country the art of non-co-operation should be studied more than any other branch of civil defence.

Can one argue that in small countries, where anonymity is difficult, the Organization Man cannot operate freely? Either he does not exist, as in simple Bulgaria, or his mechanism is fully understood, as in sophisticated Denmark. Croats, Greeks and Romanians do not fit too well into this pattern, and it is easier to diagnose the vast apathy of the great bourgeois states. Science is partly to blame. Every invention produces a counter-invention and, to match the speed of communication, there are devices for not-knowing which our ancestors never dreamt of. The press and the radio have superseded oral communications and are much easier to control and the committee habit helps by endlessly deferring and delegating. And, of course, the specialist has his sound-proof bolt-hole.

If one were to choose the three most murderous affabilities of the twentieth century, what would they be? I would give first place to: 'I'm a simple gas-fitter (engine-driver, dentist, nuclear physicist). I do my job and mind my own business.'

Less obvious, perhaps, is: 'I felt so sorry about Einstein (or poor Miss Cohen).' This enables amiable people to swallow their indignation by mincing it up into mouthfuls.

And finally, of course: 'Why rake it all up again? It only makes bad blood.'

[1962]

21

ESCAPE TO SPAIN

I have just read a sarcastic newspaper paragraph concerning 'drivelling, soft, escapist literature about Spain, devised for the professional *émigré* from the Welfare State'. I had been in the humour to drivel softly about a pleasant holiday in Spain, when this sentence reminded me of an earlier mood.

Twenty years ago Spain's problems were Europe's and passionate convictions had often to be based on slender knowledge. Today Spain's problems are primarily her own, but middle-aged people often find it hard not to feel implicated in them still. We still wonder what responsibility we must bear for what we see, and it is a land of such beauty and challenging strangeness that we analyse commonplace adventures there with less than ordinary detachment.

The frontier at Port-Bou is a very real one. Coming from Ireland through vulgar, sensible England and greedy, excitable, intelligent France, we do not adjust ourselves easily to these short, dignified people with one-track minds, who are always courteous and never make scenes about money. We never know when they are going to be very formal and when very uninhibited. The policeman at the main crossroads is puffing a cigarette as he negligently directs the traffic with his disengaged hand; the booking-office clerk has to finish chewing a mouthful of ham before she can give us her attention. But when she gives it, she gives it all. She comes out of her office to point out the platform. They are constantly yelling, but are calm when others yell. In fact, in the old Roman way, they usually manage to be excessive without compromising their dignity.

One day we sat down beside some children on the beach to watch them grilling three sardines skewered on a sugar-cane.

They had made a fire of orange-peel and driftwood and lit it with pages from *A Manual of Instructions for Policemen.* We wanted to talk to them but they were busy and had only time for yes and no. (A foreigner is either not noticed at all or else subjected to the most intense and exhaustive scrutiny.) We felt rebuffed and to restore our self-esteem pretended we had come to read what was left of the manual. We found some of the instructions so pithy that Cicero or Cato might have shaped them:

> A policeman must be gentle with the gentle.
> He must be terrible with those who seek to inspire terror.

Escapists like ourselves, with GB or EIR on our cars, seldom, of course, meet the Guardia Civil in his terrible aspect but the delinquent native must often tremble. It is a land in which maxims, old saws, oracular judgments, guide the devious course of justice more effectively than bye-laws.

In Spain's Civil War the heroes on both sides behaved as much like ancient Romans as possible, and their historians took the same liberties with what they said and did as Livy or Plutarch might have taken, recasting in a classical mould the haphazard improvizations of the chaotic struggle.

All the Anglo-Saxons in three-star hotels capitulate immediately to the archaic charm of Spain.

> What does it matter [they ask] if the electricity is cut off in Catalonia three days in the week and there is no water after eight a.m. in the suburbs of Malaga? Who cares if half of them can't read or write? Do they not read in the Book of Life? They are natural yet traditional . . . fiestas, bullfights, flamencos, gypsies, castanets.

The temptation to agree is strong. As one lies in bed, one hears before it is light the rhythmic shouts of the fishermen. 'Arriba! Ohe! Arriba!' as they drag in the two ropes of the net, ten men to each. If the weather is good, the same ritual is performed by man and beast and fish five or six times a day. Even the one-legged war casualty tugs at the rope, though he cannot be of any use, and gets his ration of fish.

It is a world with few neuroses and no artificial legs. But when the weather is too bad for the nets, the fishermen, like most of Adam's children, yearn to go to the United States. Two of them are great readers. Stretched out on the beach, one of them has a coloured comic, *Selección de Humor,* the other has *Collección Wild West*. The pages turn very slowly indeed. The price that these Garden of Eden peasants pay for their simple harmonious lives is that they are frightfully ignorant.

Having written 'ignorant', I feel ashamed; for the Spaniards seldom have that pawky know-all repressiveness of the Northern Ignoramus. It would be better to call them incurious and uncritical. Nobody knows the name or history of anything, or sees any point in knowing it. Of birds, beasts and flowers, there is only one question to be asked: 'Is it edible?' Possibly the enquiring mind is a casualty of the Civil War, which put a premium on minding your own business; or else it is a luxury of the well-to-do. Certainly its absence is very marked.

One day a fisherman let us take out of the net a large slab of brown gristle with a red claw protruding from its belly. 'You can't eat it,' he warned us. It looked like a shrivelled jellyfish that had half digested a small lobster. We put it in a wash-basin on the verandah and a queue of people passing by looked at it doubtfully. They had not seen anything like it before, but of one thing they were certain: 'No se come,' 'You can't eat it.'

After a while the slab began to expand, the gristle parted into five lumps, three strawberry, two liver-coloured, and began to poke out hundreds of polyp hands. Below them the red claws protruded more venturously and finally levered the whole slab over. Now it was all clear. There was a large shell in the middle, completely hidden by five sea anemones. In the shell lived a hermit-crab.

They were, an English friend told us, 'commensal', a co-operative dinner-party. The crab moved the anemones to fresh pastures and ate the scraps which its fellow diners caught but did not want.

Spain is full of such natural wonders. Near Algeciras we saw pearl-grey lupins two feet high, growing as parasites out of the roots of a ruined plot of garden peas. In the next field a dozen white birds sat looking at a dozen cows with the keenest anticipation; one bird to one cow. Obviously it was another co-operative dinner-party, but what were the rules? And were they small cranes? All we could learn from passers-by was that we could not eat them.

Some people have connected this Spanish incuriosity with a more ominous inability to see more than one side of any question, and with a fanatical dogmatism. I have heard odd explanations of it. One of the most ingenious blames it on the Mesa Camilla. This is a round table with a heavy table-cloth reaching to the floor, round which the whole family sits on chilly evenings, directing their toes at a charcoal brazier in the centre and wrapping the cloth round their knees. Husbands and sons, who ought to be arguing in cafés and sharpening their wits over newspapers, sit instead at the Mesa Camilla as in the stocks.

The elbow-to-elbow intimacy permits of knitting, dominoes, and gossip but forbids reading or writing. The tourist will not meet this baleful piece of furniture but we found a modified version in an old-fashioned hotel with an electric stove instead of a brazier under the table-cloth. The manager's family assembled there in the evenings with their favoured guests. If you should find yourself imprisoned at one of these tables and wish to steal unobtrusively away, see that you do not catch the flex round your ankle as you rise or you will risk burning them all alive. The voice of experience speaks.

Is reading newspapers in cafés a fair test of literacy? Possibly, where there is no other outlet for controversy. UNESCO statistics show that by this depressing standard, the Spaniards are just above Greeks and Turks and near the bottom.

There has been a huge decline in the circulation of newspapers since before the Civil War, when many opposing parties printed their views. Maybe it is not the Mesa Camilla but the shattering dullness of the Spanish newspapers, unrivalled on this side of the Iron Curtain, which has fettered the Spanish male to domesticity, dominoes and dogmatism.

In the beautiful town of Lorca, near Murcia, there is a noticeboard for tourists headed HISTORICS, ARTISTICS, AND NATIONAL MONUMENTS, and below in corresponding Hispano-English these monuments are listed. One is the Collegiatura of St Patrick. It is a fine seventeenth-century building which did not suffer during the Civil War, unlike its neighbour, the Iglesia de Santiago, whose interior was burnt out by Anarchists. It is at the top of the Calle de General Prim and near the site of an ancient temple of Jupiter of which one column remains. There are countless Baroque churches and palaces on whose battered façades fat cherubs, balancing on corkscrew columns, uphold heraldic shields above a swirl of marble drapery and foliage. One of the churches is a garage with lorries undergoing repairs in the side-chapels. There are innumerable Spanish towns as rich as Lorca in decayed magnificence, so the problem of their maintenance is almost insoluble.

I tried to discover why St Patrick of Ireland, whose other Spanish church is in Murcia, was connected with this region. The hotel manager and the bookseller told me, not very credibly, that his hand was among the sacred relics in the church. I was curious, too, about General Prim, who was said to be of Irish descent. He became a marshal and a marquess and finally, overthrowing Queen Isabella in 1868, a virtual dictator. He secured the throne for Amadeo of Savoy; an era of religious toleration was inaugurated but Prim was assassinated. One of the Prims of Kilkenny had gone out to Spain in the late eighteenth century as accountant to a wine exporter. He had sent home a large present of wine to his uncle but then disappeared. His Irish kinsmen later considered he must be the dictator's grandfather. To steer me through so much hearsay the local guidebook was essential, but the bookseller told me it was long out of print.

The more celebrated towns have, of course, guidebooks aimed at Anglo-Saxons and written in Hispano-English. This tongue is spoken and written with such confidence and spontaneity that it deserves a digression. You will meet it at its most exuberant in the official Granada guide, but many others are equally funny and several writers on Spain have filled out their chapters with long extracts. All enterprising hotels have Hispano-English menus and it is a pleasure to puzzle them out without using the Spanish crib overleaf. Vegetables of Time, Drunk Biscuit, Flawn, Spong. And was not this a good answer to get when I asked the difference between a Tangerine and the loose-skinned and pippy Mandarin? 'A Mandarin have wind under clotheses and plenty rubbish.' Even jam-pots have polyglot inscriptions. We treasured a pot of red-currant jam. It had on it a picture of red currants, but there had also to be a gesture towards the English so GOOSHBERRY was printed below it; there had then to be a gesture towards the Germans so PREISELBEEREN, which means 'cranberry', was added.

Does all this reveal the fine Spanish spirit of independence or merely that those who truly loved the Western democracies have been replaced by those who love only their pounds and dollars. The ravages of the Civil War can only slowly be repaired or even assessed. Village schoolmasters and local antiquarians were often progressives and Westernizers like General Prim. They backed the wrong side and met their doom and the confident ignoramuses who wrote the notice-board at Lorca and their like took their places. It is only by accident now that one finds traces of the extinct species. On the way to Valencia we stopped at a village café and were surprised to find some forty startling oil-paintings decorating the walls: misshapen old men with rachitic legs, starved pop-eyed children, dwarfs, crones, skeletons. Anyone could see that they had a grim originality and distinction. The barman, himself a returned *émigré*, was disinclined to betray any solidarity with the painter. He said laconically that he had been a schoolmaster but had lost his job because of his views. He painted all day and now and then changed the pictures on the walls. The barman was a bad salesman and his customers, bent over their wine and dominoes, could not look less like art-patrons. It was a tragedy of frustration and wasted talent which must have many counterparts in Spain.

After a civil war places have to be found for demobilized heroes and in Spain, as in Eastern Europe, the heroes replace the highbrows and are used as disinfectants in the highbrow institutions. Cultural institutions are looser in texture than administrative ones and it is easier to infiltrate into them a well-mannered ignoramus with a war medal. The show-places of Spain are full of heroes collecting tickets and offering misinformation. It does not matter much being told in Barcelona that a vast modern mosaic was dug up in the Greek city of Ampurias, or hearing in Sagunto some Iberian inscriptions described as Greek, but there is sadness in the thought that some enthusiast, to whom correct knowledge would have been a pride and a joy, is being excluded from his rightful post. The symptoms of grave diseases are often slight in themselves. In a desultory holiday search for information about General Prim and St Patrick's link with Murcia, I found myself in a great city library but distracted from my search by the works of Bosch Gimpera which lay on a table. He is one of the greatest of authorities on the origins of the Celtic peoples and his address to the British Association on the Celtic tribes in Spain should be, for an Irishman, of absorbing interest. I asked the librarian if he were still alive. 'Oh, yes . . . but he had to leave. He's in Mexico.' I decided to be embarrassing so I asked, 'Is he a good scholar?' There was a pause and I heard deep breathing, before in a low voice the librarian said, 'Yes!' His face flushed as red as those carnations that Spaniards, a loyal and ceremonious people, are always throwing on spots where blood has been shed.

But, of course, not all hero-curators are misplaced. I can think of a one-legged enthusiast who has the keys of a great prehistoric cave near Antequera. With its dim paintings and its three vast columns, which support the roof, it is one of the earliest of human achievements. The guide had discussed it with Professor Gordon Childe, and now, without caring that Childe notoriously held the wrong political views, he rummaged excitedly through the Visitors' Book to find the memorable name.

It is dangerous, therefore, to form a general impression from a few episodes, but one of these seemed to me conclusive. It happened to the friend in whose car we were travelling. He had wished to see some prehistoric paintings in a cave near Teruel. They are well known and have been illustrated in Garcia's great *History of Spain*, published in five volumes before the Civil War. The cave lies many miles beyond a small village up a rocky road. The village schoolmaster was not informative but asked for a lift for himself and his fiancée in the crowded car. When, with the radiator boiling, they reached the cave, they were told that some Frenchmen had come a year before with a lorry and, hacking away the paintings, had taken them to France. The schoolmaster, who had enjoyed the outing, took the news calmly. Which is the more depressing phenomenon, the dull Spanish schoolmaster or the cultivated French thief?

Nature, we are often told, intended the Spaniards to be the most individualistic of peoples and that is why to their revolutionaries Anarchism rather than Communism has always had the greater appeal. Spanish genius, which is often regional in its expression, does not thrive under a centralized government. The artificial rigid society of today is perhaps an inevitable reaction from the chaos of the Civil War and there are already signs of its relaxing. The chaos had been scarcely imaginable.

We were in a Catalan village into which there had poured successively Swedish, English, Russian, German and Italian soldiers. Each contingent had made his own language the official one and posted up manifestoes on the post office wall in a tongue unknown to everybody else. At the end of the war, in the interests of national solidarity, Catalan, which is spoken by 99 per cent of the population, was forbidden throughout Catalonia and there was a ban on Catalan books and newspapers which has not yet been lifted. Yet even at the height of the struggle the Catalans had shown a spasmodic respect for idiosyncrasies. A Russian soldier had been at the point of death. He had had nothing to say against the Anarchist burning of churches, which had seemed to him a Spanish affair, but it was his urgent wish that he should be buried upright, for according to the tenets of his faith it was necessary that he should, on the Day of Resurrection, meet his Redeemer on his feet. It was hard to do this in the shallow rocky soil but the Catalans had done it, and one of them took me to the large cemetery to find his grave. It eluded us but the makeshift tombs of the past twenty years had an eloquence of their own. The cemetery was like one of those necropolises of the Dark Ages, where misspelt epitaphs are scored hastily on fragments of the sarcophagi of defunct proconsuls. There was a street of small family vaults, sealed with concrete doors. Till the Civil War the names had been carefully carved but, ever since, the details had been scratched roughly with a nail on the moist cement.

As you drive down the prosperous Mediterranean coast of Spain it is easy to forget these omens of social decay. The road south runs through acres of staked carnations and export lettuces to Barcelona, through orange groves to Valencia, through rice fields to Castellon, where for a whole mile the track is bordered with roses and geraniums. At Elche they are thinning dates, at Motril there are sugar-canes and lemons, while inland there are valleys of flowering peach and almond and whole hillsides silvery with the leafless skeletons of fig trees. There are teeming towns rose-coloured like the rocks out of which they grow; even the troglodytes, who in their thousands make themselves neat whitewashed burrows through the dry chalky cliffs, rouse admiration rather than pity. Chains of mules come down the slopes piled so high with cypress twigs, rosemary, prunings of olive and vine, that only the mules' noses are visible. It is hard to grasp that these arid bundles are for fuel and forage and that behind the orange plantations lies a hidden Spain so unimaginably poor and inarticulate that it is only through burning and massacre that it can express itself.

The Civil War left a revulsion against violence such as no national war has ever caused, but the crime of fratricide has only had a lukewarm condemnation. Every village has its monument A LOS CAIDOS, but only those who fell on the winning side are commemorated there. Yet, if we count on the other side the dead and the exiled and those who mourn them, half the population of Spain is involved in an unrecorded bereavement. Some years ago, when a fabulous Pantheon de los Caidos was projected in the Guadarrama hills, a minister proposed that it should be dedicated to all who had died in Spain. President Azana, when the victory of the Republic had seemed probable, had spoken similarly: 'All the dead will be equal. All being Spaniards are equally our dead.'

But Spain dislikes compromises. Azana, driven to rely upon extremists for the defence of the Republic, could hardly have kept his promise. On the winning side the minister who made the conciliatory proposal lost his job.

[1958]

22

AMERICAN IMPRESSIONS

I. IN SALT LAKE CITY

The plane plunged down through the clouds and scattered the last wisps of fog that protected the burnished platter of the Great Salt Lake. It is ribbed north and south like smoothest corduroy and around its shores the salty tide has mapped out its ebb and flow in many-coloured Paisley spirals. Is one looking at water or rock or mud or salt or powdered ice? A shift in the light can turn any of these grotesque cones and curves to rose-pink or opal. The mountains that surround Salt Lake City have often been televised. There is an abundance of picture postcards and brochures about its canyons and copper mines, its glaciers and limestone caves, but the apocalyptic landscape has not yet been tamed. You can see how it must have appeared to Brigham Young and his followers as a final refuge, a sanctuary so inhospitable that no one would wish to violate it.

In a different way the city is equally arresting. After reading the fantastic history of the Mormons and their bloody progress across the continent, founding cities and then having to abandon them, one is surprised to find how demurely Brigham Young and his followers settled down in their Utah wilderness, having been driven successively from foundations in New England, Ohio and Illinois, with great brutality. His mansion, the Beehive House, is as appropriate for a Founding Father as Mount Vernon or Monticello; it is both homely and dignified and he had Jefferson's passion for experiment and ingenious contraptions. He lived there with his principal wife and her seven children and many up-to-date conveniences, a sewing machine, a 'Lady

Franklin' stove, a rocking-horse, and much evidence that his daughters sketched and embroidered.

There is a possibility that the next President of the United States will be a distinguished leader of the Mormon community. George Romney is the president of a state, ranking with a bishop of the Episcopalian Church, and at one time an active missionary in Britain. A great figure in the automobile industry, he is standing for the governorship of Michigan and, if he succeeds, has equal chances with Nixon and Rockefeller of being the Republican nominee for the Presidency. Conservative Americans of all creeds agree that he would make an honourable and dependable leader. On religious grounds only the negroes and their integrationist allies are disturbed, for the Mormons believe, like other Fundamentalists, that Noah cursed the descendants of Ham and that a dark skin is a token of God's displeasure. Mr Romney has dealt with this problem in a statesmanlike way, being conciliatory to the negroes without disrespect to Noah.

Esteemed physicists, bank directors, congressmen, adhere loyally to the beliefs which the Angel Moroni communicated to Joseph Smith in 1833 and the Angel's golden figure crowning the Mormon Temple in 16th Street is one of the landmarks of Washington. In the Book of Mormon, which ranks with the Bible as a source of truth, Moroni told how in 600 BC colonists from Jerusalem landed in Chile and like an earlier emigration from the Tower of Babel fell into sin and strife, so that God condemned the wicked portion of them to wear dark skins and, as Lamanites, to become the ancestors of the Red Indians. Finally these unworthy people at the great battle of Cumorah slaughtered their white brethren and only Moroni survived to tell their story, in many complicated and exciting chapters.

By later revelation Smith was told that mankind was permitted to be polygamous like the patriarchs of Israel. The Mormons maintain though that only 3 per cent of them ever accepted this privilege, for it was stipulated that the first wife must always give her consent and the husband had to convince his Church that he was capable of maintaining more than one family. So practised, they contend that plural marriage brought comfort rather than discord, for few women lacked a protector and society was closely knit by family kinship. It is only in deference to wordly laws that they abandoned polygamy.

Certainly today Salt Lake City seems happy and harmonious. The citizens are well-dressed, polite and competent. There are few beggars or unemployed and the statisticians say that in proportion to its population Utah has more scientists than any other state in the union, 11.7 per 10,000 to be precise. Possibly applied science will flourish in a soil that is too arid to nourish more delicate forms of art or speculation, since I have heard Utah described as an intellectual desert. Praise or blame belongs to the Mormons who still dominate Salt Lake City in a way that Quakers and Moravians have long since ceased to dominate Philadelphia and Bethlehem, their cities of refuge. I am sure that the Mormons owe most to the enforced harmony that comes to proud, ignorant people who are persecuted for their convictions. After George Romney's candidature was announced, there were photographs published of he and of his son speaking to jeering crowds in Edinburgh and at the Marble Arch.

They are, of course, immensely conservative, believing in the separation of Church and State on the federal level, because their own state is almost a Church in itself. The Church cares for the indigent, the old, the adolescents. The bishops collect tithes in food and factory products from the farmers and manufacturers and store them in great produce barns in every county. There is no need for federal officials to intervene.

Obviously there are rebels and backsliders, but the three or four whom I met were apathetic rather than sceptical. A taxi-driver said to me: 'My dad went on about it so, I got kinda bored.' But observing that I was a heretic, he swiftly went on the defensive and told me that long before the ancient Maya cities of Central America had been discovered they had been mentioned in the Book of Mormon and that geologists working in the copper mines had confirmed the truth of Moroni's revelations. More sophisticated Mormons do not, I think, concern themselves much with these scientific corroborations. When the angels intervene in human history, they are surely capable of covering up their traces, if they wish.

In the Temple precincts there is an excellent but matter-of-fact ethnological museum, in which there is no reminder that the Ute Indians, whose remains are admirably displayed, were descendants of the Lamanites, who came from Jerusalem. I could nowhere detect any trace of those symbolic or existentialist interpretations which have brought comfort to the sceptics of other confessions. About this I questioned a distinguished Mormon who had been in his time Elder, Bishop, High Priest and Patriarch, and he said, 'If what we believe is not true, then our religion is one of the biggest frauds in history.'

A friend took me to a service in a suburban temple (judging by the telephone directory, there are several hundred temples in SLC), a fine building with many offices and rooms for basketball, reading, science, gymnastics and hobbies. There were many children as well as adults, and as the service proceeded some sixteen-year-old boys began to slice up bread into small portions, while smaller boys of eleven or twelve filled up little silver cups with water. A big boy blessed them. The big boys were priests, the little boys, who then carried the bread and water round the pews, were deacons. Informality and reverence were gracefully blended. Even the babies took the consecrated bread and drank from the silver cups. Two small girls beside me, who had been quietly decorating a book called *Fun with Crayons*, put their chalks aside for a moment to take some bread and water. A young man stepped forward beside the bishop to report on his recent mission in Liverpool. He veiled his adventures in theological imagery, 'The Vineyard of the Lord and its pruning,' etc. Yet, little more than a child himself, he appeared to have converted some English children to the faith of the Latter Day Saints. These pilgrimages plainly affect the missionary more than the mission field, the Vinedresser more than the Vineyard. The missionaries seem to bring back to Salt Lake City a replenishment of that blended innocence and worldly wisdom which make it one of the most fascinating cities in the US.

[1962]

II. IN THE DEEP SOUTH

The best way to visit the Southern states is by Greyhound Bus on a tourist ticket. The Southern bus terminals have in recent years become historic battlefields, at which victories for the negro peoples as momentous as Marathon have been peaceably won. If you bus across Alabama from Atlanta to Jackson, Mississippi, you are following the route of one of the Rev. Martin Luther King's campaigns. He and his band of black and white Freedom Riders had embarked on a crusade to open for their people the Greyhound Bus white waiting-rooms, toilets and cafeterias which had hitherto been regarded as race sanctuaries. At every stop they had met embattled waitresses, policemen and bus officials, and peacefully defied them. As they approached Jackson, resistance had been toughened by telephone, there were more and more police and finally the sanctuaries were locked, to the great physical discomfort of segregationist and integrationist alike. When the crusaders reached Jackson, they were all put in gaol. But the battle had been won. You very rarely see WHITES ONLY notices now, though I was surprised to find in the fine museum of Jackson a drinking tap labelled WHITE. Yet there is progress even there, for till recently the negroes were not allowed into the museum at all. The negro leaders have become expert and assured strategists, their telephones are always ringing, they look exhausted but happy. They hatch plots from which very tiny chickens emerge, but vast possibilities of growth are envisaged.

When in Atlanta, I met Wyatt Tee Walker, Luther King's second-in-command; he had just returned, famished and sleepless but exhilarated, from Albany in Southern Georgia. He had dashed down there to give moral support to some hundreds of negroes, who had been kneeling, praying, demonstrating outside the court house in which some Freedom Riders had been condemned. 'A sandwich please from the café next door!' he said to his office boy, as he collapsed into his chair, 'And one for this gentleman too!' 'I am sorry', he added to me, 'that I can't ask you to lunch there, but it is segregated. However, we're tackling that next. I am giving them an ultimatum. If they don't desegregate within thirty days I'll organize a sit-in there.'

The next negro leader whom I met was keen-featured and vivacious like Mr Walker, and not very dark, so I decided to ask him an embarrassing question. He was the editor of a negro paper in Jackson, claiming to be 'the only negro paper in the States which is not an Uncle Tom paper'. In parenthesis, Mrs Beecher Stowe, like most conciliatory people, annoyed both sides. She wanted the negroes to be free, but expected them to be simple and merry like Uncle Tom and very deferential to the 'good' whites. So to be called 'an Uncle Tom paper' is to be damned.

My question was, 'I was told by an official of the White Citizens' Council that young negro leaders are partly white and therefore quite untypical. Is this so?' He answered quickly, 'More than 65 per cent of American negroes have white blood. I myself am part Indian and had a white grandfather.' In fact the average negro integrationist is not interested in racism and Africa. He smiles sardonically when he hears the whites talk of a basic physical repugnance between black and white, for he knows that the white man invariably took the initiative in the creation of the 65 per cent. There was indeed a celebrated annual ball at New Orleans, still mentioned in the guidebook, attended by white men and black girls only. No marriages resulted from such sociabilities but many babies, who were brought up as slaves. In the Natchez area of Mississippi many of the more educated blacks and whites have mixed blood, because of an honourable and wealthy planter who, unlike others, cared deeply for his parti-coloured offspring and left them large marriage portions, which other planter families were very ready to share.

But the tradition of a deep racial antipathy persists in the South. It is blasphemous and even dangerous to question it. A clergyman in South Carolina told me that his congregation would mostly refuse to take communion with negroes, believing that it was a violation of a natural law to eat with them. Many Southern Baptists think that the posterity of Ham was cursed by Noah and even cultured white Southerners have scruples, unknown in the North, about sharing hairdressers with negroes. 'THEY want kinks taken out of their hair, WE want kinks put in,' is a common way of laughing off this intolerance. In a crowded New Orleans bus a friend and I were sharing a seat for three with a negro, when two tired-looking elderly ladies, hung with parcels, came in. We offered them our seats but they stared ahead with silent, stony dignity, as if we had not spoken. My friend explained to me that they were full of Southern pride and loyalty. 'How glad I am', they were thinking, 'that dear Mother died before this day! What would Grandpa, who fell so gloriously at Vicksburg, have thought! Rather than lower the flag I will stand till I drop.'

As well as sit-ins, there are, of course, kneel-ins; when I was in Charleston most of the churches had been visited by bands of negroes. If they were admitted, they sat quietly in their pews and probably did not return. If they were turned away, there was a photographer present who immediately took photographs of the pious scuffle in the church porch and sent them to an integrationist newspaper. 'They're just exploiting religion for political purposes,' say the indignant segregationists. Who is right?

Two Churches stand out above all others in their consistently warm acceptance of the negro, the Roman Catholic and the Unitarian. Captious people say that it is easy for them to be tolerant, since they have so few negro adherents. I do not find this fair. The ministers of both faiths were ready to suffer criticism and obloquy for their belief that God created all men equal.

Probably there will now be no dramatic explosion of animosity or reconciliation. Most school integration is not very thorough in the South. If more than a few token black children appear in class, the whites move by degrees to some suburb, where there are no negroes with whom to integrate. Nor are the negroes all passionately integrationist, or very well organized. Both sides are unhappy and confused. I saw a ladies' hat-shop in New Orleans picketed by two earnest black students and one white. They carried banners proclaiming a boycott of the shop because of its discrimination against negro employees, but behind the banners a group of black ladies clucking happily over a selection of hats was clearly visible.

If serious trouble were to arise it would come not from the pacifist followers of Martin Luther King but from the Black Muslims. They number more than 100,000 'Black Men' in the USA. (They proudly proclaim themselves black and are not worried by the kink in their hair.) They believe that Allah sent their late leader Elijah Muhammed to help them throw off the dominion of the white. They are uncompromising and aggressive and have large resources. They thrive on racial tension and will doubtless disappear with it.

The negroes, by their numbers, are entitled, if democracy were enforced, to assume control of many of the Southern States. Their potential power is great. Their total annual income has been estimated at $20 billion, greater than the total income of Canada and greater than that of several European states. Yet people who have been humiliated and denied education do not make good rulers and their best friends do not anticipate a black Utopia. It is natural for the white Southerner to feel apprehension as the threat to his supremacy develops. He is exasperated by the tolerant detachment of the Yankees who see only the moral aspect of this complex historical tragedy.

[1962]

III. STUDENTS IN REVOLT

Time and the film industry have blurred the memory of the Vietnam War, turning it from a near-victory full of glorious episodes into a squalid conflict which America had lost and deserved to lose. First there was 'POW – The Escape' and 'The Deer Hunter', both travesties of the truth. Then in 1986 came the anti-war films, 'Platoon', 'Full Metal Jacket' and 'Hamburger Hill'. In fact, all the advanced technology of a powerful nation had been dropped on a peasant people, and the peasants had won. Four million tons of bombs had fallen on Vietnam (compared to the 80,000 by which Britain was devastated in the Second World War), killing over a million inhabitants and laying waste vast tracts of land.

I was in New York in 1968 and remember well the great anti-war parade in Central Park. We were staying near Columbia University and witnessed from close at hand the famous student revolt. I am recalling the story now because, while the ugly pointlessness of the Vietnam War is largely forgotten, so too is the student revolt against a military take-over of the universities by IDA, the Institute of Defence Analysis. The students rose in defence of the humanities, which the teaching staff, already the servants of the president and governors of the universities, could not undertake. For a brief period the students had control of their own destinies; they were free of their parents and they refused to acknowledge the authority of the businessmen who, because of their financial acumen, were essential to the administration of so vast and complex a university. The students pointed out that the men who manipulated their lives and set the tone of their educational environment were the same men who profited from the war. They planned to make the universities subserve military needs. To cope with the guerrilla tactics of the Vietcong the administration needed socio-economic software; this they hoped to secure from the departments of sociology and anthropology. Though the revolting students were defeated, they had made their case and the link with IDA appears to have been broken.

I left New York and heard no more about Columbia. I assume

the students went back to their studies and their brief period of independent thinking came to an end. No doubt many of them themselves became prosperous and sensible businessmen like President Grayson Kirk, but some will remember those happy days when they still believed that their visions of truth and justice could be realized by their own efforts. I thought of Wordsworth's 'Ode – Intimations of Immortality from Recollections of Early Childhood':

The Youth, who daily farther from the east
Must travel, still is Nature's priest,
And by the vision splendid
Is on his way attended;
At length the Man perceives it die away,
And fade into the light of common day.

i

One morning at three a.m. we were woken by people running round our block on 113th Street, and through the window on Broadway we saw mounted police riding towards Columbia. The next day I tried to find out precisely what it was all about. It is hard to be precise without being boring, and most of the pamphlets and harangues about the revolt were detailed and parochial. Yet the alternative is to see nothing but an epidemic of student violence sweeping over Europe and America, and to underestimate what is spontaneous and individual. And that is the most significant part.

Of course the Vietnam War had triggered it off, but the war is considered a public issue, which the public can take care of. Among the 87,000 New Yorkers at the great anti-war parade in Central Park, there were many Columbia students; but while the ordinary banners had inscriptions like TRADE DEAN RUSK FOR THE PUEBLO and HITLER TOO FOUGHT THE COMMUNISTS, the students' banners kept to the one theme: PRESIDENT KIRK MUST GO! STOP THE GYM! DOWN WITH IDA!

A few Marxist students (they have a magazine, *Challenge*) probably welcome the war, and the moral and intellectual confusion into which it has thrown the nation. They talk of the universities as being 'the soft underbelly of society'. Their seizure would bring about its overthrow and the dictatorship of the proletariat.

But the vast majority of the rebels does not want any dictatorship at all. They hate the Vietnam War for the same reason that the Marxists welcome it. Theirs is a humanist university; on the buildings round the campus the names of the great writers of the past are carved, Homer, Virgil, Sophocles. Modern writers whom the young revere have condemned the war as the most senseless and obscene in American history, and to most students it must seem that all the vision and generosity of educated America is in stark opposition. In one issue of *The New York Times* there are four pages of protest from the editorial staffs of the magazines of 500 universities and colleges.

It is through IDA that the war made a direct impact upon Columbia and challenged it to defend its academic freedom. The military had long been wooing academic scientists but now the institute threatened to involve the other faculties, and to turn a casual liaison with the university into a marriage. The faculty technologists had long been contributing what IDA called 'military hardware' but the war had shown 'the ideological and human superiority of guerrilla movements', and to redress the balance the hardware must be supplemented by 'socio-economic software'. That is to say: 'The motivation and morale of the Vietcong military and civilian personnel must be studied.' This could best be done at the universities, where there are social and behavioural scientists. The negro riots made it urgent that the control of 'domestic insurgency' should also be studied.

IDA, whom the students' magazines picture as a voluptuous nude to whom adoring professors bring strange parcels, knew how to flatter the bored academic. It is more interesting to have some hush-hush work of national importance than to be helping adolescents to pass exams, and her military hardware research programme was a challenge to inventive minds. . . . It was necessary to discover ways of dispersing crowds and sit-in strikes with something more subtle than truncheons. Good work had been done on tear-gas, fogs, foams, sticky blobs, but the control of humidity and temperature could be investigated in university laboratories. 'The technical problem should be to avoid heatstroke and mass-fainting, which would create both problems of porterage and public relations.'

While the science faculties were working on this, the sociologists could be considering how to break up ideological solidarities, to spread misgivings and sap courage. IDA is an innocent-looking octopus whose friendly tentacles it is very hard to elude and, at the start, she got good support from a dozen universities. In Columbia the president, Dr Grayson Kirk, and William Burden, one of the trustees, became committee-men; Professor Koopman, the mathematician, was given special leave of absence to devote his talents to military research. Dr Garwin, the physicist, paid a private visit to Vietnam, which the students linked with the impending use of tactical nuclear weapons there.

The result of all this was that in 1960 IDA was able to say in its annual report: 'Our new members are strong in the humanities and social sciences, as well as in the physical sciences and engineering. . . . The Institute thus increases its capability across the spectrum of talent.' There were also many pleasant remarks about the spirit of co-operation which the universities had shown towards the requirements of the military.

However, some of the faculty members of the twelve co-operating universities were disturbed, and dreaded some technological take-over. In the past thirty years universities have shown themselves immensely vulnerable. A small push, and they topple over to the right or to the left, and the dead weight of the 'neutral' sciences makes them lie like logs. For the 'objectivity' of the scientist has been shown to be a fraud, a mere excuse for handing out ideas to whoever pays for them. An honest intellectual is usually the first victim of aggression, and in 1968 he should be studying how to resist sticky blobs and not how to manufacture them; how to make 'the problems of porterage and public relations' as insoluble as he can, and possibly how to riot.

I heard a rebellious faculty member explaining from the steps of the Low Library that Columbia owed its name and fame to a riot, as did the United States themselves. And, indeed, the inscription on the pediment above his head said that the university had been built in the reign of George II. In 1782 the rioters had changed its name and its allegiance and turned its curriculum upside-down.

Chicago was the first university to rebel against IDA. On 15 February 1968 the *New York Post*, under the heading PROFS PULL PLUG ON THINK TANK, reported that a committee of five professors, headed by a geophysicist, recommended that the university sponsorship of IDA be withdrawn. Columbia followed by ending its institutional connection with IDA but the students protested that this was 'an outright farce' as long as President

Kirk and William Burden were officially associated with it.

The university is deteriorating as a place of learning. Petty details are being substituted for analytical thought, study is being fragmented into academic disciplines and specialities, and innumerable bureaucratic pettinesses are being perpetuated by the university, so that we may be processed into functionaries in corporate society. The university has increasingly denied us the opportunity to become creative, socially productive individuals.

We demand a permanent and democratically elected student-faculty body to join in restructuring the university and to pass binding judgment on all future disciplinary action.

But the authorities would listen to nothing. They were not humanists or scholars, and they did not understand what was happening. Columbia had grown so large and complex that no mere scholar could administer it. So inevitably the president and all the trustees were businessmen. Grayson Kirk, as well as being on the committee of IDA, was a director of Consolidated Edison, of Socony Mobil Oil and several other powerful firms; the other trustees were directors of the Chase Manhattan Bank, of Ford, the Prudential Life, the Metropolitan Life, General Foods, Lockheed Aircrafts, and a dozen similar enterprises. So we read in the students' magazine: 'The men who manipulate our lives and set the tone of our educational environment are the same men who reap profit from the war and prestige from their participation in institutions like the Asia Foundation (financed by CIA).'

The students decided to force the issue by violent action and to use what allies they could find. Because of the gymnasium and a plan to extend the university by evicting some thousands of tenants from large deteriorating buildings owned by Columbia, the neighbourhood was inflamed and its Puerto Rican and negro inhabitants ready to join forces. And, of course, the negroes had their own reasons for disliking IDA, its 'sit-in quelling hardware', and its 'socio-economic software'. Town and gown were ready to join together against the university authorities.

On 23 April five university buildings were seized and the revolt began.

ii

The participation of the negroes has made the Columbia students' revolt different from any other. The coloured students are relatively few; they keep to themselves and are not well known. When the white students made advances to them supporting black interests in Morningside Park and the apartment blocks, they could not reject them, but they may have been embarrassed. The black students are very well-behaved and do not identify themselves gladly with the transient SROs (single room occupants) who use the park. So they have co-operated in a very independent way. When they were invited to join the whites in seizing one of the five blockaded buildings, Hamilton Hall, where the dean has his offices, they showed themselves to be more serious and more committed, and at once the difference of outlook began to show itself. They had brought in arms, perhaps because they expected to be roughly handled by the police, and they were morbidly concerned about keeping everything tidy, not breaking furniture or interfering with private property. From outside, a well-known negro psychologist, Dr Kenneth Clark, was urging restraint.

The negroes paid special attention to food supplies. Their sympathizers in Harlem, the proprietors of bars and restaurants, sent in tins of food and even hot dishes to 'the soul-brothers', who lobbed many cans and loaves through the windows of the other 'liberated' buildings. But soon disagreement about tactics and aims became acute and the blacks asked the whites to leave Hamilton Hall. This the whites reluctantly did; Alexander Hamilton was deposed and his Hall rechristened Nat Turner Hall of Malcolm X College. (Turner was a negro slave, who headed a revolt over a century ago; his body had been broken up and fragments circulated round the Southern planters.)

The evicted whites then broke into the Low Library, where President Kirk had his offices, and established themselves there. Searching his desk thoroughly, they found some indelicate articles and papers which revealed he was a man like themselves, and some memoranda about the conversion of the apartment blocks. They later published the memoranda with other 'liberated documents' and under the heading 'The Peasants take over the Palace', they describe drinking the president's sherry and tossing his cigars from block to block. Meanwhile, Avery Hall was occupied by the architectural students, Fayerweather Hall by the social science students, Math Hall by the extremists, who flew the red flag and set a portrait of Karl Marx in a window. The students' journals do not tell us much about what they did during the six days of blockade. A wedding without a licence was celebrated in Fayerweather Hall; pamphlets were written and programmes planned and there were constant negotiations with the faculty. The dean was held a prisoner for twenty-four hours in his office. Sympathetic faculty members, who disapproved of IDA and the gym, tried to act as mediators, running to and fro with proposals. But for the most part the liberal faculty members are derided in the students' journals as fifth columnists tormented by worry about their jobs and families. When on the last day word reached Harlem that there was to be a 'bust' and that 'the brothers at Columbia are about to be messed over by the cops', about 150 young negroes came and yelled encouragement through the windows of Hamilton Hall. It looked as though more negroes, a real invasion, were likely to arrive, so the liberal faculty members reasoned with the students: 'Listen! We agree with much that you say. But let's keep this among ourselves. Let's exclude from the campus all those who are not *bona fide* Columbia members!' Whereupon, they excluded the reinforcements from Harlem.

That was the night of 'the Bust'. At three a.m. one thousand police, called in by the mayor and President Kirk and certainly not *bona fide* Columbia members, burst into the campus with night-sticks and handcuffs. A handful of liberal faculty members did try to dissuade them, but had to retreat badly bruised. The police swept on and in a couple of hours had battered their way into 'the liberated buildings'. Because Harlem was in an explosive state, the occupants of Hamilton Hall, which was seized first, were treated gingerly. After King's death a spark would have set off a great riot and all the buildings of Columbia would have gone up in flames. The negroes, on their part, had been busy vacuuming and tidying and none of the weapons they had brought was used. Both sides realized that this was not THE DAY; it was only a rehearsal. The militant socialists in Math Hall were also treated with care and most of the police violence was expended on the more frivolous blockaders and the sympathetic bystanders in the campus. The lesson, which *RAT*, the rebel journal, drew from this was: 'It pays to be serious and aggressive.' Seven hundred and twenty-eight arrests were made, but the police invasion of the campus turned many waverers into rebels and Grayson Kirk's 'victory' settled nothing.

A few days later I was on the campus at Columbia. The rebel students seemed to be in control of the whole university. There were strike committees at work inside and outside the buildings and busy secretaries telephoning sedition. Literature was being distributed from stalls and from the steps of the Low Library short fiery harangues galvanized large crowds. There were to be speeches like this every morning at eleven. Official lectures were boycotted and students warned that if faculty members offered 'discussions', this was a trick to lure the rebels into the classrooms; they were not to go. Instead, some fifty outdoor lectures were organized by the students, some of them on the campus, some outside St John's Cathedral. A list of Monday's 'liberation lectures' said that Mr Azim was to lecture on Hindi Urdu outside the Physics building, Mr Kaptchuk was to talk on Buddhism. There were to be talks on American poetry, behaviour analysis, on Herbert Marcuse, William Blake, and 'the Warfare State'.

Is it really so presumptuous of the students to organize their own classes? Is is possible that the president, the trustees, the university, all universities, are now anachronisms and that everything must be reshaped? Young intellectuals are kept artificially childish and then asked to throw all their weight, their lives and their brains into a conflict whose rights and wrongs have been decided for them elsewhere. The mass media, press, radio, television, overwhelming in their impact, can turn the dull-witted into conformists, while at the same time, for the inquiring, they expose the dirty little secrets of authority as never before. With a cine-camera and a tape-recorder and a Xerox machine, the most venerable certitudes can be undermined. One can trust nothing but one's own judgment and an adventurous eighteen-year-old can now claim an intellectual licence that has not existed since the War of Independence.

The old university tradition was, in fact, a free one. When Alexander Hamilton was at Columbia (then King's College), he was already, as an undergraduate, working for the revolution and reflecting on the future constitution of the United States. He issued pamphlets in defence of 'The Natural Rights of Mankind' against the propaganda of the British, and his reading had clearly followed the contours of his own mind and not that of any board of trustees. At the age of eighteen, five years younger than Cohn-Bendit, addressing himself to a pro-British pundit of the day, he had written: 'Apply yourself without delay to the study of the law of nature. I would recommend to your perusal Grotius, Puffendorf, Locke, Montesquieu and Burlemaqui. I might mention other excellent writers, but if you will attend diligently to these you will not require any others.'

He was worse than a draft-dodger because he was ready to fight his own countrymen in defence of natural rights. Before he was twenty he had outlined a basic military strategy for their defeat. He became Washington's aide-de-camp and trusted adviser.

It is difficult to believe that Hamilton would not have looked with understanding on the queer confused struggle in Hamilton Hall. The Founding Fathers were all individualists and humanists. Some of them, like Jefferson and Franklin, were pioneers in science, but it was an occupation for their leisure hours only. No one could anticipate the direction from which the new assault on the National Rights of Mankind was likely to come.

There is a bronze female reading a book in front of the Low Library, but she was so covered with rebellious placards that I could not decipher her name. Maybe she was Columbia, who threw out George II, but someone said she was Scientia, the Bitch-Goddess, who gives heart transplants with one hand and napalm with the other. For a generation now she has diverted men's minds from human problems to technical ones. She is worse than George III and now she is being found out. Allied with institutional bureaucracy, she exploits what is conformist in men and represses their Natural Rights.

The students were nowhere near as articulate about all this as young Hamilton was, but they argued that the university must be reshaped from the ground up if creative thought were to flower again. One of their manifestoes ended with a verse by Walt Whitman:

> I hear that it was charged against me that I sought to
> destroy institutions.
> But really I am neither for nor against institutions;
> What indeed have I in common with them? Or what
> with the destruction of them?

Only I will establish in the Mannahatta and in every
 city of these States, inland and seaboard,
And in the fields and woods and above every keel,
 little or large, that dents the water,
Without edifices or rules or trustees or`any argument.
The institution of the dear love of comrades.

Uncertain as the motives and methods may have been, the students had some success. When the blockade was over and picketing of classes began, over a hundred faculty members issued a collective statement. They proposed that all ties with IDA be severed, that the gym construction be abandoned and that the university be restructured to permit of student participation at all levels.

iii

'STOP THE GYM IN MORNINGSIDE PARK!' was the second of the students' battle-cries. For them Morningside, which is largely owned by Columbia, was a microcosm of New York, of all America. It was an urban community in which universal problems could be reduced to manageable dimensions and solved by direct action.

Where Morningside touches Broadway you meet people of every race and clime and colour. Shops with foreign names display exotic wares from all over the world. At first it is fascinating and stimulating. But soon this barrage of impressions becomes as unnoticeable as the sound of the traffic. There is too much; all the colours in the spectrum blend into a dirty grey. It is a cultural chaos where nothing happens because everything happens. To the east is a great jungly park that it is unsafe to walk in; to the west a great polluted river that it is unsafe to bathe in. A man whose job it was to work a garbage incinerator in an eighty-family apartment house told me he had found among the milk cartons and stale vegetables a dead baby. 'How did it get there?' I asked him. He shrugged his shoulders.

Morningside Park is a narrow strip of grass and stone which stretches for a dozen blocks behind the university and St John's Cathedral. Unattractive as it is, it is one of the principal open spaces available to the inhabitants of Harlem. On the west side it is a rocky precipice, thinly planted with stunted acacia and dogwood; on the east it is flat and bald. They call it Muggingside Park because, if you carry your cash, you may be mugged by an 'addict'.

The gymnasium project was started by Columbia in 1962; it was to be on the rocky high ground. As a gesture to the neighbourhood, which at the time seemed generous, a small portion of it, with a separate entrance, was to be set aside for the use of those who lived around. At the same time the university planned to 'improve' the neighbourhood by demolishing many of its tenement blocks and converting the rest into middle-class apartments suitable for faculty members.

But nothing much was done till lately, when a large rectangle in the park was levelled off and the mounds of rubble enclosed with a fence. In the meantime the negro leaders have become more articulate and touchy. The gym, with its separate entrance, spelt segregation and encroached on 'their' park. Nor did Columbia's plan to improve its property by throwing them out appeal to them at all.

When their allies, the white students, understood their feelings, they had a battle with the police and tore down the railings round the plot. They then made a protest march through Harlem cheering and being cheered by the negroes. 'STOP THE GYM! NO MORE JIM CROW!' And when President Kirk, at a memorial service for Martin Luther King, was eulogizing his pacifism, Mark Rudd rose up in his pew and, accusing him of hypocrisy because of the racist implications of IDA and the gymnasium, he walked out of the chapel followed by forty of his supporters.

One of the 'liberated documents' found in the president's desk (marked CONFIDENTIAL) was a memorandum about the extension of the university in Morningside. This was published during the blockade in *RAT*. One would need to be young and idealistic in order to be shocked by it. The picture it gives of a great city is dismally familiar. There is not a sentence in it to which any respectable real estate agent or urban developer would not assent. It is a simple recipe for making a 'bad' neighbourhood into a 'good' one. There were a lot of worthless people camping on a valuable property; all one had to do was to clear them out.

Cheap air travel, said the memorandum, had brought thousands of Puerto Ricans to Morningside, and during the war it had been 'discovered' by negro soldiers drafted in from other states. It was pleasanter than Harlem, but near enough to 'the brothers' to make segregation bearable. In the past ten years 1,200,000 coloured people had come to New York, the white middle classes had fled before them, and the character of Morningside had totally changed. Hunting for cheaper and cheaper rooms, the newcomers had seldom stayed in any for more than eight months. 'They had no interest in the community, and there were now more narcotic addicts in Morningside than anywhere else in New York.' The university had in the past four years made 'a massive effort' and 4000 SROs had been dislodged; now the rest must go, and 7000 occupied rooms must be demolished. A recent survey reveals that, next to Chicago, Manhattan is considered the least desirable place to live in by faculty members. If the university is to attract them it must build Class A apartments. There will be 'tensions' of course during the demolitions and conversions, but it must be remembered that the purposes of the university are 'wholly good'. What *were* these wholly good purposes? That it humanized the neighbourhood? No, that it spends money there. And the writer assesses how many million dollars the university spends in taxes, wages, scholarships, food.

The students also liberated and published a letter to the president from the chairman of the Morningside Tenants Committee. She described a Mourn-In to condemn the evictions and the abusive tactics of superintendents. They were dumping tenants' belongings on the sidewalk, and getting rid of them by turning on the heat in mid-summer, and turning it off in winter. Other letters show that she had difficulty getting a reply. The president was very busy.

And he obviously was. He seems to be a conscientious and liberally minded man. There is no evidence that he approved of cooking and freezing the tenants, or that he wrote the memorandum; and how could he be expected to run the whole neighbourhood as well as the university? The students were attacking not a man, but a system, a whole society. In Megalopolis you have to shout at the top of your voice, and make violent accusations, if you are to be heard at all.

Have they any remedy that is not visionary? I do not think so, but visions have to precede plans. Once, when Mark Rudd, the bellowing, fair-haired student leader, was cursing President

Kirk, Mayor Lindsay and the police from the steps of the Low Library, a man beside me said: 'It's pure anarchy! My boy has to pass his exams next fall. His whole career depends on it!'

And, in fact, there are more Anarchists than Communists among the students, but it is anarchy of a complicated kind. They were selling on the stalls a magazine, *Anarchos*, dedicated to 'the Transformation of Life in its entirety, which begins when Men Dare to Rule their own Lives', and I recollected that I had seen posters in a Puerto Rican part of Morningside, 'VIVA DURUTTI' (he was the Anarchist leader killed at Madrid in 1936). *Anarchos* advocated the reorganization of society by 'neighbourhood assemblies', patterned on the Athenian ecclesia. Only so could our propertied, class-ridden and centralized society be restructured. Technology must not be rejected, but steered into reverse, 'scaling down the size of our industrial complexes and their electronic components to community dimensions'. The magazine refers respectfully to the revered prophets of the world's rebellious students, William Reich and Herbert Marcuse. Marcuse is the elderly Californian professor who gave warning that technocratic governments would try to dominate and enslave the universities.

Many of the pamphlets were written when Washington and Chicago were burning after Martin Luther King's death. There is an apocalyptic phrasing about them as there is about all contemporary American writing, its novels, its plays, its journalism, a wild extravagance of self-loathing and self-contempt. It is as though they are waiting eagerly for Judgment Day, for crumbling skyscrapers and rivers of blood. Americans used to be renowned for bragging, but now they surpass all but the Hebrews in savage self-criticism.

What is your dream, white middle-class America? A new dish-washing machine, a sleek Jaguar, a motorized lawn-mower? Do you dare to babble about city-planning and clean air, while the cities and villages of Vietnam lie in shambles and the air is filled with the stench of decaying bodies? You have the nerve to talk about 'freeing' Saigon, whose soul you demoralized and crushed long before your guns had shattered its buildings. In its shanty cheapness and florid vulgarity, in its blackmarkets and brothels, in its corrupted venial officials and sadistic police, in its garish neon lights and squalid streets, it has become the authentic image of New York, Chicago and Los Angeles. . . . The only pure and clean thing in Saigon is the armed guerrilla lurking behind a window.

Take care, white middle-class America, the war is coming home. Your youth may not permit itself to be sacrificed hypocritically to your computerized God of War. Your black house-cleaners may revolt. Your stinking cities may burn in the flames of insurrection!

When you are young and arrogant, it is exhilarating to be a Jeremiah, because in your heart you believe you can prevent what you predict. The students seemed cheerful and pragmatic. By limiting their objectives they had achieved two things. They had made the authorities thoroughly uncomfortable about IDA, and spoilt the plans for the new gymnasium.

[1968]

IV. THE BOB JONES UNIVERSITY

I constantly see in the newspapers contemptuous little gibes at the Bob Jones University. Since I must be one of the few Irishmen actually to have been there, I would like to add to the picture. Mr Tom Luby writes that it is 'bogus' and suggests that a book about Orange Ulster, *America's Debt to Ulster*, which emanated from it must be nonsense. Well, I found it an awful place, but then I dislike all modern universities and modernized ancient ones. Built like airports, they function like factories for processing lively children into civil servants and narrow 'experts'. By those standards, BJU is perfectly normal.

I saw it by accident. I was staying with a friend in the large and hideous industrial town of Greenville, South Carolina, when one of her after-dinner guests said to me, 'The President of Ulster was in Greenville last month and Bob Jones [the Third] is going to preach the Easter sermon for him in Belfast.' I sorted that one out and asked her to show me BJU before I left. My hostess and her friends were Episcopalians but they regarded BJU as an adornment to the town. It is a mark of distinction to have a university, and leading citizens had seduced Bob Jones from Tennessee by offering 200 acres of land in an important location. They told me of the huge 'amphitorium' which houses 7000, what an 'aristocratic' figure Miss Jones presented at the numerous civic functions she graced, and how well-behaved the students all were:

They are clean-living, they never have scruffy long hair or take drugs or drink; student riots would be unthinkable and . . . [a pause to think of a telling indication of their quality] they always wear ties at symphony concerts. They have very dogmatic views, of course, but then in these days of laxity and permissiveness . . .

On the way to the station I made a brief tour of the university. The 'amphitorium' was as monstrous as I had been told, and there were acres of lawn, fountains, begonias, laboratories and other academic appurtenances. It did not seem to me any more or less frightful than other modern academies, but my train was soon due and the rest of this account stems from the *Bob Jones University Bulletin* of 255 closely printed pages.

One of the arguments for calling it 'bogus' is that it does not belong to 'any educational association, regional or national'. On page 8 Bob Jones III takes a header in to this rather stagnant pond and comes up composed: 'It is our sincere conviction that BJU can do more for the cause of the Lord Jesus Christ by not holding organic membership in any such association, though our finances, our equipment, our academic standards would fully qualify us.'

A brief inspection of the university and a long perusal of the *Bulletin* convinced me that it is rich and well equipped. What about academic standards? These are harder to assess. A little over a thousand courses are listed, including 'Advanced Hebrew Grammar', 'Botanical Taxonomy', 'Coaching Soccer', 'Elementary Sumero-Akkadian', 'Parasitology' and 'Papyrology'. There are also many European History courses, so I doubt whether *America's Debt to Ulster*, which Bob Jones it seems has written with Ian Paisley, can be as inaccurate as Mr Luby claims. He is annoyed with the authors for saying that 'Orangemen' played a leading part in the American Revolution of 1776, 'because the Orange Order was not set up for another twenty years'. This is a quibble. July the Twelfth and the Relief of Londonderry had been annually celebrated before 1795 and, whatever they called themselves, Ulstermen played a prodigious part in the creation of the United States and in building into the Constitution Orange William's civil and religious liberties. Ulstermen have a right to be proud.

To quote further from the prospectus, they have '42 flourishing literary societies', a library of 150,000 books, a 'collection of Sacred Art' containing pictures by Tintoretto, Titian, Rembrandt,

Rubens and Van Dyck, a museum in which thousands of visitors are given guided tours each year, a radio station 'for the winning of souls round the globe', a printing press and a film studio for roughly the same purpose, and an abundance of athletical playgrounds, gymnasia, pavilions. Unless the religion which informs these activities is 'bogus', all the rest seems (to me depressingly) normal. The religion is shared by the majority of Christians, black and white, in the Southern States, for it is Fundamentalist and the Southern Baptist Church is the citadel of biblical Fundamentalism.

So why all this chatter about Paisley's bogus doctorate? The university draws its pupils from 80 of the 243 American Protestant sects, each of which, like Paisleyism, started as a breakaway from some parent Church, which at first angrily repudiated and then finally accepted it. The sects later seldom quarrel; the 19 distinct sects of the Baptists, who are particularly prone to schism, live together now in perfect amity, and many of them get their ministers from BJU, where, according to the prospectus, approximately a thousand students study for the Church or some other religious post every year.

Dean Sperry of Harvard, who wrote the classic book on religion in America, deplores the anti-intellectualism of the Fundamentalist ministers and their mistrust of biblical criticism. 'The inspiration of the Holy Spirit', he writes, 'is invoked to do duty for book-learning.' That of course is the level on which Paisleyism should be attacked, but it never is, for here in the Republic there is an equal mistrust of intellectualism and biblical criticism. Insults and bombs are much easier to handle.

My friends in Greenville praised the Fundamentalists for their nice behaviour; they often have a simple goodness and piety that shames one (everyone ought to read Thornton Wilder's novel *Heaven's My Destination*). Most important of all, they pay for their own doctrines, for the amphitorium, for the global winning of souls. Like most American Protestants they are staunch supporters of the separation of Church and State, which derives from Jefferson's Statute of Religious Freedom in Virginia. They ask no one else to pay for the inculcation of what they believe.

The Fundamentalists are old-fashioned, very resolute people, but no more bogus than anyone else whose views we do not share. Their record of resistance to Hitler, Stalin and Franco is better than that of any of the established Churches (consider also, for example, the Russian Baptists and the Jehovah's Witnesses in Nazi concentration camps). It would be wrong for us to underestimate their strength, their sincerity, or their iron determination on either side of the Atlantic.

[1977]